D0487513

Industrial
Archaeology
in the
British Isles

Elek Archaeology and Anthropology

General Editor: J. V. S. Megaw
Professor of Archaeology in the
University of Leicester

Already published

The Environment of Early Man in the British Isles
John G. Evans

The Roman Forts of the Saxon Shore
Stephen Johnson

Science and Society in Prehistoric Britain
Euan W. MacKie

Greek Architects at Work
J. J. Coulton

Parthian Art
Malcolm A. R. Colledge

Industrial Archaeology in the British Isles

John Butt

Professor of Economic History
University of Strathclyde

and

Ian Donnachie

Staff Tutor in History
The Open University

Paul Elek London

First published in Great Britain in 1979 by
Paul Elek Ltd
54–58 Caledonian Road, London N1 9RN

© John Butt and Ian Donnachie 1979

ISBN 0 236 40157 2

Printed in Great Britain by
Unwin Brothers Limited
The Gresham Press, Old Woking, Surrey

Contents

Plates

List of figures

Preface

There is widespread and growing interest in industrial archaeology, as witness the range of literature and of museums devoted
to the subject. We hope that this volume will provide both an
introduction to the subject and an examination of some of the
achievements in recording and conservation undertaken at the
local level throughout the British Isles. Part of our purpose is
also to synthesize as much of the regional and local material as
is immediately relevant.

Because industrial archaeology is an inter-disciplinary subject
its toolbag of approaches and techniques should not be too closely
prescribed. However, we have tried to examine the archaeology
of industry in its historical context, and at the same time to
emphasize what we consider to be the contemporary relevance
of this surviving heritage. Partly as a consequence of the increasing awareness of environmental conservation and partly as agents
of the process, architects and planners have had to think more
deeply about how to treat the country's relics. Even though we
do not personally believe that preservation schemes in themselves represent the main *raison d'être* of industrial archaeology,
we think it necessary to pay careful attention to them.

We believe that in the future field recording and excavation
will give way to general interpretation. Perhaps the main difference between our book and those of earlier writers is our attempt
at this sort of interpretation, looking at the British Isles as a
whole. Of course, we could not claim to be definitive within the
confines of a single volume. Industrial archaeology is still a very
young discipline and there are many real and exciting discoveries
to be made.

Acknowledgements

Many people and organizations have helped us in the preparation
of this book. Our principal debt is to our colleague and friend,
John Hume, who provided us with many illustrations and his
usual good advice. Special thanks are also due to Gavin Bowie,
Christopher Cox, Douglas Hague, Jeremy Lowe, David Palmer,
Neil Sinclair, and Bill Thompson for help with illustrations. The
compilation of the Irish section of the gazetteer was greatly
assisted by An Foras Forbartha Teoranta, The National Institute
for Physical Planning and Construction Research, Dublin, in
particular Ken Mawhinney, Secretary of the Irish Society for
Industrial Archaeology.

For permission to reproduce illustrations we are grateful to:
Gavin Bowie, 7; Peter Clarke, 91; Christopher Cox, 63; Department
of the Environment, 9; Eastbourne and District Preservation
Society, 2; The Faversham Society, 52; John Hume, 4, 6, 8, 12, 13,
15, 16, 17, 18, 20, 22, 25, 27, 28, 30, 31, 33, 34, 35, 37, 38, 39, 40,
43, 44, 45, 46, 48, 49, 50, 51, 53, 54, 55, 56, 57, 58, 61, 65, 66, 67,
68, 69, 70, 76, 79, 80, 83, 84, 85, 86, 87, 88, 89; Ironbridge Gorge
Museum Trust, 29, 59; Lancashire Museum Services, 24; Jeremy
Lowe, 91, Fig. 2; David Palmer, 32, 95; Royal Commission on
Ancient and Historical Monuments in Scotland (National Build-
ings Record of Scotland), Fig. 6; Royal Commission on Ancient
and Historical Monuments in Wales, 72, 73; Walter Stephen, Fig.
5; W. J. Thompson, 21; David Tomlin, 74; Gordon Tucker, 90;
Tyne and Wear County Council Museums (Monkwearmouth
Station Museum), 78; Tyne and Wear Industrial Monuments,
Sunderland, Fig. 7.

The Open University kindly gave a research grant to visit
Ireland and to help with travelling expenses. Miss Ann Douglas
of Paul Elek was forbearing with us. Finally, we wish to thank
Mrs Elizabeth Thrippleton, who coped admirably with our
manuscript.

1
Introduction: Scope and Definitions

Although it is not commonly realized, the practice of Industrial Archaeology—the study and recording of industrial monuments and other artefacts—is far from being a recent development and indeed pre-dates the evolution of separate disciplines like Economic History, Historical Geography or the History of Technology. Engineers and scientists of all specializations had from the late nineteenth century investigated the history of technology, often combining archival and archaeological data in papers to their learned journals.[1] In 1919 the Newcomen Society was founded specifically with the objective of publishing research on the history of technology;[2] members of the Newcomen, in turn, pioneered the development of industrial archaeology after the Second World War. One of them, Rex Wailes, had worked for many years on the subject of English windmills, and his classic text,[3] published in 1954, was an inspiration to those working on other fields and a preliminary to his appointment as consultant to the Industrial Monuments Survey in 1963, an undertaking jointly sponsored by the Council for British Archaeology and the Ministry of Public Buildings and Works.

Local historians and antiquarians had for many years contained within their ranks individuals interested in industrial history, and some of these published papers which demonstrate both a traditional historical approach and also evidence of field surveys. John Postlethwaite published in 1877 his *Mines and Mining in the English Lake District*, in which, among other things, he gives authoritative descriptions of mining methods and equipment over several centuries.[4] The following year, Isaac Fletcher's paper, 'The Archaeology of the West Cumberland Coal Trade', appeared in the *Transactions of the Cumberland and Westmorland Antiquarian and Archaeological Society*, a body which maintained a continuous interest in the history and archaeology of the regional economy. William Ivison Macadam, in a modestly titled paper, 'Notes on the Ancient Iron Industry of Scotland', published in the *Proceedings of the Society of Antiquaries of Scotland* in 1887, anticipated the development of post-medieval archaeology as well as industrial archaeology for he catalogued, using evidence from the field as well as documentary material, the principal sites of ironworking in Scotland in the period between 1500 and 1750.

As Arthur Raistrick makes clear, university extra-mural departments contained individuals in the 1920s and 1930s who taught courses and conducted field studies in what we would now call industrial archaeology.[5] Professor J. D. Chambers was one of several tutors who recognized the importance and value of our industrial heritage, for he aroused the enthusiasm of his students in economic history by taking them round old framework knitters' cottages and other places of industrial interest in Nottinghamshire. In Manchester there is a tradition that the late Professor Arthur Redford actually used the term 'industrial archaeology' in the 1940s to describe the physical remains of past industrial activity.[6] After the war the phrase was re-coined by Professor Donald Dudley of the University of Birmingham in the early 1950s and widely put into circulation by Michael Rix, whose specialization in architectural history made him a particularly authoritative voice in favour of conservation.[7] Inspired by an awareness that industrialization in Britain was a unique phenomenon and that everywhere demolition and redevelopment was proceeding, a participatory audience for extra-mural industrial archaeology classes and short courses evolved in the 1950s and 1960s, and eventually specialist tutors were appointed in the universities of Hull and Newcastle upon Tyne.

Preceding this movement was the longstanding concern of museums for the artefacts of industrialization.[8] The foundation of the Science Museum in London following the Great Exhibition of 1851 was an indication that Victorian society appreciated that technology had historic as well as profit-making value. In 1854 the Royal Scottish Museum was founded in Edinburgh as 'The Industrial Museum of Scotland',[9] and in Ulster and Wales national collections illustrating the history of technology were gradually accumulated. Municipalities followed the example set by central government, and today very few cities do not boast specialist exhibits, often of more than local significance.[10] In recent years experimentation in the organization and presentation of material, commonly stimulated by a knowledge of international examples, has been the order of the day. The most radical development has been the specialist museum, for instance the Windmill Museum in Wimbledon, the National Railway Museum at York, or the Gladstone Pottery Museum in Stoke. Specialist industrial exhibits have become a feature of many museums, for example, the splendid watch-maker's workshop in the Liverpool Museum. One of the most exciting recent developments has been the open-air museum, the two principal examples being at Ironbridge and Beamish.[11] Less elaborate and often privately financed ventures can be found in most areas of the British Isles. Two examples from Cornwall—supported by a growing band of visitors—are the Wendron Forge Museum and the English China Clays Museum at Wheal Martyn.[12]

The boom in conservation and the tourism associated with it have little to do with the academic study of industrial archaeology, but they do explain the remarkable growth in lay interest which made it possible for public policy on preservation to be amended so as to include industrial monuments. Industrial archaeology shares with traditional archaeology a policy-forming role: it is concerned with selective preservation so that later generations may have the opportunity to understand the culture of earlier industrialization; its practitioners and supporters, therefore, attempted, with success, to change government and civil service attitudes towards industrial remains.[13] The stress is increasingly on how to put obsolete buildings to use: the Maltings in Ship Lane, Ely, demonstrate how a community can gain a pleasant public hall from a large building consigned to redundancy by industrial change; craftsmen and 'week-enders' are beginning to move back into villages such as New Lanark, previously subject to sharp decline in population. Many private bodies administer individual industrial sites in different parts of the British Isles, and their commendable efforts have demonstrated to official quarters what can be done with a little imagination and a great deal of enthusiasm. At Ryhope (Sunderland) water-pumping beam engines have been restored;[14] at Sticklepath (near Okehampton) a metalworking project has been resurrected from an early-nineteenth-century scythe-making venture.[15] These are merely two examples of a widespread effort at industrial archaeological conservation.

Before the Second World War the Vintage Car Club had demonstrated that part of the motivation of conservation was recreational participation—finding pleasure in what had been previously work for others. Well before the title of industrial archaeology stuck or institutional status was sought for it, the late L. T. C. (Tom) Rolt was heavily committed to this recreational approach, as parts of his autobiography reveal.[16] Just before the outbreak of the war he had decided to live on the canal narrow boat *Cressy*, travelling the neglected and commonly weed-stricken inland waterways and living frugally upon the proceeds of his writing. The manuscript of his justly celebrated first book, *Narrow Boat*, went the rounds of publishers and then into a suitcase under his bed for two years before its appearance in 1944 inaugurated a new era of canal conservation associated with the later formation of the Inland Waterways Association. *Railway Adventure* (1953) tells how Tom Rolt became involved with the Talyllyn Railway preservation project; railways have since gripped the popular imagination, and societies concerned to operate steam locomotives using volunteer labour are now numerous.

Industrial archaeology is more than a study of the remains of manufacturing industry. It is concerned with *all* the physical relics of economic growth: warehouses and workshops as well as 'factories; windmills and water wheels as well as steam engines, gas engines, turbines, generators and internal combustion engines; rural trades, crafts and agricultural implements, as well as urban industrial remains; transport and other public utilities; workers' housing and other social relics. Although some of its practitioners may dislike the title, it is conveniently short and is now justified by common usage. This simple label has helped to establish the image and character of the study, for industrial archaeology—in our judgement—has already gone through the process of creating an informed readership and a greater public awareness of industrial monuments in our environment. Yet the phenomenal growth in interest in industrial archaeology since the 1950s has also been accompanied by extensive and unresolved debate about its nature, intellectual boundaries and usefulness.[17] A mixture of sincerity and acrimony prevents the universal acceptance of any definition. This may be a sign of vitality, the only means by which the issues may ultimately be clarified.

The study of the past using the evidence provided by physical remains—buildings and artefacts—is a well-established part of archaeology. Industrial archaeology is essentially a field study concerned with elucidating industrial history. First and foremost, it involves the location, surveying and recording of the sites and structures of industrial activity. Chapter 2 discusses the techniques likely to prove useful in the field and the nature of sources which may be of help before and after fieldwork is undertaken. However, industrial archaeology also comprehends a wider range of activities and objectives arising from its primary purpose. Once sites and structures have been located and adequately recorded, interpretation becomes the fundamental aspect of the study. Fieldwork is not an end in itself but the beginning of an end.[18] Interpretation means assessing the significance of what has been located and recorded, and, in turn, this task demands that documentary and/or oral evidence should be added to and weighed against what has been discovered in the field. Some investigators proceed from documents to field study, others from field study to documents and interviews. An interplay between all the available forms of evidence is vital if the best results are to be achieved. Field study and conventional research should walk hand in hand.

A number of problems require discussion before our definition is complete. The first concerns the nature of industrial history and raises the relationship of industrial archaeology to archaeology in general. Most industrial archaeologists have concentrated their efforts on physical remains of the time-span since 1700 and commonly stopped at 1914. There really should be no rigid limiting dates to the study, a plea eloquently made by Arthur Raistrick in 1972: Roman leadmining, medieval bloomeries and twentieth-century cinemas are equally fit subjects for investigation.[19] However, it is the case that before 1950 field studies relating to industry after 1700 were very few and that departments of archaeology were sometimes reluctant to admit the validity of medieval archaeology, never mind later branches such as the archaeology of the Industrial Revolution. Moreover, the sheer weight of the surviving evidence relating to the process of industrialization is likely to coerce most investigators towards the study of the physical remains of the last three centuries. Nonetheless, it is much more important that investigation and interpretation of the industrial past should proceed than that practitioners should quarrel over what they believe to be their province in chronology.

A more vexed question, perhaps, is what constitutes industrial history. We have not included a detailed historical study of agricultural techniques and progress but are more concerned in Chapter 4 with the processing of primary commodities and rural industries. Rural archaeology itself is likely to extend its time boundaries in the future just as archaeology in general has already done. Transport, housing, and recreation might not be included in any narrow definition of industrial history, but the industrial archaeologist needs a wide remit, for his objective should be to interpret the experience at work and at leisure of industrial workers and their employers.

The relationship of industrial archaeology to archaeology is closer than is generally supposed and ought to be closer still. Like his colleague in any other branch of archaeology, the industrial archaeologist is concerned to use physical remains to remedy the deficiencies of the existing record, to complement other historical evidence, and to assist in the testing of current orthodox interpretations of past cultures.[20] He should be equally circumspect in his methods of working and in the standards of his research reports; in particular, measured drawings and photographs should be of the highest quality because they are an indispensable part of any accurate record and may form the basis for comparative studies at a later date. The standards of recording in industrial archaeology need to be improved, a fact particularly recognized by the Association for Industrial Archaeology (established in 1974) which has, as one of its objects, the worthy aim of raising the general level of research reports. More traditional archaeology met these problems long ago; that they have been so successfully surmounted may be a consequence of the passage of time and professionalization rather than a tribute to individual genius.

One great advantage accrues to the industrial archaeologist: he is not usually so dependent upon careful excavation and stratigraphy as his colleague in other branches of archaeology. This was often regarded as a defect by hide-bound archaeologists who tended to confuse these techniques with the substance and nature of archaeology. Because structures survive above ground, it was commonly felt that the new infant industrial archaeology could not properly have the same parentage (or, at best, the same side of the blanket) as its older brothers such as prehistoric archaeology or Romano-British archaeology. Attitudes have greatly changed in the last fifteen years, but further co-operation between specialists in different periods of archaeology could do nothing but good for the study as a whole.

The fact that archaeology is divided for the purposes of specialization by periods rather than by themes—and that industrial archaeology is concerned with a theme—has commonly been paraded as a major problem. This is really a gross simplification of a very complex issue.[21] Technology and production do not change uniformly; advances in one industry or even in one sector of an industry were not accompanied contemporaneously by changes elsewhere. Diffusion of the changes in technique may cross time barriers imposed for scholarly convenience. For instance, in tanning, the medieval archaeologist, post-medieval archaeologist and industrial archaeologist might well find much common practice; in ironworking, pottery, glassmaking or lime-burning, the technical pedigree might be even longer. Tracing the diffusion of new techniques cannot simply be a matter for one specialist archaeologist or another, for it is difficult to be certain how long obsolescence may take. Side by side with up-to-date producers it is likely that more primitive units survived; traditional documentary methods of research reveal that, for example, the charcoal-fired furnace survived into the age of cheap steel. We believe that industrial archaeology cannot have rigid time constraints placed upon it; they only impede purposeful scholarship. If the archaeology of industry were strictly confined to the period since 1700, the intellectual losses would be significant.

Nor do we exclude the likelihood that excavation and stratigraphy may sooner or later become more significant techniques of the industrial archaeologist. His colleagues in post-medieval archaeology have already demonstrated the possibilities for unravelling the history of glassmaking and pottery,[22] and the Historical Metallurgy Group has transcended all the time barriers which periodization entails, excavation being a fundamental preliminary stage in the preparation of its exceedingly valuable reports on the iron industry.[23] With just one reference to a glassmaker in a local parish register in 1600, it was decided to excavate in a field called Glass Hey Field in the neighbourhood of Ormskirk, Lancashire, in 1968. This uncovered the remains of a wood-fired furnace, the only definite evidence of glassmaking having taken place in that part of the country at that time. Ruth Hurst Vose, who was responsible for this discovery, later went on to use a similar technique to unearth the first coal-fired furnace in the north-west, dating from c. 1615, at Glasshouse Fold near Stockport between 1969 and 1973.[24] The products of the early-nineteenth-century Bellevue Pottery in Hull are now much better known as a consequence of an excavation in 1970 when the principal find was a cellar full of wasters. A greater number of patterns was revealed, a fact of major importance since much Hull pottery was not marked.[25] Open-cast operations in the coal industry have from time to time exposed older workings, and Dr Alan Griffin has made excellent use of this fortuitous 'excavation' to demonstrate, among other things, the low rate of extraction in some Derbyshire seams in the mid eighteenth century.[26]

Perhaps of greater significance in this discussion is the fact that industrial activity does not and did not take place in some vacuum or enclave in society. To understand any society at any time, as Marx has taught us, we must try to assess its technology and economy; equally, its political and social organization is an engine which may alter production. Any archaeologist worthy of his salt must, therefore, take an interest in as many aspects of a culture that he has chosen to study as he can reasonably manage; this is true also of historians and it may be an equally binding dictum for other branches of scholarship.[27] Rigid time zones, in fact, have little validity for many branches of archaeology if our knowledge and comprehension of the past is to increase. If industrial archaeologists concentrate upon the interpretation of the industrial landscape as their prime function, willy-nilly they must take a broad view of the historical development of the society which produced it. In the last analysis, industrial archaeology is a significant historical source to be used alongside other, more traditional, historical sources, and with the same care and scholarship exercised by traditional archaeologists and other historical fieldworkers.

2
Sources and Techniques

Because Industrial Archaeology is something of a hybrid discipline it inevitably uses a wide range of sources and techniques drawn from a variety of other subject areas. Principal among these are History, Archaeology, Geography, the History of Technology, Engineering, and Architecture. These and others—presented in no particular order of priority in the foregoing list—have much to offer industrial archaeology by way of approaches to research and practical recording in the field. Some industrial archaeologists are experts in one or more of these fields, but the majority simply learn from practical experience as they go along. There are several useful books that provide general guidance, including the various works of Kenneth Hudson, a pioneer of the subject, Angus Buchanan's *Industrial Archaeology in Britain*, Arthur Raistrick's *Industrial Archaeology: An Historical Survey*, and Neil Cossons' *The B.P. Book of Industrial Archaeology*.[1] There is a growing number of large-format books which provide excellent visual introductions to industrial archaeology—and the subject is essentially visual since most of the buildings are above ground—notably Brian Bracegirdle's *The Archaeology of the Industrial Revolution* and Anthony Burton's *Remains of a Revolution*.[2]

The techniques of industrial archaeology have received considerable attention over the past decade or so, both in memoirs and through papers published in *Industrial Archaeology* and its successor *Industrial Archaeology Review*, notably the 'Aids to Recording' series. There are two invaluable studies which ought to be mentioned as major contributions to the practice of industrial archaeology. The first, called simply *Techniques of Industrial Archaeology*, is the work of the late J. P. M. Pannell, formerly engineer to Southampton Harbour Board.[3] Pannell gives practical advice on the best methods of approach to background material in the form of written, printed and verbal sources; on maps, plans and pictures. Elementary surveying is explained and demonstrated by a detailed description of an actual survey on an industrial site. Measuring and drawing machines, plant and buildings are also covered in some detail, while there are excellent sections on materials of construction and on the development of design in industrial machinery and buildings. The second and more recent study, *Fieldwork in Industrial Archaeology* (1975), by the notable industrial archaeologist and architect, J. Kenneth Major, is a useful guide to all aspects of field recording.[4] Major outlines the scope of the subject and the many practical skills the industrial archaeologist needs when working in the field, from measured drawing and photography to research, recording and publication. Much of Major's work is based on actual field surveys of such sites as a brick and tile works, several corn mills, a cooperage, a brewhouse, and a horse wheel—among others. One of Major's concerns is the emergency survey which often has to be undertaken quickly because of pressures of demolition and redevelopment, always a problem in the past and likely to continue so, despite the increasing awareness of how important many industrial sites are.

All of the sources and techniques at the disposal of the industrial archaeologist can hardly be summarized here, but those who wish more detailed guidance should refer either to the works of Pannell and Major, or to the many articles and papers in the journals cited in the Bibliography. For regional and local sources, and sites, reference can be made to existing publications on industrial archaeology. Few areas have not already received some attention, though in some instances there is as yet no comprehensive survey of industrial sites. The scope for further work—both nationally and locally—remains enormous and no one with an enthusiasm for the subject need be intimidated either by existing publications or by the idea that they are somehow not expert enough to make their own contribution, however elementary it might seem.

Sources

The aim of this section is to provide some indication of the range of sources for industrial archaeology available in local libraries and record offices. It also deals briefly with oral evidence, which can often be of great value in trying to piece together fragmentary data about a site or building. Conventional research is sometimes a very necessary prelude to fieldwork and recording, while this in turn can lead on to more detailed documentary analysis, for example of one particular site or perhaps of a whole locality. Among the more important for such studies dealt with here are (1) maps and plans, (2) printed secondary sources, (3) prints and photographs, (4) estate, legal and business records, and (5) oral evidence. This list is far from exhaustive and numerous other sources may prove just as valuable.

1 Maps and plans

Since the industrial archaeologist is concerned with changes through time in a locality or a specific site, maps and plans are among the most important tools available. They provide the essential frame of reference for both field recording and conventional documentary research, as well as being of great importance at the report or publication stage.[5]

(a) **Eighteenth- and nineteenth-century small and medium scale maps.** Britain and Ireland were both extensively mapped after the middle of the eighteenth century, as a consequence of general economic development, improved communications and the need for greater information about land values, boundaries, mineral and water rights. There are therefore many useful maps from this period, giving a great variety of detail on roads, bridges, tolls, ferries, harbours, mills, mines and quarries. Useful comparisons can often be made between local town or parish maps and the· more comprehensive county maps, which are again available for most parts of the country. Many of the county maps, on a scale of approximately one inch to one mile, were produced between 1770 and 1825, therefore providing a useful picture of the changing agricultural and industrial landscape. A typical map of the period, John Ainslie's *The Stewartry of Kirkcudbright* (1797), marks turnpike and other roads, bridges, toll-houses, milestones, quarries, kilns and mills of every description.

Town plans at varying scales are also generally available after 1770, and these can provide a great deal more detail about the location and layout of industrial plant, water courses, weirs, harbour installations and related features. At the beginning of the nineteenth century borough maps were produced to accompany evidence gathered for Royal Commissions on Boundaries, and these can often be usefully compared with the first Ordnance Survey Six Inch series for the locality concerned.

Other promising sources under this head include estate, road, canal, and railway maps. Transport maps are often found in route guides and directories, which were a necessary accompaniment to travel at the time. Canals and turnpikes are well represented, a particularly good example being John Cary's *Survey of the High Roads from London* (1790), which marks many interesting wayside features. Later, during the nineteenth century, the railway companies produced similar guides, and the Victorian pride in industrial achievement means that a great deal of interesting data can be obtained from these sources.

(b) Ordnance Survey maps. The first O.S. maps of Britain were surveyed at the beginning of the nineteenth century on the one inch to one mile scale, starting with Kent (1801) and Essex (1805). The survey was later extended to cover the whole of England and Wales (completed by 1873), while Scotland and Ireland were completely mapped somewhat later. The one-inch O.S. maps can be very informative to the industrial archaeologist. Railways, tramroads, collieries, quarries, mills and other plant are marked, and regular revisions mean that comparisons can be made through time. Other points of reference, including Rate Books and Valuation Rolls and census records, can provide additional information on dating. Even more useful is the Six-Inch series which was started in Ireland, and after 1840 extended to unsurveyed territory in northern England and Scotland. With their scale of six inches to a mile these maps are now more than adequate for most field research in industrial archaeology. For example, they show the type of threshing mill installed at a farm (horse, water or steam powered), or the basic layout of a more complex site, like an ironworks or limestone quarry. In common with later maps the first Six Inch series marks a disused or derelict plant, for example, 'Old Mill' or 'Old Kiln'. The existence of such sites can therefore be checked on earlier maps of the locality or in the appropriate entries of gazetteers, topographical dictionaries, the *Victoria County Histories* (for England) or the *Statistical Accounts* (for Scotland).[6]

Also of great value in relation to studies of the industrial archaeology of mining and quarrying are nineteenth-century geological maps, again drawn mainly to a scale of one inch to one mile. The Geological Survey of Great Britain began in the 1830s and most of the country was covered by the 1880s. The Geological Memoirs which accompany many of the sheets are extremely valuable, as are later memoirs dealing with specific minerals and mining areas in greater detail.

(c) Plans. By far the most detailed profile of an industrial complex, building or machinery can be obtained from the large-scale plans or measured drawings of architects, surveyors and engineers. There are growing collections of estate, architectural, industrial and engineering plans in the national collections, and in county and local record offices, as well as in many university libraries. A comprehensive collection of plans will cover most industries, with mining and railways often being best represented. One finds sometimes that plans have been extracted from business archives or legal processes, so that it is often possible to relate references in business or estate records to the relevant plans and drawings. A typical set of late-eighteenth-century estate plans might provide data on a local limestone quarry and kilns, corn, threshing and timber mills, dams, sluices, leats or lades—as well as detailed drawings of buildings and machinery. Later plans, including the O.S. series at 1 : 2500 scale, will indicate subsequent changes and developments. Machine drawings are clearly of immense value and can help in the reconstruction and preservation of historic machinery (for example, a water wheel or steam engine) either *in situ* or after removal to a museum. Most record offices maintain a detailed index of map and plan holdings.

2 Printed secondary sources

The range of secondary material on industrial and economic history is considerable and few working in the area of industrial archaeology could expect to have a detailed knowledge of the whole field. Nevertheless, the industrial archaeologist needs to have a good working knowledge of the district he is studying—particularly the economic and social background. Some might well argue that industrial and technical developments can be studied for their own sake, but the archaeology of industry certainly means a great deal more when seen in its historical context, national or local.

Major bibliographies of local and national topography are an obvious starting point in an unfamiliar area, though it is often quicker to go straight to the local collection in the library or record office to find what is immediately relevant to one's interests. A good overview of the history of a locality can invariably be obtained from the *Victoria County History* series (England), the *Statistical Accounts* (of Scotland), and similarly comprehensive volumes for Wales and Ireland. The parish or borough entries in such series vary greatly in quantity and quality, but the footnotes at least sometimes give good leads to economic or social conditions, the development of industry, and perhaps of particular firms in the area. Local histories themselves also vary in quality; some Victorian studies of local industrial development are of outstanding value, others are overtly concerned with antiquities or local dignitaries. It is very important to know the basic local sources, and research of this kind in the library will repay many dividends.

Gazetteers are another major source. Some of the early-nineteenth-century examples are of considerable interest to the industrial archaeologist, for instance Constable and Murray's *Gazetteer of Scotland* (1806), and Samuel Lewis's *Topographical Dictionary of Ireland* (1837). From later in the century is *The National Gazetteer of Gt Britain and Ireland*, published in various editions during the 1860–80s. This gazetteer and a variety of *Ordnance Gazetteers* covering Britain and Ireland, are of great interest—local detail is often considerable, particularly on economic and industrial matters. Guide books are in a similar category: nineteenth-century works of this kind usually contain industrial material. Many were published by railway or steamship companies.

Directories vary widely in quality but provide an essential aid to the industrial archaeologist in building up a profile of the economy of a community. Some pre-1800 commercial directories are available for the main towns, though they are not always reliable. Typical are the *Western and Midland Directory* (1784) and the *Universal British Directory* (1790–8). The best comprehensive volumes are those of *Pigot's Commercial Directory* (first published 1815), covering most of the country. Organized by county and town they provide details of local industries and craftsmen (like nailers, weavers and millwrights), even in the most modest village. From later in the nineteenth century are *Kelly's Directories* and the *Post Office Directories*. A combination of directory and guide book was provided by William White, and among the most valuable county directories in this series are those for Devon, Essex, Norfolk, Suffolk and Yorkshire. Trade journals and directories, such as *The Brewers' Almanack*, provide information on the development of specific industries during the latter half of the nineteenth and early twentieth centuries in particular. Newspapers also provide useful data on local industries and economic conditions, and should certainly be checked carefully for items on trading conditions, new buildings, and such events as accidents, which throw light on working conditions and machinery employed.

Another extremely useful source for the industrial archaeologist is the local Rate Book or Valuation Roll, which dates back in most places to the mid nineteenth century. Some of the early ones are in manuscript form, but the majority are in printed volumes. Local libraries may well have old rolls covering their areas. The Valuation Roll is a useful complement to earlier manuscript rolls (including hearth or poll tax returns) and provides details of ownership, function and rateable value. The roll usually indicates the nature of industry carried on, and whether the trade is discontinued, or the building derelict. Change in ownership or use can also be checked against earlier or later rolls, as well as in commercial or trade directories and large-scale maps or plans.

Parliamentary papers cover the whole field of nineteenth-century industry and are of outstanding value to both the industrial archaeologist and the local historian. The papers can be consulted in the major civic libraries or in the various university libraries. Individual volumes or sets of volumes in the massive Irish Universities Press reprint of the papers are also readily available together with index volumes. Several guides to the use of parliamentary papers can be consulted, and additionally most of the series have been indexed.[7] For most years or sessions an annual index exists, and there is also a useful general index of commissions, select committees, accounts and papers. It would be impossible to provide a detailed list of sources for industrial history, but some of the most valuable papers cover roads, canals, railways, ports, harbours, factories, water power, textile mills, distilleries, breweries, mines and quarries. Two regional studies, *The Industrial Archaeology of County Down* and *The Industrial Archaeology of Galloway*, have made particular use of parliamentary papers and these provide some indication of the data that can be obtained from this valuable source.[8]

3 Prints and photographs

Old prints and photographs are invaluable sources of information about buildings, and the social detail of old street or industrial scenes. Like maps, they can be used to date buildings, and to build up a chronology of changes on industrial sites. Some of the early-nineteenth-century topographical prints are immensely interesting and useful. Those of William Daniell—well known for their accuracy and detail (Plate 1)—are collected in *A Picturesque Voyage Round the Coast of Great Britain* (1814–22), while other notable nineteenth-century artists and engravers produced excellent industrial views all over the country. Apart from national sources, the local library, record office or art gallery usually maintains a collection and index.

There are some important and growing collections of archive photographs, in both public and private hands. Again, record offices maintain collections which are likely to reflect industrial and social conditions in the area. Agencies like the National Monuments Record and the Royal Commission on Ancient and Historic Monuments also have archive photographs drawn from a wide variety of sources. Old photographs are presently arousing much interest and there are many excellent books of nineteenth- and early-twentieth-century material available. Some of the larger

Plate 1 Black Marble Quarry, near Red Wharf Bay, Anglesey.
Engraving by William Daniell.

and older-established engineering firms maintained photographic records of their output over the years.

Finally a word about air photographs—as yet a little-exploited
source in industrial archaeology. There are many sites where air
photographs can assist in identifying features not visible from
the ground—especially long-abandoned sites which have been
little disturbed. Excavation of industrial sites will undoubtedly
become increasingly important in the future, and the use of air
photographs will become more significant.

4 Estate, legal and business archives

These are increasingly important sources for research into industrial history and industrial archaeology. The largest collections
are housed in national repositories, such as the Public Record
Office, the Scottish Record Office, and the major libraries and

record offices of Wales, Northern Ireland and the Republic of Ireland, but there are growing archives in most local record offices. Indeed, the local archive is an obvious place to start looking for local material, and it is also likely to hold indexes or catalogues of nationally held records of local interest. Many such records remain in private hands, but have been surveyed by the National Register of Archives or the Historical Manuscripts Commission, whose survey reports can be readily consulted locally. The National Railway Museum and the Scottish Record Office maintain large collections of railway archives.

Landowners were responsible for many economic developments during the eighteenth and nineteenth centuries, and consequently estate papers are of great value to the historian of the period. Although many archives are still maintained in private hands, large collections have been deposited in record offices. A typical estate archive might include material on mills, water power (always the subject of dispute), textile mills, collieries, metal-mines, turnpike roads, canals, railways and planned villages. A great many of the case studies published in *Industrial Archaeology* and *Industrial Archaeology Review* provide indications of how field study and documentary research on estate papers have been linked to build up detailed pictures of industrial and social changes in the century 1750–1850. The scope of such archives is often considerable, and extends in many cases beyond the immediate needs or concerns of the industrial archaeologist. In such instances the real test for the successful researcher lies in finding his or her way to the most immediately relevant data—not always the easiest task.[9]

Business and legal records are perhaps more difficult to use, but nevertheless are becoming increasingly popular with industrial archaeologists. Certainly more groundwork and background information is required before one uses them. Yet solid research in such archives can often provide a wealth of material on business history and technical developments. This is particularly so if a firm went into liquidation and the legal trustees were careful enough to gather up all the account and letter books. A large collection of business archives might also contain maps, plans, and catalogues of the firm's products. The national record offices maintain indexes to such legal cases, but anyone embarking on research in these archives would be well advised to consult the appropriate staff, who are only too willing to assist.

In the Guildhall Library in London there is an extensive cache of fire insurance records dating from the early eighteenth century. These relate particularly to the Sun Fire Insurance Company which insured many industrial buildings throughout Britain. Before 1800 provincial insurance companies did not exist on any scale, and so this collection of policy registers is an invaluable source for those concerned with industrial buildings dating back to the eighteenth century. Searching can be a long and tedious business but the insurance records will give many details about the building or buildings, together with details relating to machinery and equipment.

5 Oral evidence

Oral evidence has its limitations, but it is nevertheless most valuable to have the memories or recollections of former workers in a mine or mill, or local inhabitants with a knowledge of past working and living conditions. Most local societies and groups active in the industrial archaeology field have given some attention to the recording and publication of local memories which are likely to prove of considerable interest and value in the future. It always makes sense to use local knowledge of a building or site; even a garbled memory can help piece together a picture of a vibrant community long abandoned.

Techniques

It must be obvious that the fieldworker interested in the physical evidence of the industrial past requires a wide range of talents, but at the same time there is plenty of room for a variety of approaches. Enthusiasm coupled with a willingness to work in the fresh air on cold winter days are probably the best qualifications at the outset! Winter and spring are, in fact, good seasons to undertake fieldwork on old industrial buildings, because the site is much less likely to be hidden by trees and undergrowth and hence is more readily photographed. Like other forms of environment study, fieldwork in industrial archaeology requires a minimum of equipment before one can start. Assuming one has carried out the necessary preparatory research and has some clear idea of the questions one wishes to ask, fieldwork is likely to prove worth while. It may provide some of the answers to the initial set of questions and ought certainly to raise new ones. If preparatory work is inadequate, much of the effort which goes into any field exercise is likely to be useless.

First, a brief word about equipment. Listed below under (A) is really essential equipment for a simple field survey not involving much in the way of measuring, under (B) the minimum of equipment for undertaking basic measured drawings of industrial buildings or sites—and probably generally useful for most field-work—and under (C) obvious personal accessories:

(A) clip-board
firm polythene cover for above
hard-back notebook
loose-leaf paper
graph paper (squared for measured drawings)
pens/pencils
ruler
rubber
camera

(B) folding measuring rod (2 m or 6 ft)
steel tape measure
cloth tape measure (15 m or 30 m)
ranging rod

(C) solid footwear
rubber boots
warm and waterproof clothes, as required
hard hat (very useful, and often necessary)

Most of the things mentioned in list (C) may seem pretty obvious, and will be recognized as essential if exploring a dark and damp factory or mine (where care must clearly be taken). As Ken Major has indicated, 'experience will show the industrial archaeologist how much equipment he needs to take into the field. He should remember what he would feel like if he discovered a horse wheel for raising ore out of a mine some three or four miles from where he left his camera and tape!'[10]

Relevant maps, as previously indicated, are absolutely essential, the chosen map scales being appropriate to the breadth or depth of local research. A familiarity with the standard scale Ordnance Survey maps is almost a prerequisite for any fieldwork. The current series are:

(A) small-scale   — 1 : 50,000 (First Series)
                      1 : 25,000 (Second Series)
(B) medium scale — 1 : 10,000 (Metric)
                      1 : 10,560 (Imperial)
(C) large scale   — 1 : 2,500 (Metric/Imperial)

The 1 : 50,000 series (at a scale of 2 cm to 1 km) is the metric replacement for the old one inch to one mile series, and is suitable for a wide variety of general fieldwork, while the medium and large scale maps (on the old imperial scale of 2½ inches, 6 inches, and 25 inches to 1 mile) are appropriate for study involving such details as field boundaries, railway embankments or cuttings, streets, and individual buildings. Certainly valuable assets to any historical field study are photocopies of relevant eighteenth- and nineteenth-century maps (such as those previously described), which allow immediate comparison of the modern landscape or existing physical evidence with past topography. In this connection contemporary air photographs can also be useful in the field, if copies can be obtained. A good working knowledge of the National Grid Reference system is essential in pinpointing locations.

In a preliminary location survey the most important points to note are (a) the type of site (colliery, ironworks, corn mill, worker's house, etc.), (b) its size, condition and construction, (c) its age (roughly), (d) its location (parish, town, street, Grid Reference, etc.), and (e) an estimate of its importance compared with other similar sites, or its importance in the locality (if any). The Council for British Archaeology (C.B.A.) has produced a standard record card for industrial archaeological studies, an example of which is reproduced in Fig. 1. Using these cards it is possible to build up a simple index of a particular group or type of sites. A separate card should be completed for each site, the data being transferred from a field notebook. Other information—such as photographs or photocopies of maps, if small enough—can be filed with the card. In industrial archaeology, as in all aspects of archaeological or historical investigation, negative evidence is important. The demolition or disappearance through decay of a site is worthy of record, as is the absence of typical features in a surviving site.

Several points are worth considering about all sites, and the following are some of the basic questions one might ask at the earliest stage of a field investigation on a new site:

1 Why was this building or installation made in this particular place?
   (a) Convenience of supply of raw materials (for example, grain, iron ore, water)?
   (b) Availability of power (for example, wind, water, steam, electric)?
   (c) Availability of fuel (for example, timber, coal, gas, oil, electricity)?

NATURE OF SITE (Factory,mine,etc.)			COUNTY	REF. No.
GRID REFERENCE OR LOCATION.	INDUSTRY.	DATING.	PARISH/TOWNSHIP.	DATE OF REPORT.

DESCRIPTION: dimensions; present condition; architectural features etc.

(Further remarks or photo/sketch may be recorded on the back)

MACHINERY AND FITTINGS.

DANGER OF DEMOLITION OR DAMAGE.

PRINTED, MANUSCRIPT OR PHOTOGRAPHIC RECORDS.

REPORTER'S NAME AND ADDRESS:-

Return to:-

INSTITUTION OR SOCIETY:-

INDUSTRIAL ARCHAEOLOGY REPORT CARD.

Fig. 1   Industrial archaeology standard report card.

(d) Near markets for product? (Particularly true of urban industries)

(e) Availability of labour (for example, provision of workers' housing and other facilities)?

(f) Good communications (for example, tramroad, canal, turnpike)?

2 Is this site part of a group of similar or related sites (for example, spinning and weaving mills; flint mill and pottery; saw-mills and furniture works; mines on the same mineral field)?

Is it one of a number of sites connected by a common power supply (for example, a river, local electric power station)?

3 Do any documentary records survive on the site, or in a central archive? If so, are there plans of the site? (This can save much time spent in measuring and drawing.)

4 Is there a photographic record of the site? The owning firm may have such a record. If none exists, general views should be supplemented by detailed views, and a sketch may be necessary to link photographs with no obvious connection.

More detailed recording of such features as buildings or workers' housing (Fig. 2) will necessitate the use of camera and

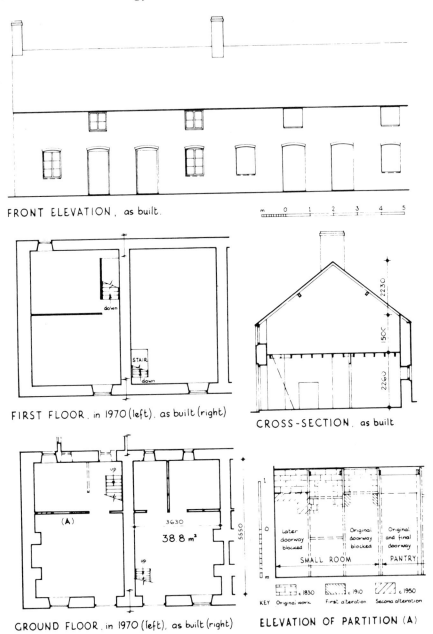

FRONT ELEVATION, as built.

FIRST FLOOR, in 1970 (left), as built (right)

CROSS-SECTION, as built

GROUND FLOOR, in 1970 (left), as built (right)

ELEVATION OF PARTITION (A)

Fig. 2 Drawing of Blaenavon Lower New Rank housing (after Lowe, 1972).

measuring tape. Simple measured drawings, diagrams and sketches are invaluable and add considerably to the value of the record. The main constructional or architectural details to note about any building are:

1 *Exterior*: overall dimensions (measured if possible), constructional materials (brick, stone, tiles, slate), number of storeys, number of windows in each storey (including attic dormers, etc.), type of windows (wood, cast-iron frame, multi-paned), type of roof (gabled, hipped, mansard, flat, etc.), chimneys (if any), other architectural features, such as additions, ornament, etc.

2 *Interior*: construction of vertical members (cast-iron, wood, concrete, steel girder, etc.), horizontal members (cast-iron, wood, etc.), flooring (wood, tiles, concrete), dimensions of any uprights, distance centre-to-centre, design of roof-trusses, thickness of walls, type (spiral, orthodox) and position of staircases (interior, exterior), overall layout (doors, cupboards, fireplaces, etc., in dwellings).

In the recording of machinery it is essential to note the type of machine clearly (for example, a spinning mule, lathe, portable steam engine, circular saw, etc.), the maker, date and machine number (often on a plate fixed to the machine, if the recorder is fortunate). Older machinery is often made of wood, and in places like corn mills or farm threshing mills, often anonymous, though certainly made by local millwrights who might be pinpointed in directories or valuation rolls. Machinery is best photographed in detail, because detailed measured drawing calls for considerable expertise. But straightforward measurement of overall dimensions ought to be possible, and a sketch on squared paper could be useful. The type of power transmission (see pp. 25–6) should also be noted, such as direct drive from a water wheel, lineshaft from a central steam engine, individual drive from an electric motor, etc.).

Some of the details that ought to be recorded of specific industrial buildings and sites, of power installations, and of workers' housing is indicated as follows:

1 Recording specific industries
The following list is not exhaustive, but covers the basic types of buildings and sites likely to be discovered, and the sort of detail the industrial archaeologist needs to look out for.

(a) *Textiles.* Note type of fibre processed (cotton, wool, flax, jute, nylon, etc.), processes used (bleaching, spinning, weaving, carding, etc.), number of machines, and type of product (yarn, ropes, tweed, etc.).

(b) *Agriculture.*
(i) *Farms.* Note type of farming (dairy, arable, etc.), construction and layout of farm steading, farming machinery, including method of driving (horse-gin, steam engine, water wheel, oil engine), cheese presses and lofts, whin crushers, threshing mills.
(ii) *Grain mills.* Note type of power installation (wind, water, steam, oil or gas engine, electricity), type of machinery (stones, rollers, etc.).
(iii) Grain stores.
(iv) *Lime-kilns.* Note type (one draw, two draw, three draw, etc.), number, size, associated quarries, crushing equipment, tramways.

(c) *Brewing.* Note type of mash tuns, coolers, fermenting vats, type of product, whether malting floors and kilns associated.

(d) *Distilling.* Note type of mash tuns, coolers, fermenting vats, stills (pot or patent), malting floors and kilns, bonded warehouse, excise offices.

(e) *Canals.* Note number and construction of locks, aqueducts, overbridges, tunnels, wharves, warehouses, dry-docks, slipways, lock- and bridge-keepers' houses.

(f) *Roads.* Note toll-houses, bridges, type of construction (can often be seen when trenches are cut for cables and pipes).

(g) *Railways.* Note earthworks, bridges, tunnels, stations, signal boxes, signals, track construction, gauge (if not standard), rolling stock (if not British Railways), engine sheds, water towers and columns.

(h) *Harbours.* Note layout, type of construction, materials of construction (rubble, concrete, wood, iron, etc.), lighthouses, cranes, warehouses, railway connections, customs houses, type of traffic (import, coastal, coal, fishing, etc.), if connected with any particular industry (oil, aluminium, etc.).

(i) *Mining.* Note product (coal, iron ore, slate, etc.), type of mine (pit, inclined shaft, day level, etc.), pithead buildings, winding machinery, associated railways or tramways, spoil heap.

(j) *Pottery, glass and brick making.* Note product (earthenware, tile drains, bottles, refractory brick, etc.), ancillary buildings and machinery (pug mills, moulding machines, etc.), source of raw material (mine, quarry, etc.), associated railways or tramways, type of kiln (bottle, tunnel, compartmented, etc.).

(k) *Iron-smelting works.* Note blast furnaces, blowing engines and houses, furnace-banks, hot blast stoves, pig-beds or casting machine, slag heaps and type of slag, associated railways or tramways.

(l) *Foundries.* Note cupolas, cranes, heat-treatment ovens, pattern shops, type of product, metal used (iron, brass, etc.).

(m) *Forges.* Note furnace or hearths, blowers or bellows, power hammers (steam, compressed air, belt driven, tilt, etc.), drop forges, handworking, type of product (shovels, axles, etc.).

(n) *Engineering works.* Note unusually high roofs, doors, gantry cranes, machine tools, sometimes associated foundry or forge type of product (engines, machinery, motor-cars, etc.).

(o) *Shipbuilding.* Note slipways, cranes, sheer-legs, fitting-out basins, associated workshops (carpenters, electricians, etc.).

(p) *Chemical industries.* Note machinery for crushing and grinding, filtering, evaporating, pumping, crystallizing. Note also distillation columns, storage tanks, lead chambers (for sulphuric acid), type of product.

(q) *Gasworks.* Note retorts (horizontal or vertical), condensers, purifiers, gas-holders, producers (if retorts gas-fired), coke tramways, and railways.

(r) *Papermaking.* Note pulp boilers, beaters, Fourdrinier machines (one, two, or three wire), calendars, type of product.

2 Recording power installations

As indicated in Chapter 3 power installations are likely to be discovered in almost every industrial plant, and accurate recording is therefore of great importance.

(a) *Wind.* Record type of mill (post or tower), material of construction (wood, stone), number of sails, type of sail (patent-weight operated, spring operated), purpose (threshing mill, grain mill, drainage, etc.).

(b) *Water.* Record type of wheel (overshot, breastshot, etc.); clock-face convention may be used (overshot=12 o'clock, undershot=5 o'clock, etc.). Note whether buckets or paddles used, materials of construction, if driven from rim (externally or internally) or axle. Note construction of leat or lade, whether weir used or dam. If water turbine used, record type, size, head of water, horsepower.

(c) *Steam.* Record type of engine (horizontal, vertical, beam, etc.), whether simple compound, triple or quadruple expansion, if high or slow speed, type of boilers used (Cornish, Lancashire, or water-tube), operating pressure, and fuel used—if solid, whether hand or stoker fired. If steam turbine used, record type, horsepower.

(d) *Internal combustion engine.* Record type of engine (horizontal, vertical, V, Deltic, turbine); if reciprocating, record number of cylinders and type of cycle (2 stroke or 4 stroke), type of fuel used (oil, petrol, gas).

(e) *Electric.* Record type of current (A.C. or D.C.; if A.C. whether 3 phase or single phase), voltage, horsepower of motors, whether individual motors or central unit, whether current produced on the premises or taken from mains supply. If produced on the premises, what is the prime mover.

3 Recording workers' housing

Houses specially built for workers are common, especially where industries grew up far from existing communities. These houses could form part of a planned company village (e.g. New Lanark, Blaenavon, Saltaire), or could be merely isolated rows. In either case they are the legitimate concern of industrial archaeologists. In the company village, not only the houses, but shops, churches and communal facilities are worth recording as part of the industrial community. One can learn a great deal about employers from the type of development they sponsored or permitted. The layout of the houses (rows or cottages) should be recorded, and, if possible, the interior of a typical house. Nineteenth century housing is disappearing rapidly due to slum clearance projects, and speedy recording is essential.

For those with limited knowledge of industrial buildings site recognition will come only with experience. There are, for example, many different types of kiln—for grain drying and malting, for pottery, glass, brick and tile making, and for lime-burning. This applies to most other categories of industrial site. Different areas of the country had their own local styles of industrial building usually linked to local materials, to some extent reflecting vernacular architecture in the district. The best way to identify the various categories and styles is to look at existing industrial archaeology surveys covering the appropriate localities, many of which are listed in the Bibliography.

Photography requires particular skills, which are not always found in the industrial archaeologist. Brian Bracegirdle, a professional photographer and teacher of the subject, has devoted considerable study to the photography of industrial buildings, and those with an interest in accurate recording are urged to look at his publications. Bracegirdle considers that first-rate recording of industrial sites and buildings will not be achieved by having *either* a photographer *or* an industrial archaeologist; one must either be both, or both must be present when the photographs are being taken. He draws attention to a number of points which will go a long way towards assisting the production of good industrial photographs:

(a) The first step to a dramatic improvement in quality when making records of a site for industrial archaeology is to leave the camera in the car (or otherwise out of reach) until the entire site has been explored and a list made in the field notebook of the pictures to be made and various angles required.

(b) The second step is never to hand-hold a camera for any picture, but always to support the camera on a good tripod and use a cable-release. This has two effects—first, it makes the photographer more critical in choosing exactly the right view-point, and second, it improves the sharpness of the pictures.

(c) For work indoors, the use of the camera with shutter open at 'B' while giving several directed flashes from different positions away from the camera gives an improvement in quality of about ten times.

(d) When working by available light indoors, possibly in the absence of a flash for any fill-in, it is vital to compress the time range of the subject. This is achieved by using a film speed index of one-quarter that stated by the manufacturer, so as to strongly over-expose, and then cutting the development by shortening the time and by dilution.

(e) The use of scales (for example, a ranging rod or metre stick) is important, particularly with smaller objects of no obvious size. These scales should not be more obtrusive than the object itself.[11]

In the preparation of a report for publication there are many points that command attention. The first is to check the conventions used in the publication: the 'house-style', typography, layout, presentation of maps, diagrams and photographs. Most journals (even local ones) will be glad to advise on the acceptability of different forms of illustration. Maps and diagrams should be clear and uncluttered, with a linear scale, and north point as appropriate. The location of all sites mentioned in the text should be indicated by National Grid references, and it is sometimes helpful to give map sheet numbers in addition. Photographs need to be black and white, preferably hard, sharp prints, which reproduce best. Major devotes a useful chapter to the publication of the results of fieldwork, while advice on the preparation of maps and diagrams can be obtained from a variety of sources, notably in the excellent work of Hodgkiss.[12]

A working archive of material on industrial archaeology is still in the process of formation. Much of the country has already been surveyed in a preliminary fashion, and the results published or otherwise made available. Yet the scope for recording remains enormous, the possibilities for local research abound, and the opportunities for conservation and preservation of industrial buildings as part of the historic environment are infinite. As a new subject drawing on a wide range of expertise there is room for almost everyone with an enthusiasm for the industrial past. The real lifeblood of the subject—apart from its expanding academic wing—will probably remain at the grass roots, in local societies, local recording and preservation. Indeed, there are many who would argue that these activities demonstrate the real success of industrial archaeology. The work previously undertaken has set a broad pattern of standards in fieldwork and recording which can be built on and improved. The studies on which this book draws so heavily are perhaps the best indication we can give the reader of what can be achieved using a variety of sources and field techniques, many of which we have been unable to mention here for lack of space.

3
Power and Prime Movers

The development of prime movers largely dictated the pace and scale of all the major industrial developments which occurred during the main period that is the concern of the industrial archaeologist. Few industrial buildings or sites that he or she is likely to survey and record are without one or more of the main prime movers—animal, wind, water, steam or electric power—and therefore an understanding of them is essential. It might be thought that when animal, wind and water were the main forms of motive power the scale of operations must have been limited. Yet in the eighteenth and nineteenth centuries very large plant—in textile mills, iron forges or lead mines, for example—was driven with considerable efficiency by water wheels. Pre-steam-power technology remained of great importance long after the Industrial Revolution. Although little water and wind powered plant was built after the mid nineteenth century many earlier installations were still at work, even into the present century. In general, however, water and wind power were first succeeded by steam or water turbines and then latterly by electricity. The actual chronology is perhaps best dealt with separately in the individual sections on each prime mover.

Animal power

Animal power—mainly but not exclusively horsepower—was applied to haulage in mines and quarries on a considerable scale, as well as driving farm machinery like threshing mills. Horsepower was cheap and flexible, for horse-driven machinery could invariably be used where water was unobtainable and a windmill impracticable. The use of horsepower in collieries, mines and quarries continued within living memory, but mainly for haulage. During the nineteenth century steam engines were gradually introduced to drive winding gear or raise drainage buckets. Horsepower was used on the farm until relatively recently—indeed, the introduction of the combine-harvester probably dealt the final blow during the 1920s and 30s to a decline begun by the use of portable steam threshers in the mid nineteenth century. Many horse mills can still be found on farms throughout the countryside; the various types are described in Chapter 4. Other applications, such as water raising and driving machinery in industrial plant like breweries, were also of some importance, and would repay local investigation.[1]

Wind power

Windmills are of great antiquity though the majority found in the British Isles are of post-medieval origin, and mainly eighteenth and nineteenth century. Windmills had a multitude of functions, the most common by far being the driving of corn mills. They were also widely used, as in the Netherlands, for pumping water and for drainage. This was important not only in low-lying districts like East Anglia and the Fenlands, but also in mines and quarries where windmills could be readily constructed. Windmills were also used to drive grinding plant, for example crushing lead ore, or flint for pottery manufacture. Threshing mills were occasionally powered by wind, but with horse or steam as standby. Though windmills could still be found at work until relatively recently—and many fine examples have been restored to working order—the majority had gradually fallen out of use during the latter half of the nineteenth and early part of the present centuries.[2]

Despite many regional variations, three main types of windmill can be identified: the most primitive and probably oldest, the post mill; the smock mill, most commonly found in south-east England; and the tower mill, which in all its varieties was undoubtedly the most popular of the three. Other types which do not strictly conform to any of these patterns, such as the farm windmills of Orkney, were built, but there are few remains to be seen. The post mill, known in England by the late thirteenth century, consists of a wooden box-like superstructure supported on a fixed post, so that the whole mill can be turned to catch any available wind. The sweeps or sails—four in number—are generally made of wood and cloth, while the machinery—adapted mainly for corn milling—is housed in the superstructure. Subsequent developments include the tripod post mill (which, as its name suggests, was supported by three posts) and the turret post mill, a much more substantial structure again supported on a central pivot. The turret post mill was the logical development of earlier types, though despite its larger dimensions it still needed to be manoeuvred into the wind from the ground. Common to these earlier designs was the tiller beam, which could be pushed round by hand, winched by a capstan or harnessed to a horse. From the mid eighteenth century fantails or small wind-vanes were fixed at right angles to the main sails to turn them into the wind, though these are more commonly found on smock and tower mills. Fantails were sometimes fitted to the tiller beam of post mills. The oldest working post mill in England, built in 1665, can be seen at Outwood, Surrey, while there are numerous other fine examples elsewhere, especially in south-eastern England.

Smock mills—sometimes called frock mills—are either octag-onal or twelve-sided structures built of wooden frames covered with clapper-boarding. They resemble post mills in that only the top portion of the mill revolved, but in other respects they are similar in external and internal fitments to tower mills. Smock mills—so called because their sloping sides give them the appear-ance of a countryman's smock—often have a painted or tarred base and a white-painted superstructure. The oldest smock mill in the country is located at Lacey Green, Bucks.; it dates from the mid seventeenth century and was moved to its present site in 1821. The Union Mill at Cranbrook, Kent (TQ779360)* is one of the finest and probably the tallest smock mill in England. Built in 1814 it is more than 70 ft (21 m) high and was in use until 1950.

The ultimate development of windmill engineering is seen in eighteenth- and nineteenth-century tower mills. The mill consists of a round or octagonal brick or stone tower—generally between 30 ft and 50 ft (9–15 m) high, tapering towards the top—which housed all of the necessary machinery. The boat-shaped or domed top (called the windcap) is the only part of the tower that revolves. This supports the sails, and power is transmitted to the millstones through a series of gear wheels. Tower mills were generally fitted with fantails to keep the sails turned into the wind. Polegate windmill (TQ581041) at Eastbourne is a first-rate example, built in 1817 and restored in 1967 by the Eastbourne and District Preservation Society. The red-brick tower, partly hung with tile, is 47 ft (14 m) high with an internal diameter of 21 ft (6.4 m) at ground level and 14 ft (4.2 m) at the top. A 7 ft (2 m) high cap surmounts the tower and is topped by a spike finial. The cap turns on a cast-iron track and there is a fine five-bladed fantail. Much of the internal machinery has been renewed, and an adjoining storeroom is set out as a milling museum.

*Where appropriate, National or Irish Grid references are given.

The sweeps are set turning when weather conditions permit (Plate 2).[3]

In other areas distinctive types of windmill were built, mostly simple modifications of the tower pattern. Many of the mills constructed in the north and west of England, on Anglesey, in Scotland and Ireland, tended to be squat stone-built towers surmounted by a windcap. Many of the Scottish examples (and a few in Ireland) were constructed over a vaulted chamber or cellar, which supported the base of the tower and at the same time provided the miller with extra storage space.[4] The surveys so far undertaken on windmills outside the south of England would seem to support the impression that local millwrights adapted standard designs to suit local conditions—building windmills as they built watermills, largely on the strength of experience. Much the same might be said of windmills built on farms to drive threshing machines or pump water from wells. The more modern form of windmill—the windpump—is well worth recording whenever discovered because most have fallen into disuse. It is readily recognized, having a small wind-vane like a fantail on a metal pylon, and is mainly used for drainage and raising water for livestock. Windpumps were built by local agricultural engineers and implement-makers: consequently many varieties were developed.[5]

Windmills had several drawbacks and it is easy to understand why they were superseded by other modes of power. First, the wind could not be relied upon to provide a constant source of power. The mill might stand idle for days on end in a period of calm weather, and conversely in stormy conditions might be badly damaged or even set ablaze if struck by lightning. Second, although the windmill probably generated enough power to drive a few sets of millstones, or to pump water from one level to another, it could not be harnessed on a large enough scale to drive bigger and more sophisticated machinery. Third, wind power was not particularly flexible, for the majority of mills had to be constructed on elevated sites to catch the wind. Clearly this did not facilitate widespread industrial application. These drawbacks resulted in the widespread use of standby power, particularly after the start of the nineteenth century when small stationary steam engines became more cheaply available. Some windmills still have an engine house and chimney stack alongside.

Windmills have been the subject of detailed study and in most areas of the country mills have been surveyed and recorded. The pioneer was Rex Wailes who has devoted a lifetime of study to

Plate 2   Polegate windmill, following renovation by Eastbourne
and District Preservation Society in 1967. Notice the arrangement
of sweeps and fantail.

both wind and water mills, while others have followed up his work at local level.[6] Indeed the scope for further investigation is considerable, particularly more detailed surveys of some of the lesser relics, which have hitherto been neglected. Despite all that has already been achieved in the field of preservation there are still many interesting examples which merit restoration, for example in East Anglia.

Water power

Water power was of far greater importance than wind power, and this particular phase of technological development in the driving of machinery has left an enormous legacy of sites and buildings worth recording. Water power was used from the medieval period to drive a wide variety of plant, including corn, saw, and fulling mills. Later water wheels were applied more widely in the drainage of mines and collieries, and to work machinery in iron forges. In the early stages of industrialization during the eighteenth century water power was the prime mover for numerous industries. Much of the pre-1800 plant that the industrial archaeologist is likely to investigate would probably have relied on water wheels, and at many sites remote from coal supplies water wheels or turbines continued to be important until the present century. The textile industries used water wheels on a large scale, for the majority of wool, cotton, linen and other mills built in the early stages of the Industrial Revolution were located on river and stream sites where power was readily available. This can be seen in the development and archaeology of the woollen industry in the West Country, the West Riding and the Scottish Borders; in the cotton industry, particularly the cotton-spinning mills of Derbyshire, Lancashire and the west of Scotland; and in the linen trade of Ulster and the eastern Scottish Lowlands. At the same period water wheels were adapted to a multitude of functions in collieries, metal-mines and quarries, notably haulage and drainage. The scale of some of these installations was often formidable, and although it would be difficult to match the sheer size of the Lady Isabella water wheel at the Laxey Glen mines on the Isle of Man against many other relics of her type, there is much else of interest in the old metal-mining and quarrying districts of the country, as later examples here indicate. Water power was also used extensively in ironworks to drive bellows in furnaces and tilt hammers and rolling mills in forges and foundries—seen well in the charcoal ironworks of

Ulverston and Argyll, and in the substantial remains at Coalbrookdale.

A variety of means was used both to channel water where it was required and to conserve it in ponds or reservoirs. In the first instance water was dammed back behind a weir and led off by means of a sluice to the mill leat (or 'lade' in Scotland and elsewhere in the north). At the other end of the leat another sluice-gate controlled the flow to the wheel, which, in the breast and overshot types, was generally supplied by a flume or trough. The design of weirs—a study in its own right—evolved from straight structures (of wood and stone) simply built from one bank to the other, to those curved or angled to channel water to the leat with minimal loss. Larger weirs also served to dam back the river or stream, creating a useful reservoir of water (Plate 3). Where a series of mills and weirs was built along a watercourse, efficient use of available resources was of great importance. This often called for skill in both siting and construction of plant, especially in slow-moving water where natural falls did not provide good heads of water and obvious sites for mills. Nixon describes a number of Derbyshire examples on the Derwent and

Plate 3   The great weir of the former cotton mills at Blantyre running across the River Clyde, *c.* 1780.

its tributaries where there are numerous great weirs and dams, typical of larger installations needed to drive textile mills and similar plant.[7] The same techniques can be seen in the construction of dams, ponds and reservoirs for storing water to supplement natural reservoirs where these existed. The hammer ponds of the Wealden iron industry are among the most important relics of this former woodland activity, with large earthen dams built across streams to create reservoirs and provide adequate power for the forges.[8] Wherever water power was used natural or man-made reservoirs of this type will be found, if the flow of water from the river itself was not adequate. In all water-power installations flood waters could be directed away from the wheels by sluices and overflow or side channels. A tailrace carried off the water to the main stream after it had served its purpose.

During a long period of development it was natural that many attempts were made to improve the efficiency of the vertical water wheel, and there are therefore several distinct types to be found. The primary factor in determining the character of the wheel—undershot, breastshot, or overshot—was the height at which the water was applied to the wheel. Probably the earliest wheels were undershot, with paddles or float boards dipping into a flowing river or stream and, like the horizontal wheels of northern Scotland and of Ireland, moved by the force of the water alone. Later, by confining the water to a channel no wider than the wheel, more efficient use could be made of available power. A further development, which we have already noted, was the construction of a mill leat or lade at a higher level than the main stream, taken off some distance upstream of the mill itself. A suitable head of water could also be obtained by using tributaries at points where they fell into the main stream. By these and other means the water could be projected on to the wheel at different points above or below the axle level. The breastshot wheel was usually fitted with buckets rather than paddles or float boards and had built-up rims to retain the water. Thus the wheel was moved by reaction and weight of water, this being sufficient to start momentum. Some primitive Scottish examples, consisting of a single cast-iron ring supporting paddles, were appropriately known as 'start and awa' wheels'. According to the point where the water fell on the breast wheel it was additionally described as 'low breast' or 'high breast'—the latter sometimes 'pitchback'—though there is considerable variation in terminology, which only local knowledge can improve upon. Finally, there is the overshot wheel, where the water is carried by flume to the top of the wheel—a type widely adopted where geography allowed. The relative merits of each type gave rise to considerable controversy, though it was generally agreed that where only a small quantity of water was available, and a fall great enough to place the wheel beneath it could be developed, then the overshot arrangement would be preferred. Where the head of water was smaller, the breast wheel was considered most suitable (Plate 4). The undershot wheel depended solely on the impulse of the water and was often the only type suitable for installation along the banks of slow-moving rivers in areas of low relief.[9]

An enormous range of interesting water wheels and water-power installations can still be seen in most parts of the country, and widespread opportunities exist to examine the different types described. It would be wrong to suggest that a particular type of installation predominates in a specific area, for one can often find great diversity. It is worth remembering that millwrights often followed standard designs found in pattern books (like *The Useful Millwright* or *The Young Millwright's Apprentice*) but adapted them to suit local conditions. Many of the wheels one is likely to discover are of nineteenth-century origin, for a great deal of

Plate 4 Breastshot water wheel at Meadow Hill, Castletown, Isle of Man (SC266691). This imposing limestone mill group was served by a lade from an embanked millpond; the sluice-gates can be seen in the foreground. The wheel is now disused.

refurbishing and reconstruction took place then, especially in the substitution of iron for wood. As this discussion shows, much more than the details of the wheel and its construction needs to be recorded, particularly the construction of the leat or lade, whether a weir or dam is used, the type of drive to the internal machinery (either from the axle via a spur wheel, or from the rim either externally or internally). In the recording of different types of wheel the clock convention is often very useful, for example, '12 o'clock' admirably describes the overshot wheel.[10]

In several parts of the country, particularly the eastern and southern coasts of England, conditions were ideal for the construction and operation of tidemills. Tidemills are generally restricted to low-lying areas around the coast where shallow creeks provide ideal sites. A dam is built across the inlet which has an opening with swing gates which will only open inwards. The incoming tide pushes the gates open and fills the millpond. When the tide ebbs, it closes the gates and traps the water, which can only run out through a sluice built to channel it through the mill. The escaping water turns a water wheel to power the mill. Sometimes the millponds are large—up to thirteen acres—to compensate for the low head of water available. Despite this, tidemills can only be worked for a few hours a day, the actual time varying with tidal conditions. Three or four hours has to elapse after high tide to allow the water to recede sufficiently to create a head of water, and once the water in the pond has been used the miller has to wait for the next tide to resume work.[11] The general layout and internal arrangements resemble those of ordinary water mills. Only a few tidemills survive in anything like original condition: these and the sites of others have been examined in some detail by Wailes and others.[12] A typical example, which has fortunately been restored, is the Eling tidemill (SU365125) in Hampshire (Plate 5). This brick tidemill is built on the seaward side of Eling Causeway which carries a road and toll gate across Eling Creek and acts as the mill dam. The pond, badly silted when visited, is fed by Bartlet Water, but tidal flow from the creek provides most of the water supply. Inside the building are two water wheels placed side by side on different shafts below ground level. Two pairs of stones, two belt shafts, drive gears and the sack hoist all work off the vertical shaft. The grain bins on the second floor are on both sides of the walkway from end to end of the building. Like Eling most tidemills were grain mills.[13]

Another form of water-driven prime mover, the water-pressure engine or hydraulic pump, was fairly widely used in mines and

Plate 5   Eling tidemill, near Southampton (SU365125), showing
restoration work in progress. There are two water wheels side by
side under the ground floor in the middle of the building.

quarries during the eighteenth and nineteenth centuries. The
water-pressure beam engine, as Nixon indicates, was important
in pioneering the use of high pressures and contributed to the
development of the steam engine after the expiry of Watt's
patents made more extensive innovation possible. The engine
worked by the pressure of a head of water (usually provided by
a cistern placed at a higher level than the engine) upon a piston
and could be either single or double acting. Several interesting
relics survive, notably the water-bucket pumps at Wanlockhead,
Dumfriesshire, which have been excavated and described in some
detail by Downs-Rose and Harvey. The best preserved at
NS870131 consists of a fine dressed stone pillar supporting a
wooden beam with iron fittings. It is now in the guardianship of
the Department of the Environment as a historic industrial monument (Plate 6). At the nearby Bay Mine site there is the stone
column of another water engine and the pit of a large water
wheel.[14]

Water turbines were known from the eighteenth century, but
were not used even on a limited scale until the middle of the

Plate 6   Water-bucket engine at Straitsteps lead mine,
Wanlockhead, Dumfriesshire.

following century. Among the pioneers was James Whitelaw, a
Scottish engineer, who installed his first turbine, developing
only a few horsepower, near Paisley in 1839. Subsequently many
more Whitelaw-type reaction turbines were installed elsewhere,
mainly to drive threshing or grain mills. Another engineer, James
Thomson, adapted French designs to produce a Vortex turbine,

which was installed in some numbers after 1850. Many other designs—including the American Francis-types—were adopted, but in general terms turbines remained relatively rare despite their obvious advantages over conventional water wheels.[15] Turbines were often installed by enthusiastic landowners to drive machinery on their estates or to generate electricity. One such was Lord Armstrong, the Tyneside shipbuilder, who had several turbines on his estate at Cragside near Rothbury (Northumberland). The saw-mill (NU066027) is driven by a turbine, as is the thresher and other equipment.[16] In other instances turbines replaced water wheels in grain mills and other plant, where the power required was modest, or conditions were particularly suited to retaining a water-power installation rather than converting to steam.

Two areas in particular have interesting associations with the development of water turbines, Cumbria and Ulster, and both preserve some interesting examples of early installations. One of the leading makers, Gilbert Gilkes and Gordon is based in Kendal. The firm's first turbine built in 1856 is on view in their main machine shop. Not surprisingly many of their products were installed locally, a good example being at Staveley Gatefoot Mills (SD467983) which is a 29 hp vertical-shaft Gilkes turbine.[17] A number of Ulster engineers were also pioneer turbine builders and a great number of turbines were installed in the Province, including some large ones for the generation of electricity. These have been listed and described by Gribbon in his study of water power in Ulster.[18] After the 1880s in Ulster, as elsewhere, turbines were more widely used to generate electric power (see pp. 223–4).

Steam power

Steam power more than any other motive force is traditionally regarded as the great prime mover of the Industrial Revolution. Certainly, there can be little doubt that it was of enormous importance to nineteenth-century industry and transport, and has therefore left substantial relics to interest the industrial archaeologist. The development of the steam engine pre-dates the classic industrialization era by at least a century. Significantly the early engines developed by Thomas Newcomen at the beginning of the eighteenth century were built at Cornish tin mines and at Midland collieries. When the patent rights on the less successful engine invented by Thomas Savery ultimately expired about 1733, many 'common engines' on the Newcomen model were built in mining districts. What was described as a 'surprising machine for raising water by fire' soon had many exponents despite its insatiable appetite for coal and its relative inefficiency. A veritable succession of engineers, including John Smeaton, was responsible for a number of improvements, mainly in materials and accuracy of construction. Even so, the atmospheric engines were thermally very inefficient and remained so until 1765 when James Watt began his experiments with the separate condenser. The condensing engine patent was obtained in 1769, and in 1775 Watt was granted rights for twenty-five years, covering both England and Scotland. His partnership with Matthew Boulton dated from the same period, and while production of Boulton and Watt improved atmospheric engines went ahead, Watt himself began the development of the rotative engine. The first rotative engine—installed in 1783—drove a tilt hammer in the Bradley Forge of John Wilkinson. This opened the way to more widespread use of rotary motion to drive machinery of many kinds, notably in textile mills, collieries, metal-mines and ironworks.[19] Subsequently, the nineteenth century saw the development of many types of steam engine including the compound, vertical and horizontal engines. These and others have been described for industrial archaeologists by George Watkins, who has devoted a lifetime of study and research to the history of steam power. We will deal here with some of the commonest types likely to be found, and with some means of applying steam power in different plant.[20]

The Cornish pump, a single-acting non-rotative beam engine, probably comes nearest in actual appearance to the early atmospheric engines of the eighteenth century. It was developed, as its name suggests, to provide economical power in metal mines where fuel was expensive. The steam was admitted above the piston, which, as it descended, lifted through the beam the heavy pump rods in the shaft. The steam was then cut off and the stroke completed by the momentum of the pump rods. Then an equilibrium valve was opened, allowing steam to pass from the upper to the lower side of the piston. The heavy rods then descended, thus raising the water by ram pumps attached to the rods. After this stroke the valve was closed, and with the piston at the top of the cylinder the next cycle could proceed. The Cornish engine was used widely for water pumping not only in mines but also in waterworks. An interesting example, currently under restoration, can be seen at Prestongrange (NT373737) East Lothian, where it forms the focal point of a museum of mining. It was built by Harvey of Hayle in 1874 to pump water from 800 ft

(244 m). The beam weighs more than 30 tons and is 33 ft (10 m) long by 6 ft (1.8 m) deep at the centre, the fulcrum being 18 ft (5.5 m) from the steam end. The cylinder is 70 in. (177 cm) in diameter. The normal speed was 3½ strokes per minute and the pumping capacity was 650 gallons per minute allowing an efficiency of 70 per cent. The engine was enlarged in 1895 and continued to be fully operational until 1954.[21]

The single cylinder 'house-built' rotative beam engine was another common type, widely used for pumping and in mills. It was still being manufactured for use in waterworks as late as the 1880s. The cross girder under the centre of the beam was actually built into the walls of the engine house—hence the term 'house-built'. Most of the major parts, like the cylinder, the iron columns supporting the beam, and the crankshaft bearings, were fixed to the foundations. In mills it was common to find the drive taken off by spur gearing to another shaft which would transmit power to the machinery, while in waterworks the pumps were generally arranged on either side of the beam centre. The compound beam engine brought further refinements, particularly substantial reduction in heat loss, by placing the high and low pressure cylinders at the same end of the beam. The pistons therefore moved together, but the stress on the centre of the beam was considerable. Many small versions of this type were installed in corn mills, while some large ones were installed in waterworks. The Ryhope Pumping Station at Sunderland preserves two fine 100 hp double-acting rotative beam engines built by R. and W. Hawthorne of Newcastle upon Tyne in 1867–70 and capable of delivering 40,000 gallons of water per hour. The engines are splendid examples of Victorian engineering design (see Fig. 7, p. 218), with finely restrained ornamentation, particularly on the parallel linkages, valve chests and valve gear. The beam of each engine is of double construction, measuring some 33 ft (10 m) between the pump rod centres, and weighing approximately 22 tons. Originally the engines ran at 10 r.p.m., lifting water in two stages to be discharged to the surface reservoir. The original six Cornish boilers were replaced by three Lancashire types in 1908.[22]

Other important beam-engine types include the McNaught (which dates from 1845) and the 'A-frame' model, so called because of the 'A'-shaped frames used to support the beam centre bearings. The former (Plate 7) was widely used after the mid nineteenth century and had the advantage of working at higher pressures than previously. It was very efficient, and gave greatly increased power output with reduced fuel consumption. After 1870 most beam engines installed in mills were of this type. The

Plate 7   No. 1 beam engine at Jameson's Bow Street distillery,
Dublin.

latter was one of several designs developed to meet the demand
for a cheap and easily constructed engine. Unlike the Ryhope
engine and many others, the 'A-frame' models were often completely devoid of ornament and were purely functional.

'Inverted' engines had the cylinder placed above the crankshaft, and the more familiar term 'vertical' was later applied to
these types. In the typical vertical engine the crankshaft was
overhead with the cylinder on or below the floor. The vertical
engine was widely used, especially in Yorkshire textile mills and
to drive colliery winding engines in County Durham. Many of
the larger engines were later fitted with high pressure cylinders
to make them more efficient.

The horizontal engine was extremely popular and was used to
power machinery universally after 1845. Richard Trevithick built
a horizontal engine in 1802, but there were problems with heavy
wear on the cylinder and for many years engineers were reluctant
to use the model. Most of the later models were single cylinder,

non-condensing, slide valve types, although twin cylinder models of up to 120 hp were also built. Other types of horizontal engine included the tandem compound engine, the cross compound engine, and the triple expansion engine, which were made in a variety of powers. Larger ones were used in cotton mills, rolling mills and other plant. Very large triple expansion engines with four cylinders of up to 3,500 hp were installed in textile mills, and up to 6,000 hp in generating stations following the introduction of electric power. The ultimate development in this connection was the steam turbine, which also had numerous industrial applications.

Several semi-portable and portable engines were developed, mainly to provide greater flexibility than the static types. The combined vertical boiler and engine was very compact and of simple design, so that it could be easily erected and maintained. Most produced only a small amount of power and were ideally suited for installation in country mills (such as corn or bobbin mills) or to drive threshing and other machinery on farms. An under-type, which had the engine placed underneath the barrel of the boiler, was altogether larger; some could produce up to 150 hp. Portable engines had many applications, for the whole power unit could be moved from site to site, again particularly in the country, where they drove saw-mills and other farm mills. The traction engine was an even more mobile version of the portable engine. A general purpose machine, it commonly drove portable threshing machines, as well as performing a multitude of industrial functions.

The colliery winding engine merits a special mention, since it is a common relic in colliery districts—although many have been lost in recent years. Many different types of engine were used to drive colliery winding gear, including the beam, double tandem compound, vertical, diagonal, and the double cylinder horizontal engine. The last was commonly used toward the end of the last century, the rope drum being placed between the cranks. These engines needed to be very powerful and to run at both fast and slow speeds. Adequate brakes were clearly of great importance, for complete control by the engineman was essential in winding men and materials; over-wind safety devices gradually became standard to eliminate the worst effects of human error. A good example of the mid nineteenth century vertical colliery winding engine has been re-erected at the North of England Open Air Museum at Beamish, while in South Wales the remains of beam engines and a later engine house at Glyn Pits (ST265999) near Pontypool, dating from 1845, are of considerable interest. The engine was a double-acting single cylinder engine pumping from a shaft 186 yds (170 m) deep and delivering water to a roadway 85 yds (78 m) from the surface.[23] The winding engine raised cages from a similar depth. There are several interesting north Staffordshire examples, notably the preserved engine house and headgear at Hanley Deep Pit (SJ885484), now an outstanding feature of Hanley Central Forest Park.[24]

Other aspects of steam power technology are of concern to the industrial archaeologist, including the recording of drive mechanisms and the different types of boilers used to raise steam for the plant previously described. Much will be said in subsequent chapters of power transmission and driving mechanisms in a variety of industrial plant, the four main ones being (1) direct drive, (2) toothed gear drive, (3) rope drive, (4) belt drive. Direct drive, as the description suggests, involved taking power directly from the steam engine. This was done by coupling the main driving shaft of the plant to the engine's crankshaft, while smaller machines were driven from line shafts worked by rope drive or belts. Wall engines were low-powered, rarely exceeding 100 hp, and often much less. Toothed gear drive involved the use of a 'second motion' or underground shaft which carried power to a vertical shaft reaching up through the floors in the mill. Bevel wheels on each floor allowed power to be taken off where required. Rope drive was common in mills large and small, and consisted of circular fibre ropes, which ran in v-shaped grooves turned in the driving by pulley wheels. Separate rope drives carried power to various floors of the mill. The system was efficient and economic—often ropes lasted thirty years. Flat belt drive was also universal and consisted of leather or fabric fixed with a metal fastener. Large belts were used to drive line shafts, with smaller belts carrying power off to the machines or other equipment as required, seen at best in textile mills. Small belts were widely used in wind and water mills, and in such plant as bobbin mills.[25]

The opportunities to survey and record steam-power installations have been sadly reduced in recent years, though much has already been achieved through the work of enthusiasts like George Watkins at the Centre for the Study of the History of Technology at Bath University. His work over many years has resulted in an invaluable archive on the history of the steam engine and of steam power. On both subjects he is an international expert—industrial archaeologists can learn much from his publications. At the same time other enthusiasts have been actively involved in the conservation and restoration of historic steam engines, and the list of preserved engines is still growing. As with much else in industrial archaeology awareness of just how important such artefacts can be has done a great deal to encourage practical conservation.

Electrical power

The generation of electricity will be reviewed later in the context of public services and utilities. Electric power was not adopted widely in industrial plant until the close of the nineteenth century, though small-scale use of water turbines and steam engines to generate electricity was quite common from the 1880s. The industrial archaeologist is likely to come across electric-power installations in a variety of plant and where these are clearly of historic interest details should be recorded. Electric motors, as Angus Buchanan has indicated, have been applied to almost everything requiring power, so the scope for recording both now and in the future is considerable.[26]

Other means of power, such as the gas engine and the internal combustion engine, ought to be mentioned. The gas engine was developed successfully in the 1870s and was adopted where small amounts of power were required, for example, in sewage pumping stations. Small gas engines were also installed in mills to replace water or wind power. The internal combustion engine with its use of oil fuels had more widespread application, and in the long term created its own important archaeology. This development is perhaps more properly regarded as transport history, though clearly there are many artefacts of outstanding interest to the industrial archaeologist.

Power is a dominant theme in industrial archaeology and it is therefore of great importance for practitioners of the subject to have an understanding of the main types and their respective chronologies. Power installations are often of great interest in themselves, and water and wind mills are amongst the most attractive features likely to be found. Despite the detailed survey work already undertaken much remains to be done, and in the field of preservation there are limitless possibilities for those with the enthusiasm and determination.

4
Agriculture, Processing and Rural Crafts

Agriculture, primary processing and rural industries have left an important and widespread legacy which in its own way constitutes a major part of the country's industrial archaeology. There were few areas of the British Isles which were unaffected by an important Agricultural Revolution that accompanied the process of industrialization during the eighteenth and nineteenth centuries. Innovation was just as critical to successful entrepreneurship in agriculture and related processing activities as it was in other industries, and therefore many technological developments took place in the countryside particularly in the period 1750–1850. New plant and buildings appeared on the land and many existing installations were reconstructed and updated. Model farms incorporating the latest equipment—such as dairies, grain mills and threshing machines—were designed and built by enthusiastic 'improvers' with an eye to the future and an awareness for efficiency and saving labour. This is not to say that farm mechanization was universal before the turn of the present century, for in many districts, particularly the more remote where subsistence farming lasted longest, the old ways survived into the age of 'the electric'. A great many features of interest to the industrial archaeologist can be found on the farm: the farm buildings themselves (often arranged in a courtyard layout); early machinery and processing plant, such as implements and dairy equipment; and a wide variety of farm mills, mainly winnowers or threshing mills.

The primary processing industries—milling, tanning, brewing and distilling—owed their rapid eighteenth-century expansion to the increased demand produced by a rapidly growing population. Here too the new technology was important, although perhaps less so than the existing techniques which were increased in scale. Investment in primary processing industries was a logical consequence of capitalist farming on the part of landowners, and hence plant was built in or near estate villages or in market towns. Given adequate transport facilities wider markets could be exploited, and it was not long before the processing industries began to expand in urban centres themselves. Much larger plant was therefore constructed, well illustrated in the development of urban breweries during the classic Industrial Revolution period. The most interesting remains to the industrial archaeologist are grain mills (mainly water, wind and steam powered) with their ancillary equipment like kilns and granaries, tanneries and leatherworks, breweries, distilleries and maltings. Other important plant concerned the processing of hops and sugar beet and the manufacture of cider and mineral waters.

Many traditional crafts helped to maintain the fabric of the community in days gone by and although by no means all are the direct concern of industrial archaeology, some at least command attention because of the tools and skills used. One activity of considerable importance was woodworking and timber crafts. Timber was certainly of prime significance as a building material, in the construction of machinery and in the manufacture of a wide variety of products ranging from bobbins to barrels. Sawmills and woodworking plant generally are of considerable interest. They are most often found in areas with good timber supplies close at hand, for example Galloway or Cumbria, both of which also had ready markets for their products in the textile mills of the west of Scotland and Lancashire. Apart from burning, timber was widely used as an industrial raw material—for instance, in the production of charcoal for iron smelting or the manufacture of gunpowder and as a tanning agent. The millwright made extensive use of both timber and iron in the construction of much of the machinery in mills and other plant and hence his particular craft is of some concern to the industrial archaeologist. Agriculture and many of the processing trades required simple metal machinery and tools—mainly provided by country smithies or small forges in nearby market towns. Wayside smithies also had an important function servicing turnpike road traffic (see pp. 165–8).

Some would no doubt argue that much of what we have described as 'rural archaeology' has little to offer the industrial archaeologist. But we take the view that agriculture is in itself an industry of major importance which played a critical role in the economic growth of Britain during the past two hundred years. Not only should we regard agriculture as an industry in its own right, but we ought to have equivalent respect for its particular terminology. Both the industry and its historic artefacts are worth recording, as many pioneers and present practitioners in the industrial archaeological field have found. Major surveys have been undertaken of mills and other features in different parts of the country, while many of the existing regional surveys devote attention to agriculture and related industries. Yet many relics still remain to be surveyed and recorded in both countryside and town and the scope for further work is therefore considerable.

Farm buildings

Farm architecture and the layout of buildings in and around the farm are of considerable interest to the industrial archaeologist. Traditional farm buildings can be found in great numbers in different parts of the country, each area having its own distinctive style and use of raw materials. The vernacular architecture of, for example, the West Riding or Cumbria, is seen both in the farmhouse and in farm buildings like the byre, hay loft, granary, and dairy.[1] When mills of various kinds came to be built on farms, they too were constructed in the vernacular architecture of the district with simple modifications to accommodate machinery including threshers, horse wheels and water wheels. The earlier farmsteads retain much of interest, particularly in their outbuildings. In the north of Scotland and elsewhere many farmsteads were equipped with primitive corn kilns for drying grain, features seen at their best in Caithness and Orkney.[2] More sophisticated kilns—akin to those in maltings—were later incorporated in corn mills, particularly in the wetter parts of the country. In the richer cereal lands of south-east Britain the granary was often the most important building—plenty of pre-Agricultural Revolution examples can still be found.[3]

New farm buildings were necessary in the late eighteenth and early nineteenth centuries not just because existing buildings were old-fashioned and inefficient, but because of the rearrangement of estates and farms taking place at the time. Well-designed buildings were an important aspect of estate management, and some splendid farm buildings were constructed by improving landowners and farmers. The buildings on the average farm fall into three groups: those to house livestock—stables, byres, cowsheds and piggeries; those used for storing crops, such as barns and granaries; and the house for the farmer or steward.[4] A quadrangular layout was popular on many 'model' farms, with separate units for various functions, notably the housing of stock and poultry (Fig. 3).[5] The threshing mill was also generally incorporated in the layout. The agricultural revival of the mid nineteenth century saw the construction of fine Victorian farm buildings, some of which applied technical developments of the

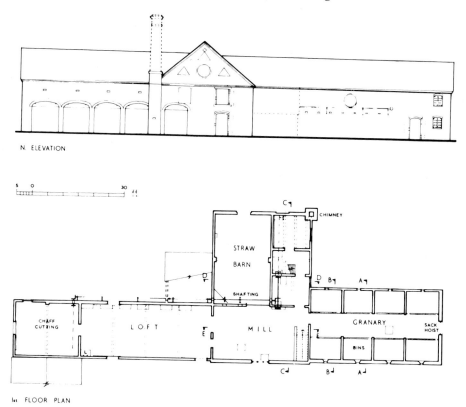

N. ELEVATION

1st FLOOR PLAN

Fig. 3 Threshing barn and associated buildings, Drayton Manor,
Penkridge, Staffordshire (after Peters, 1969).

period such as the use of steam power or electricity in various
farm processes. Few were on the scale of that at Buscot Park
(Berkshire) but many examples of less ambitious 'model' farms
can be found and are worth recording.[6] But the main concern of
the industrial archaeologist is farm machinery, to which we now
turn.

Threshing mills driven by horse, water, wind, and steam power
can be found on farms throughout the countryside, especially in
the west and north. Although the threshing machine invented
by Andrew Meikle, the East Lothian millwright, had its precur-
sors, the mill which he perfected in 1786 quickly spread throughout Scotland and the north of England. Rotary motion held the
key to success, and Meikle's patented machine incorporated
revolving drums which knocked the grain free of the straw and
chaff. The great advantage of the Meikle machine was its relative

cheapness and adaptability to various forms of power. It could be driven by horse levers, water wheel, wind power, and after the 1800s by a stationary steam engine. Simpler, and cheaper, versions were subsequently developed (some worked by hand) and are commonly found in the south and east. The threshing mill itself is readily identifiable, consisting of a rectangular single or two-storied barn housing the machine, and, if the prime mover was enclosed, an appended structure containing it. The cheapest and probably most flexible power was provided by horses, so horse wheel houses (sometimes called 'gins' or 'gangs') are very common. They can be found in a variety of shapes and sizes—circular, hexagonal, octagonal—fully or partially enclosed with roofs supported on stone or iron columns. An example from Berwick Hill (Northumberland) now at the North of England Open Air Museum at Beamish is fairly typical, having a diameter of about 25 ft (7.5 m), stone built and roofed in slate. Up to six horses could be harnessed to the wheel and power was transmitted by gearing to the thresher in the adjoining barn.[7] Many of the open varieties found in the south were worked at ground level. Water power was also widely used to drive threshing machines and the installations are akin to those in water-driven corn mills. The water wheel is often located on a gable end of the mill, the drive being again by gearing through the wall to the machine. In some instances the wheel is enclosed in a lean-to structure. Wind power was not commonly used to drive threshers because it was so expensive, but even so a number of examples of farm mills using wind survive. When small stationary steam engines became more efficient and readily available they were installed in considerable numbers on the larger farms to drive threshing machines and other equipment. The engine house with its chimney stack is often an incongruous sight in the middle of the countryside and although many good examples can be found they are individually worth detailed record. The East Lothian Farm Survey carried out in 1968 identified 27 steam-powered threshing and other mills out of the 130 or so recorded—not surprising in an area where coal could be cheaply obtained.[8] Here, as elsewhere, the cautious farmer had two prime movers, in event of breakdown or, in the case of water power, drought or severe frost. Many interesting surveys of these features have already been undertaken and they provide an indication of the scope that exists elsewhere for further investigations.[9]

Dairying has left its own peculiar buildings with a wide range of artefacts now more readily found in folk museums than on the farm. The farm dairy would be equipped with a butter churn and cheese press and in parts of the country where cheesemaking was a speciality many would have a cheese-loft. Butter churns and cheese presses are readily identified: the former is generally a round wooden barrel-like vessel with a plunger or handle; the latter, a device for pressing cheeses as they mature, consists of two heavy stone or flat iron plates manipulated by turning a screw (Plate 8). When railways penetrated the countryside after 1850 the larger commercial dairy and creamery became more common, often established in redundant grain mills near the railway. Examples in areas like Devon, Somerset, Derbyshire and Dumfries and Galloway date from the 1870s and 80s and were originally steam-powered.[10]

Plate 8   Cheese press at Reay, Caithness.

A building type peculiar to Kent and parts of Sussex is the oast-house used to dry hops, an important flavouring agent in beer. The oast-house, equipped with its kiln, was stone or brick built, often circular and topped by a conical roof, wooden ventilator and wind-vane. The furnace was at ground level with the drying room and cooling floors above. An adjacent storeroom housed a press which was used to pack the dried hops into sacks prior to despatch for the brewery. The majority of surviving oast-houses date from the mid nineteenth century and many have been wholly or partially converted to dwellings.

Elsewhere, changing economic fortunes have helped to create rural industrial archaeology. Such has been the contraction of glass-house horticulture in recent years that large acreages of hothouses have had to be abondoned. Influenced by the close proximity of urban markets, large-scale expansion dates from the 1880s, principally for the growth of tomatoes, lettuces, cucumbers and flowers. The most important concentrations of glass-houses included the Lea Valley, western Essex, north-west Kent, Hampshire, parts of Lancashire, and the Clyde Valley south of Glasgow. Glass-houses were heated by steam, which was also used to sterilize the soil before planting. Many old houses still preserve a boiler house, steam engine and chimney stack.

One final crop and processing activity which merits mention is sugar-beet. Sugar was first produced commercially from beet in France during the Napoleonic Wars when hostilities restricted cane-sugar supplies from the West Indies. Experiments in extraction began in Britain c. 1830 and the first large-scale plant was opened in 1912. Sugar-beet works are typified by that at Cupar (NO390150) in Fife—recently closed—which has a large concrete storage silo adjacent to the extraction works.

Mills and milling

Milling was undoubtedly the most widespread processing industry and there are therefore opportunities to investigate old mills in most parts of the country. Many mill sites are of great antiquity, but most survivals are of eighteenth- or nineteenth-century origin, since mill building and reconstruction coincided with peaks of activity in agriculture, particularly in the century 1750–1850. Although milling was traditionally a rural industry, larger mills were also built in the towns and at ports, the latter being especially significant in the second half of the nineteenth century with the increase in grain imports from abroad. The larger mills are often found adjacent to granaries, warehouses and other stores in former grain centres. Few other generalizations on chronology can safely be made, except perhaps to emphasize the great variations from one part of the country to another. In many country areas of the north and west, mills of the type common in the south of England since the medieval period were not constructed until the late eighteenth century, but conversely mills in some remote districts remained in use long after those in the more economically advanced areas had been abandoned. There were almost as many stages in the decline of mills and milling as there had been in their development; only careful research and field-work will reveal the pattern in one particular locality.

Before examining the two main types of corn mill—the water mill and the windmill—we ought to mention the traditional horizontal mills of the Northern Isles, the Western Highlands, the Isle of Man, and of Ireland. This was a logical development of the hand mill (or rotary quern) driven by a horizontal water wheel resembling a primitive turbine. One of the best surviving examples at Dounby (Plate 9) on Orkney is in the care of the Department of the Environment. It consists of two compartments: an upper, housing the hopper, millstones and flour box; and a lower chamber containing the horizontal mill wheel.[11] Other restored examples are to be found in Shetland and the Western Isles, while Bowie has described two interesting Irish examples from County Roscommon and County Mayo which both retain substantially original features including the wheels.[12]

The general arrangement of plant and machinery is common to most grain mills, no matter what form of power was adopted. The machinery consists of a prime mover (water wheel, windmill, steam or other engine), linked by driving mechanism and gearing to the milling equipment, usually stones or rollers. Power is also provided for ancillary equipment like sieves and bruisers, and to operate hoists for lifting sacks and other gear. The layout of a typical large country mill is well illustrated by an example at Sutton upon Derwent (SE704474), surveyed by Allison in 1970. The mill range of brick and tile with stone dressings is three storeys high with lofts above. Iron columns support the first and second floors. The two undershot water wheels survive, together with the hubs of both pit wheels, the majority of driving machinery being located at semi-basement and ground level. The mill had seven pairs of stones, four driven from one wheel and three from the other, to which power was supplied by drive shafts. The lofts provided storage space for sacks, and a group of adjacent buildings included a drying kiln.[13] The same plan was followed

Plate 9   Click mill at Dounby, Orkney (HY325228), showing (*above*)
the exterior with wheel pit in right basement, and (*opposite*)
interior, with hopper stones and flour box at ground-floor level.

in more modest water mills and in windmills where space was
limited. These smaller mills abound and often possess original
fixtures. Most were two storeys high, built of sandstone and
roofed in pantiles, as Preston Mill, East Lothian (NT595779), now
in the care of the National Trust for Scotland and restored to full
working order (Plate 10). In this instance a circular corn kiln is
detached from the main mill range. A six-spoke, wood and iron
low-breast wheel drives two pairs of stones, and also powers
ancillary equipment including sieves and a hoist. The wheel is
located in one gable, while inside the mill the spur wheel and
most of the other gearing is housed in a wooden gear cupboard—a
common safety feature. The circular brick-lined kiln is joined to
the mill by a small wooden bridge. Charcoal or wood and later
coke was burned in a small furnace at ground level, the hot air
rising to a drying floor of perforated iron tiles at the level above.[14]

The same general layout can be seen in a windmill, though
often under more cramped conditions in the smaller examples.
Most of the key features are illustrated by the finely-preserved
windmill at Ballycopeland, County Down (Plate 11)—saved for

posterity through the foresight of its last miller, who gave it to the then Northern Ireland government in 1935. Guardianship was assumed by the Ministry of Finance in 1937 and extensive repairs were carried out, particularly to the windcap, fantail and sails. The existence of dry rot and woodworm caused the virtual renewal in 1958 of the main flooring and internal machinery, which was carefully copied from the original in new timber. At the same time an engine house built for a steam engine was

Plate 10   Preston Mill, East Lothian, with the millpond in the foreground and the circular, pantiled kiln behind. The main mill range may be seen on the right.

demolished and the exterior of the mill restored to its original finish in modern materials. Ballycopeland was built some time after 1788 in the era of widespread corn production and mill reconstruction during the French and Napoleonic Wars. It is a typical tower windmill of the period, probably built by local craftsmen using designs from the north of England. The tower is 33 ft (10 m) high with an external ground diameter of 22 ft (6.8 m) tapering to 17 ft (5 m) at the top on walls 2 ft (61 cm) thick. The mill has a wooden, boat-shaped revolving cap with an

Plate 11   Ballycopeland windmill, County Down (O.S. 6/579761),
the only complete windmill surviving in this county, ceased
working in 1915 and is now preserved.

automatic fantail and four great patent sails. Of the under-drift
type, the mill has hopper, stone, gear (or drive) and ground
floors—all maintained and equipped as they would have been in
its working days. There are three sets of millstones including
pairs from Derbyshire and Germany. Ballycopeland exhibits
numerous features of a mill constructed at a period when windmill technology had reached its peak. It is certainly the best
preserved and most complete example of the type once common
in East Anglia, northern England, Scotland and Ireland, and

59

found elsewhere in large numbers where tower mills were constructed.[15]

Water and wind mills have been the subject of detailed field research and recording in most parts of the country. The majority of regional and local studies on industrial archaeology provide details of the most significant molinological features, while many areas have been covered by specialist studies such as those undertaken in the English counties by Wailes and others, and published in the *Transactions of the Newcomen Society*. The existence of these and other surveys need not deter the industrial archaeologist with an enthusiasm for water and wind mills, for much needs to be done to record features where detailed surveys have not yet been undertaken, and to up-date work completed some years ago.[16]

Tanning, leatherworking and related industries

From the medieval period onward tanning and leather processing were important and widespread industries, a consequence both of the importance of leather as a raw material and the significant part sheep and cattle played in the agrarian economy. Tanning developed early in the main market centres of the countryside and the industry remained dispersed in small units until the beginning of the nineteenth century, when—like so many agricultural processing industries—it became increasingly concentrated in larger factory units. The actual techniques of tanning were more complex than might be realized, although the materials required were simple enough—water and a tanning agent like bark. An early-nineteenth-century description of tanning indicates that it could be a long-term business, anything from six to eighteen months depending on the quality and weight of leather involved.[17] The hides were laid out in heaps in the tan-yard, prior to being hung in a smokehouse or kiln, and afterwards stripped of hair. The tanning then began, skins being washed at frequent intervals and moved from one tan-pit to another—fresh water and bark being added in the process. When tanning was complete the leather was hung on poles to dry—outside in the tan-yard during fair weather or in drying rooms at other times—and then smoothed with wooden hammers akin to those used in fulling. The description gives some clues to the type of plant and building in which tanning was undertaken. The typical country tannery would often be located near the local cattle market or slaughterhouse, probably on the banks of a river or stream or adjacent to convenient wells for ease of water supply needed for the various processes. The tan-yard would have rows of pits or vats with a watercourse, pipes and pumps to carry water where required. The tannery or tan-house would be a long, low building of no more than two storeys, the ground floor being of stone or brick and the upper floor timber-framed and slatted to allow for ventilation and free circulation of air within the drying house and stores. If the tannery was equipped with steel rolling mills and wooden beaters it might well have a water wheel or steam engine to provide the necessary power. Elsewhere in the tan-yard would be a bark store and probably a mill for grinding the bark. In towns where tanning was important the skinning processes were carried on in separate plant, so that cleaned skins could go directly to the tanneries.

Tanning was important in many parts of the country, notably the West Country, Northamptonshire, Cumbria, central Scotland and Ireland, although in most towns of any size elsewhere the trade was represented. Cumbria developed a successful tanning trade because of the local availability of both hides and tan-bark, but most of the units were small. In 1850 there were no fewer than 33 tanneries producing 60,000 tanned hides per annum in Northern Cumbria alone, and a further 57 tanneries in southern Lakeland, 21 of which were in the Furness district and 23 in the town of Kendal. One such tannery at Yarl Well, Dalton-in-Furness comprised in 1821 a large tan-yard containing 23 bark pits, 5 scouring pits, 2 lime pits, a large water pit, bark-house, drying house, and a bark mill powered by water wheel.[18] Few small tanneries of this type survive, though there is a number of larger plant dating from the eighteenth century. Starmer has indicated the scope for investigation in Northamptonshire, where the leather, boot and shoe industries are still of considerable importance, while Hudson and Hume have surveyed remains in their respective areas of southern England and the Scottish Lowlands.[19] The fact is that tannery buildings and machinery tend to be destroyed very quickly after they fall idle—mainly because of the offensive nature of the trade and its effluents. So where any relics survive they are well worth recording.

Of some interest are the related trades of soap and glue manufacture, as well as a variety of leatherworking crafts. Soap-boiling was an important consumer industry by the eighteenth century, the soap itself being manufactured by boiling tallow with caustic potash derived from the ash of wood, bracken or seaweed. Soap-making, like tanning, was at first widely dispersed but became increasingly concentrated in larger units at seaports due to the increased use of imported raw materials. By 1851 two-thirds of all soap manufactured in England was produced in Liverpool, London and Bristol, and country soap-makers were gradually disappearing. Hardly anything remains of this once important industry and the industrial archaeologist will probably have to be content with noting place names associated with soap-making.[20]

Leatherworking was almost as widespread as tanning and soap-boiling, for as well as being an important item in the manufacture of footwear, clothing, saddlery, etc., leather was used in the construction of machinery, for example belt drives and bellows. Footwear manufacture was originally an exclusively domestic trade, as was the case in Northampton, Norwich and Street before the mid nineteenth century. With the development of the sewing machine the scene was set for the development of factory production. Many of the Victorian industrial buildings in Northampton were originally built for boot and shoe manufacture. Bearing in mind that these were built mainly during the third quarter of the nineteenth century when much of the industry moved into the factories, it is hardly surprising that there are comparatively few signs of domestic workshops in the immediate environs of the town. But the boot and shoe makers' shops are still to be seen in other Northamptonshire towns and villages—in Long Buckby domestic craftsmen were still at work in the traditional way in 1969.[21] The organization of the West Country gloving industry closely resembled that of boot and shoe making during the nineteenth century and was widely distributed throughout Hampshire, Wiltshire, Somerset and Dorset.

The drink industries

The drink industries—notably brewing, distilling, cider-making and mineral water manufacture—have left an interesting archaeology and series of relics. Malting was an important ancillary activity to both brewing and distilling. It was sometimes carried on in separate plant, much of it of considerable interest to the industrial archaeologist. Brewing, distilling and cider-making were all three esentially craft activities until the mid eighteenth century. Brewing—already an industry of consequence in England, the Lowlands of Scotland, and around Dublin in Ireland by 1750—was one of the first to experience large-scale factory production. Nevertheless, many small country breweries continued to brew in market towns all over the country. Distilling followed, with factory-style production well established in Scotland and Ireland by the 1800s. As with brewing, fiscal policy encouraged such developments since it was easier to collect excise from a limited number of large distilleries, than from the countless (often illicit) stills which dominated the trade before the end of the eighteenth century. Cider-making was locally important in the south of England, particularly in Devon, Somerset and Hereford. The majority of plant was located on farms in the orchard country and factory production was not established until the mid nineteenth century. Mineral water manufacture originated from the bottling of natural spring water before the general availability of pure drinking water in towns. Carbonized minerals were introduced in the early part of the nineteenth century and some of the firms operating in the industry at the present time can trace their origins back to that period.

Brewing is essentially a flow process and therefore the typical brewery—even the small unit such as Clinch's brewery on the Isle of Man—is a tall building of three or more storeys so that gravity can be used as much as possible in the movement of grain and liquid from stage to stage (Plate 12). In the larger breweries buildings are often ranged around a courtyard and include the brewhouse itself, maltings, stores, cooperage, stables and office. Water supply was of prime importance and the well is often a central feature in the brewery premises. The brewhouse equipment consists of a malt mill, water storage tanks, coppers, mash tuns, fermenting tuns and cooling plant. Most nineteenth-century breweries of any size had a steam engine to drive machinery and pump water from the well and for cooling purposes. Few working breweries are likely to preserve original equipment, but despite many losses through demolition or closure brought about by amalgamation, there are still many interesting breweries around the country.

London quickly established itself as one of the major centres of English brewing and it therefore holds much to interest the industrial archaeologist. Two of the major plants date from the mid eighteenth century: the famous Chiswell Street Brewery of Whitbread (TQ326819), the only brewery in the city, has buildings dating from 1750 and a Porter Tun room built in 1773; while Truman's Brewery in Brick Lane (TQ338820) dates in part from 1756. Another fine survival is the Ram Brewery, Wandsworth (TQ256747) of Young and Company, where several eighteenth- and nineteenth-century buildings of interest remain (Plate 13). Here the mashing and milling machinery is driven by one of two simple beam engines—one of 16 hp dating from 1835, the

Plate 12 Clinch's Lake Brewery, built 1779 on the North Quay at Douglas, Isle of Man, was extensively altered *c.* 1868. The height of the building is typical of breweries, where gravity was used to facilitate the movement of materials from floor to floor.

other 20 hp built in 1867—both by Wentworth and Sons of Wandsworth. The brewery is famous for its stud of Shire horses which are still used for local deliveries. Finally, the Anchor Brewery, Southwark (TQ324803), mainly nineteenth century in origin, preserves a number of interesting buildings in its large complex.[22]

Plate 13 One of two Woolf compound rotative beam engines (1835 and 1867) at the Ram Brewery of Young and Company in Wandsworth, London.

Although London eventually dominated the brewing industry in England it would be invidious to overlook the archaeological possibilities in the other great brewing centres—notably, Burton upon Trent, Edinburgh and Dublin. In Burton despite widespread demolitions and alterations there are many features worth noting, including the Albion Brewery (SK231233), an impressive red-brick building with adjacent cooperage (now the engineer's shop) and stables (now stores). The brewers Mann, Crossman and Paulin built workers' housing near by as well as community facilities, for example a church and hotel. There are many buildings of interest in the Bass Breweries' complex, especially the Middle Brewery (SK247232) of 1853, New Brewery (246230) of 1864, and a series of maltings in Wetmore Road (252236) and at Shobnall (234229). The Clarence Street Brewery (241225) of 1883 incorporates maltings with an odd octagonal kiln.[23] The Edinburgh breweries and maltings have also undergone considerable change in recent years; however, the St Ann's Brewery, Holyrood (NT269741), St Leonards Brewery (264730) and Caledonian Brewery (231720) among others are substantially original, though the first two are presently used as stores. Some eighteenth- and nineteenth-century buildings survive in the Scottish and Newcastle Brewery complexes at Holyrood and Fountainbridge, while Drybrough's Brewery at Peffer Bank (287717) is an excellent example of Victorian brewery architecture.[24] Guinness's James's Street Brewery in Dublin is one of the largest of its kind in the British Isles. Originally established in the mid eighteenth century, it grew dramatically in the next 150 years through the brewing of the fine dark porter for which it is still famous. The brewery had its own quay on the River Liffey and also a dock on an arm of the Grand Canal. Although the plant is modern, many eighteenth- and nineteenth-century buildings remain. Something of the history of the firm can be seen in the Guinness Museum—the major museum of the brewing industry.[25]

Although distilling has undergone as many changes as brewing, some original eighteenth- and nineteenth-century plant can still be found in the Scottish Highlands and Islands, and in Ireland. The distillery often resembles the brewery in its arrangement of buildings round a courtyard. These consist of the still-house, maltings, cooperage, offices, excise officer's house, and the dominant feature of many distilleries, the bonded warehouse, used to store maturing whisky. Examples can be found in profusion in the north-east Lowlands of Scotland, where Speyside in particular is at the heart of malt whisky production (Plate 14). Butt lists the most interesting ones in the area. Of the distilleries

Plate 14   Benriach Glenlivet distillery, Speyside, one of the finest
examples with its pagoda kiln of the old malt whisky distilleries of
this area.

in the Lowlands proper those around Glasgow, Edinburgh and Falkirk are representative of larger units, while elsewhere other distilleries date from the early nineteenth century.[26] Bladnoch near Wigtown (NX421543) in Galloway was established in 1817 and rebuilt in 1878. It still produces a Lowland malt, mostly for blending.[27] Many interesting distillery buildings exist in Ireland, for example, the Powers's Distillery, Dublin, described by Bowie.[28]

Cider production is a significant industry in southern England and was formerly a small-scale country craft in apple orchard districts like Devon, Somerset, Hereford and Worcester. One of the skills required in cider-making lies in the blending of different varieties of apple. Formerly this was done in circular stone mills, round which a horse would be driven pulling a stone to crush the apples. Some of these presses or troughs still survive in the cider-making areas, relics of the golden age of home-made cider. Minchinton describes some of the relics to be found in Devon. Sidmouth Museum has an old farm-type cider press, and at Woodbury (SY012873) four old presses were reported working. Factory-style production dates mainly from the mid nineteenth century, although Henley's cider factory at Abbotskerswell (SX853691), which was one of the first commercial plant of its kind, is of the late-eighteenth-century origin.[29]

Timber and related crafts

The timber and woodworking trades have left many remains of interest to the industrial archaeologist, particularly in woodland areas like the Weald, Forest of Dean, Cumbria, Galloway, Argyll, and Ireland. Inevitably some of the most important activities of the woodland itself—like timber cutting or charcoal burning—have left few features of note. The history of these activities is beginning to be charted, particularly in relation to the early development of the iron industry in most of the districts mentioned. Much of the actual archaeology, however, is associated with timber sawing and woodworking in mills driven by water wheels or steam engines. Circular saws driven by water power were first built at the close of the eighteenth century, mainly by landowners or ironmasters harvesting natural stands of timber on their estates. Larger sawmills—driven by water power and steam power—were built at the ports to deal with increasing supplies of foreign timber shipped mainly from North America and the Baltic. Cardiff, for example, was one of many ports which developed an extensive timber trade with saw-mills and related flooring and furniture manufacture. Timber was of prime importance in many industries, in engineering and ship-building, as well as in the general construction and building trades.

As the work of Marshall and Davies-Shiel indicates, Cumbria was an important area of woodland industries and timber work-ing, especially charcoal burning, bark stripping, potash manu-facture, coopering and wood turning—crafts common to other woodland districts. Bobbin manufacture was probably the most significant wood-using industry in Lakeland and rose in response to the demands of the textile trades of Lancashire and the West Riding during the late eighteenth century. Cumbria produced half the requirements of textile mills throughout Britain by 1850. Most bobbin mills were originally waterpowered and equipped with saws, lathes and other turning machines for the production of bobbins, rollers, tool handles and boxes. Many other wooden fitments were made, such as spindles, pulleys and reels. The buildings were mostly of two storeys and identifiable by the nearby coppice drying shed of the same height with a slated ridged roof supported on the long sides by two rows of drystone pillars. The mill was often converted from another function, perhaps a flax, fulling or corn mill. Power was transmitted from the water wheel to a vertical shaft within the mill and by a line shaft and belts to rows of lathes mounted on heavy timbers. One such mill, Stott Park near Finsthwaite, is still working much as described, though water power has long been superseded by electricity.[30]

A variety of other timber-working crafts are of interest to the industrial archaeologist, ranging from the large-scale use of wood in engineering and millwrighting, to the smaller-scale produc-tion of such items as barrels and clogs. Much of the machinery that survives in pre-nineteenth-century plant, like corn mills or textile mills, is constructed of wood. Although millwrights increasingly worked with a combination of wood and iron after 1800, timber itself remained of considerable importance in machine building long after. The production of barrels was of significance in all fishing ports, and in centres of brewing and distilling. Cooperages could be found in great numbers in such places, as a glance at any nineteenth-century local trade directory will show. For example, even at the end of the last century almost a hundred cooperages flourished in Liverpool, as Grant has indicated. The 'wet' cooper made watertight casks for beer, rum, whisky, oils, syrup and treacle, while the 'dry' cooper made lighter casks for storing flour, biscuits, paint, dyes, fruit and the like.[31] Clog-making had obvious associations with leatherworking and was particularly important in country districts and textile towns, where clogs were worn instead of boots or shoes.

In many parts of Britain and Ireland agriculture and the processing of farm products were and remain the most important industries. Economic and technical changes, however, have produced an archaeology of enormous interest and value which occupies a position of major importance in the national heritage. Much has already been done by state agencies and local preservation groups to record and conserve typical examples of country mills. The whole field of vernacular architecture—including farm buildings, mills and other features—is attracting an increasing amount of attention and there seems little doubt that industrial archaeology can continue to make an important contribution to this study. In other instances, such as that of tanning and leatherworking, it may almost be too late to record old plant and techniques, but much remains to be discovered about the history and development of this important industry. Brewing and distilling have been reasonably well documented, and despite recent losses through demolition there is still a great deal of interest to be seen. Timber working would certainly repay more detailed local investigation in many districts.

5
Textiles

Textile production was a basic economic activity from darkest antiquity, essential for survival in the climatic circumstances of the British Isles and, therefore, always associated with peasant households as a domestic skill. Unlike other similar activities—such as the preparation of food and drink—manufacturing cloth became a 'putting-out' industry and remained fundamentally so till the onset of power-driven factory production in the eighteenth century. The peasant's household commonly combined work in agriculture with textile manufacture, supplying products to relatively distant markets via an intricate network of middlemen. The raw material, animal or plant fibre, was put out by merchants for spinning and associated preparatory processes and then later distributed to weavers who made up yarn and thread into fabrics. This organization involved extensive division of labour but, assuming a relatively constant supply of workers and no drastic increase in demand for their products, it acquired a positive state of equilibrium with few technical innovations and no sustained incentive to lower costs or raise productivity.[1]

In this pre-industrial society the merchant required a minimum of fixed capital since buildings and equipment were provided by the peasant household and, in turn, the rural family needed no trading capital for raw materials and credit were available from the merchant. Of course, there were infinite variations from this simplistic model, and it would be patently mistaken to assume that the textile industries under the so-called domestic system made no economic progress. Yet the general picture of British textiles before the eighteenth century is of a traditional group of industries with a few simple tools and machines and very low power requirements; gains in productivity were probably made cumulatively over a long period in response to slow upward movements in demand but there is no record of sensational technical change from the thirteenth century onwards.

This family economy came under attack in the eighteenth and nineteenth centuries as mechanized factory production invaded most branches of the textile industry, and horse, water and steam power gradually reduced the physical burden of production for human beings. This is not to suggest that the factory system was a universal benefactor: there are those who gain and those who lose from any important change in methods of production. However, we should not fall into the trap of imagining that pre-industrial Britain was peopled by sturdy yeomen living idyllically off the fat of the land and relaxing in summertime with Morris dances, jigs and ceilidhs. Reality was more likely to consist of poor diet, hard work, and primitive housing conditions.[2]

Only the most substantial physical remains of pre-industrial textile production are likely to have survived—wool merchants' and clothiers' houses, for instance, in places like Cirencester, Fairford and Chipping Campden in the Cotswolds or at Lavenham in Suffolk. More commonly, weavers and other textile outworkers increased in numbers in the late eighteenth and early nineteenth centuries, and their houses with workshops survive in relatively substantial but diminishing numbers. Silk weavers' houses survive in the Spitalfields area of London (E1) notably in Fournier Street and in the surrounding neighbourhood (Plate 15). These four-storey dwellings have garrets with excellent window lighting where the handlooms were located, and these were typical arrangements also in places like Bethnal Green and Mile End, for more than fifty thousand people in the East End were dependent on silk weaving in 1831. In Macclesfield (Cheshire) and Leek (Staffordshire) three-storey silk weavers' houses still survive in what were main centres of the industry. Free trade brought disaster to the trade from the 1860s, but French and eastern competition presented problems earlier.

The woollen districts of Yorkshire and the West Country provide similar examples. At High Kinders, Greenfield, Saddleworth (West Yorkshire), the clothier's house dating from 1642 was gradually extended as handloom weaving became more prosperous in the eighteenth century; and more labour was concentrated into the range of buildings, before the power loom finally triumphed in the 1880s. In the Colne valley there were about 170 clothiers c. 1750, most of them living at Golcar where recently local people have established the Colne Valley Museum in three weavers' cottages. Blanket weaving in the Dewsbury area was dominated by small-scale operators in 1841, according to Thomas Cook, one of the founders of Dewsbury Mills, and many of the Pennine villages lived by the handloom, although weaving was generally combined with farming.

In Gloucestershire, Wiltshire and Somerset the concentration of labour into the clothiers' premises began relatively early. Raw materials which went into the characteristic super-fine broad-

Plate 15 Silk weavers' dwellings and loom-shops, Fournier Street, Spitalfields, London E1, *c.* 1740.

cloths produced in this region were often expensive, and embezzlement was a business problem commonly encountered and impossible to control outside the master's workshop. Quality control was necessary if markets were to be retained and expanded; close supervision was, therefore, a prerequisite. Complaints about the unwillingness of weavers to work regularly in good times were commonplace in the late seventeenth and early eighteenth centuries, and clothiers attempted to keep piece-rates as low as possible. Clashes between labour and capital—as for instance in 1726–7—did not simply arise as a consequence of the application of labour-saving machinery but because of the incipient capitalism which the clothiers attempted to operate, disregarding attempts by Justices of the Peace to enforce fair wage rates.[3] Courtfield House at Trowbridge conceals within an impressive external appearance back quarters with weavers' windows where no doubt the clothier supervised his workforce and attempted to enforce his discipline.[4] Workshops separate from the clothier's house were once common enough in Trowbridge and the surrounding area but are now more difficult to identify with certainty. Weavers' houses, however, still survive in fair numbers, for example, in Yerbury Street, Trowbridge and near Staverton Church, two miles away.[5]

In the East Midlands the hosiery industry persisted as a handicraft well into the nineteenth century, and William Lee's stocking frame (perfected c. 1589–99) was easily assimilated into the domestic system. By 1844 there were about 48,500 stocking frames in Britain, of which nearly 44,000 were in the East Midlands in an area bounded roughly by Mansfield in the north and the Nottinghamshire boundaries with Warwickshire and Northamptonshire in the south. Technically, it was difficult to apply steam power to the stocking frame, but the persistence of the domestic system was almost certainly due to the fact that labour was plentiful and cheap, and therefore there was little incentive to adopt labour-saving techniques. The industry was run from the main towns—Leicester, Loughborough, Nottingham, Derby, and Mansfield—where the employers maintained their warehouses. Framework knitters' cottages and workshops with characteristically long windows may be seen in several places, for instance behind the Britannia Inn at Kegworth, but quite commonly domestic architecture was altered to take account of stocking knitting as, for example, at Sutton Bonington where the oldest house (1663) had windows placed in the gable and at Calverton, the birthplace of the industry, where the ground floor was usually the workroom level.[6]

In linen districts where the cotton industry also was often gradually established, the variety in the type of workroom within or outside the house was considerable. The National Trust for Scotland has restored a cottage at Kilbarchan which was built in 1723 for a linen weaver and draper, and this Renfrewshire village has a number of textile workshops dating from the early nineteenth century. At Dairsie (Fife), once known as Osnaburgh, substantial numbers of single-storey weavers' cottages survive, many with the usual double window. The Fife Folk Museum at Ceres consists of two former linen weavers' cottages, one with a double window, and a weigh-house dating from the seventeenth century. Ayrshire has a number of examples of cotton weavers' cottages: in Girvan and at Crosshill, for instance.[7]

Undoubtedly the richest group of remains exists in Lancashire, where there are also relics of outworking in the clothing trades such as hat-makers' houses and workshops.[8] W. J. Smith in his excellent study of south-east Lancashire and the adjoining Pennines indicates that there was extensive adaptation and improvisation in providing or extending workrooms within houses. Sometimes, as in the more northerly Kendal district, knitting or spinning galleries (for wool) or first-floor balconies were built of wood facing into the farmyard and so placed to avoid the prevailing winds. In Rochdale back-to-back houses often had a top working floor which was common to the whole row or terrace.[9] Basements or cellars were often used as loom-shops as, for instance, at Royton (Lancashire) or in Caithness Row at New Lanark. It seems reasonable to suppose that common working areas whether in lofts or basements were the true ancestors of the early factories before the size of spinning machinery began to impose a new economic logic upon the design of industrial buildings.

The silk industry in the early eighteenth century was the first of the textile industries to face a shortage of suitable thread, and Dutch water-driven silk-throwing machinery was introduced to Derby in 1704 by Thomas Cotchett who employed a local engineer, George Sorocold, to design his mill (SK354365) and build a 13½ ft (4 m) water wheel. Although this early enterprise ended in bankruptcy in 1713, a fresh attempt at silk spinning in Derby was made by Thomas Lombe and his brother John in 1721, again with Sorocold as the engineer, but this time the machinery was based on Italian models which were carefully copied, apparently after John Lombe had visited Leghorn, one of the most advanced centres of the silk industry. From Derby the factory silk industry spread, after Lombe's patent (taken out in 1718) expired in 1732, to Congleton, Macclesfield, Leek, Sheffield, Watford, Manchester, Leigh, Stockport, Salford, and Braintree in Essex.[10] A particularly interesting survival is the Whitchurch silk mill (SU463479) on the River Test in Hampshire which dates from 1815 and is still in operation.[11]

The limitations placed upon the market by the selling price of imported raw silk impeded the rapid growth of the industry, and cotton, wool and flax were the fibres which later formed the basis of substantial industrial progress. Cotton emerged as the most significant of these for a number of reasons. It was a more tractable fibre than either flax or wool, and in consequence machine spinning of it could be more readily achieved. Relative to wool and flax, raw cotton prices tended to fall because of the availability of supplies, principally in the West Indies and later, as a result of the spread of the plantation economy, in the

American South. Demand was more elastic for cotton goods, particularly in the later eighteenth century, and fashionable society had earlier pioneered changes in the market through the purchase of high-costing Indian cotton goods imported by the East India Company. As the price of cotton goods was reduced, the domestic market, already expanding because of an increase in population, boomed; moreover, foreign consumers in the Americas, Europe, Africa and finally in the Middle and Far East readily accepted British cotton yarns and well-finished piece goods.[12]

Superior British technology only became a significant feature in the cotton industry's progress from about the middle of the eighteenth century, and the flame of technical improvement was only ignited then because spinning capacity was an obvious bottleneck made narrower by the gradual diffusion of Kay's flying shuttle (1733) which raised the level of productivity in weaving. The technical disequilibrium between spinning and weaving even before Kay's invention was such that four or five spinners were necessary to keep one weaver fully employed. Lewis Paul and John Wyatt in 1738 patented what were to be in other hands the successful working principles of improved spinning. Their machine depended upon pairs of rollers drawing out the fibres of the raw material, and although they were commercially unsuccessful, Richard Arkwright's water-frame (1769) was based upon the same principles.[13] Earlier, c. 1764, James Hargreaves, a weaver of Stanhill near Blackburn, had built a hand machine for spinning initially with eight spindles which he patented with improvements in 1770. His patent did not survive, and Hargreave's spinning jenny was widely applied in the Midlands and Lancashire.[14] Yarn produced by Arkwright's frame was better than that produced on the jenny, but Hargreave's machine required little capital and could be readily made by local craftsmen; it, therefore, gave the putting-out system in Lancashire an additional lease of life and was used to produce weft yarns, complementing the supply of warps made on Arkwright's frame.

The cost of fine cottons was greatly reduced by the introduction of Samuel Crompton's spinning mule (1779)[15] which combined the best points of the jenny and frame. Yet the mule's greater capital cost retarded its application vis-à-vis the jenny. However, the first mules had thirty spindles, and this number was soon greatly increased. By 1792 William Kelly of New Lanark had applied water power to the mule, and within ten years mules with nearly five hundred spindles were in operation. These larger mules together with Arkwright's frames were best exploited in large-scale factories, and the supply of power, already by the 1770s an important consideration in the location of the cotton industry, became fundamental.

Arkwright's factory in Nottingham (a converted house) used a horse-gin in 1769; such capstans were commonly used in the early stages of factory development because they were cheap to install and particularly suited to driving a few machines in adapted premises.[16] Water power, however, was the real basis for the early development of the purpose-built factory, and sites able to provide 25 horsepower or more remained competitive well after steam power had been applied to spinning (Plate 16). Cromford, where Arkwright established his most famous factory,

Plate 16 Tutbury Mill (SK113394), Rocester, Staffordshire, one of Richard Arkwright's cotton-spinning ventures (1781–2), now demolished.

New Lanark under David Dale and his famous son-in-law, Robert Owen, Stanley, Deanston, Masson, 'Parsley' Peel's mills at Burton-on-Trent, and Tamworth were all built to exploit the water-frame, but the cotton industry included many relatively small establishments as late as the 1830s and 1840s.[17]

Entrepreneurs such as Owen and Peel also took up Crompton's mule, and it seems that by c. 1800 the application of the water-frame had reached a plateau. Meanwhile, the number of mule spindles increased from about 50,000 in 1788 to 4.6 million in 1811.[18] Capital flowed freely into cotton spinning, but Arkwright-type mills for 1,000 spindles cost in most areas no more than £3,000. In places like Stockport, where mule spinning was taken up by many small firms, premises and machinery were generally insured for much less.[19] The survival of small firms is difficult to chart and not easy to explain, but it seems that there were diseconomies of scale operating in large firms until *c.* 1840 which a few years of good profits could offset but not cure.[20] However, the mortality rate among small firms was very considerable.

Large firms such as Arkwright's, or Greg's at Styal in Cheshire, often had to establish communities as well as mills, and from a green-field site had to create anew a social organization. At Cromford there is more relating to the community than to the mills: apart from an elaborate lade system and a cut-down version of Arkwright's first mill (which was built to a height of six storeys), the best survivals are the Greyhound Inn and the housing in North Street.

Near by at Belper, Jedediah Strutt's mills tell us more about early factory building. The first mill here was built in 1778; the second, North Mill, in 1786, and the West Mill was added in 1795. Fire was a great hazard in the industry when timber was the main building material for internal construction and lubricants were liberally applied to primitive machinery which frequently overheated; Strutt's North Mill was burned down in January 1803. His new mill was built on the best fire-proof principles: placed parallel to the river, the main range, six storeys high, is fifteen bays long with a wing of six bays at right angles. Up to first-floor level, it is built of stone, and above that of brick to the slate roof; the windows are spaced regularly along the building at each storey. Inside the construction is exceedingly interesting with shallow brick arches running from iron beams placed on iron pillars. On these arches a brick floor was laid, and the pillars are held together with iron ties. In the basement huge stone supports assist in strengthening the pillars which bear the weight of the structure above.

Samuel Greg came to Styal in Cheshire from Belfast in 1784, and on the banks of the River Bollin established the Quarry Bank mills at a cost of £16,000. Local farm buildings were converted into houses for incoming workers, but Greg had to construct more housing and also a dormitory for pauper apprentices (Plate 17). Peter Ewart, an engineer of considerable skill, joined the firm in 1796 and kept machinery and plant layout as up-to-date as his partner allowed (Plate 18). This mill group and village is probably the best example in England of the water-power phase of the cotton industry.

The industry in the early nineteenth century was widely dispersed over fifteen counties of the country, not to mention in

Plate 17   One of the blocks of houses at Styal Mill (SJ834830),
Cheshire, built by the Gregs for incoming workers.

Ireland and Scotland.[21] The Scottish examples going back to the
1780s are particularly fine. Arkwright's influence was paramount
in the early years of that decade; irritated by his reception among
the Lancashire manufacturers, he threatened to use Scotland as
a razor to their throat; his tour in 1783–4 was something of a
triumphal progress as he picked up partners such as David Dale
and George Dempster without difficulty—no doubt on the
strength of his water-frame which until 1785 was still under
patent.[22] New Lanark, Deanston, Catrine and Stanley, all villages
created by cottonmasters, owe their existence to Arkwright's
determination to spread the technique of warp-spinning to
Scotland.

Of these planned villages, undoubtedly the most significant
for industrial and social history is New Lanark (Plate 19).[23] The
Falls of Clyde so impressed Arkwright during his tour of the
Clyde valley with David Dale in 1783 that he thought he would
be able to turn Lanark into a new Manchester. Dale and he went
into partnership, and the ground for the mills and village was
obtained from the Lord Justice Clerk, Lord Braxfield, for a feu
(or fee) duty of £32.50 per annum; the Lanark Incorporation of
Shoemakers owned part of the land upon which houses were
built, and a feu duty of £17.39 was paid to them.

Work was begun on a lade, and a tunnel driven through a
hillside to tap the waters of the Clyde. Part-way across the river

Plate 19 *(above)* The planned village at New Lanark (1783–1825), showing (from left to right) the school, cotton mills, 'institution for the formation of character', and tenement housing.

Plate 18 *(opposite)* Large direct-drive water turbine in the basement of Styal cotton mill. The grooved pulley for rope drive can be seen on the left. In the right foreground is a smaller turbine. Both are now disused.

a weir was built to raise the water level going through the lade to the mill wheels. Stone was quarried for the mills downstream, and the first one was in operation by March 1786. Before the second mill was built, the first was destroyed by fire on 9 October 1788. Dale, undeterred, had replaced it by 1789, and this five-storey building, cut down to three storeys and a basement, still survives as a monument to his enterprise, now being used by Metal Extraction Ltd. Originally this mill resembled Arkwright's Masson Mill (1783), with its Palladian windows in the stair bay, and this feature was copied at several other Scottish mills—Woodside in Aberdeen, Catrine (Ayrshire) and Spinning-dale (Sutherland).

Over the next seven years a building labour force of ninety was kept constantly at work until four mills and houses for more than two hundred families had been completed. No. 4 mill was first occupied as a warehouse and workshop, with the upper floors used as a lodging house for pauper apprentices; today there is simply a space where it once stood, for it was burned to the ground in 1883. The first two mills were used for warp-spinning (i.e. on Arkwright water-frames) and No. 3 and No. 4 were eventually devoted to mule-spinning. No. 3 mill, further to demonstrate the danger of fire, was in 1819 badly damaged in a blaze and only rebuilt c. 1825 by Robert Owen.

Owen had gained experience in Manchester as manager for Peter Drinkwater, a fustian merchant, and as a partner in the Chorlton Twist Company, before he came to New Lanark as managing partner of David Dale's mill and later his son-in-law.[24] Owen's association with New Lanark mills was highly profitable; with three sets of partners he made respectively £90,000, £109,871, and £192,915. However, his record as a profit-maker has assumed less significance as generations have passed, although no doubt it served to draw attention to his talents. His interest in environmental psychology and his educational practices have absorbed the attention of many historians; others have attempted to assess him as either a founding father of scientific management or of Utopian socialism.[25] The industrial archaeologist can visit the village today and see his school, his Institution for the Formation of Character, the truck shop (which co-operators often mistakenly imagine was the ancestor of modern co-operative societies) and the workers' housing. Much energy and considerable resources are being applied to the conservation of the village, but the task is truly daunting.

During Owen's lifetime the cotton industry became dependent upon steam power and concentrated increasingly in Lancashire and in the Glasgow–Paisley area. Geoffrey Hay examined Houldsworth's cotton mill in Glasgow (NS578651) which was built in 1804–5 and demolished in 1970; like Strutt's North Mill at Belper it was an experimental building but only partly of fireproof construction; its source of power was a Boulton and Watt engine which also exhausted through the structural columns, thus providing central heating for the whole mill.[26] The application of steam power to the loom and also to the self-acting mule encouraged further concentration of production, especially in Lancashire (Plate 20), but the typical integrated plant with its tall spinning mills and single-storey weaving sheds was also found in the woollen and linen industries, to which the new inventions were gradually applied.

In Oldham and also in the Bolton area some very fine late-nineteenth-century cotton mills survive. Kearsley spinning mill,

Plate 20   A Manchester cotton mill off London Road, seven storeys high, of classic design. Very few now survive in the city.

for instance, is a very fine example dating from the late 1890s; the Laburnum Spinning Company mill, Atherton, located beside the Hindley-Pendlebury section of the Lancashire and Yorkshire Railway dates from 1895 and is still at work; only part of the Swan Lane Spinning Mill, Bolton (c. 1900), which once proudly boasted that it had more spindles under one roof than any other mill in the world, is now spinning; the noble façade of the Beehive Mill, Bolton, now conceals the operations of a mail-order business (Plate 21).[27]

If the expansion of the cotton industry and its continued progress until c. 1900 was the most spectacular single development, the other textile industries also made remarkable progress. Regional specialization, however, was very much the order of the day. Increasingly Ulster, for instance, dominated flax spinning, and the Irish linen industry exerted its advantages over other areas without entirely subjugating them. Dundee became

Plate 21 The impressive frontage of Beehive Mill No. 1/2 (1895) at Bolton, looking south. The complex is now used by a mail-order firm.

'Juteopolis' between 1830 and 1870, and its only real rivals eventually developed in India, often as a consequence of Scottish investment. The woollen industry, so ancient and influential, gave ground only reluctantly to these parvenus, and in the West Country, Yorkshire and Scotland, there are many memorials from the factory age.

Yorkshire increasingly dominated the woollen and worsted industry of the British Isles, as factory organization became commonplace.[28] By 1835 there were 1,332 mills employing over 71,000 workers and using over 23,000 hp, possibly representing a capital investment of about £4.6 million. Yorkshire's share was 610 mills, over 40,000 employees and a fixed capital of over £2 million. The 1790s were a critical decade for industrial concentration in woollens, and an increase in yarn output from jennies was the basis for the sustained growth in the production of broad and narrow cloth. The mule and power loom were very slow to be applied in the industry; the main early developments were in preparatory machines particularly for carding and scribbling. In worsted production, substantial change became relatively common in the 1830s, but it was not until the 1850s and 1860s that

Plate 22　The gigantic mohair mills built by Titus Salt at Saltaire,
Yorkshire and completed *c.* 1860. Note the Italianate features
typical of grander textile-mill design in many districts.

the power loom was applied on any great scale to the Yorkshire
industry.

In general, the industrial archaeologist may soon have better
luck in the less famous centres of the Yorkshire trade, for places
like Bradford, Leeds, and Halifax have been subject to redevelopment. In this process small mill buildings—and some
large—have been bulldozed below their original foundation
levels. However, to follow the Hebden Beck down to Hebden
Bridge or to visit Holmfirth, is well worth while. A major site is
undoubtedly Saltaire (SE140381), a model mill village founded
by Titus Salt (1803–76),[29] near Bradford, and developed mainly
between 1850 and 1880 (Plate 22). Manningham Mill, dating

Plate 23   Higher Mill, Holcombe, Helmshore, built *c.* 1789 by the
Turner family, woollen-cloth finishers, and now a museum devoted
to the history of all textiles.

from 1873, is the best Bradford mill still standing and was built
by Samuel Cunliffe Lister (1815–1906). Much of interest relating
to the North of England woollen industry can be seen at the
Bradford industrial museum and at Helmshore (SD777214) where
relics of the cotton industry have also been carefully preserved
(Plates 23 and 24).

Plate 24   The fulling stocks at Helmshore seen through the 17 ft
(5.2 m) diameter water wheel.

In other parts of the country, there are many reminders of the
woollen industry. Although the West Country, for instance,
gradually lost its primacy which it had to some extent shared
uneasily with Norwich and East Anglia, there are many remains
in Gloucestershire,[30] Wiltshire and Somerset.[31] Marling and Evans
fire-proof mill at Kings Stanley near Stroud (SO813043) is probably the most important architecturally and dates from c. 1812,[32]
but there are several sites worthy of a visit, such as West Lavington
fulling mill which probably dates from the late sixteenth or early
seventeenth century, Avon Mills at Malmesbury (now an antique
shop), and Quemerford-in-Calne which began as a woollen mill
but was then converted into a corn mill as the Calne trade began
to fail.

In the Borders of Scotland there are a number of fine mills,
and the Scottish fancy trade in tweed has been extensively

researched by Dr Gulvin.[33] The main period of expansion occurred in the two generations after 1830, and Netherdale Mill (NT494360), Galashiels, Ettrick Mill (NT473293), Selkirk, and Nithsdale Mills (NX976754) in Dumfries are excellent examples.[34] In the north at Elgin, Newmill woollen mill (NJ225631) is a particularly attractive complex dating from 1797 and including a five-bay weaving block built in 1916.[35] Glasgow possesses an architectural marvel in Templeton's carpet factory (NS603641), which includes William Leiper's very colourful block (1888–92) built in tribute to the Doge's palace in Venice.[36]

Because the woollen industry was present in so many districts of Britain, remains may be expected in regions which have no present-day connection with this activity. At Bradford-on-Avon rubber manufacture took over existing woollen mills, and this is merely one example of the versatility of many textile buildings. Representative of a long-departed country craft is the small blanket mill at St John's on the Isle of Man (Plate 25); such buildings employing a handful of workers lasted well into the age of great factory complexes.

The linen industry also has its memorials, mainly in Scotland and Ulster, but the number has been much depleted over the last ten years. Scutching the flax was once carried out in a large number of water-powered lint mills; the most significant early remains are to be found in Scotland at Invervar, Perthshire (NN665483),[37] and Lintmill of Boyne, near Portsoy, Banffshire (NJ608646),[38] and in Ulster at Ballyaughran[39] on the east bank of the River Bann, County Down (O.S. map 48 ref. 222313). The concentration of labour into linen 'manufactories' proceeded from the early eighteenth century in Scotland,[40] and at Caputh, Perthshire (NO108409), the 'Muckle Hoose' is an example dating from 1767.[41] Kendrew and Porthouse developed a linen yarn-spinning process in the 1780s which was rapidly pirated in the east of Scotland and Ulster; the diffusion of technology was accompanied also by a rapid increase in the number of water-driven mills, especially in Angus, Perthshire, Aberdeenshire, and Fife. Fine specimens can be seen at Blairgowrie, Perthshire,[42] and at Seapatrick, County Down, (O.S. map 27, ref. 118476).[43]

From the coarse linen industry and its technology gradually emerged Dundee's specialization in jute in the 1840s. Rapid development occurred, especially during the Crimean War and the American Civil War, when the demand for sacking and bagging was exceedingly buoyant. Many mills were built, fire proof and jack arch in construction; Baxter's Dens works (NO408309), Eagle Mills (NO409312) and Logie works

Plate 25   Small country blanket mill at St John's, Isle of Man. Wool processing was a speciality of this area and still retains a place in the local economy.

(NO392303) are perhaps the best surviving examples in the city.[45] The industry spread to Arbroath, Brechin, Blairgowrie, and Montrose, and interesting buildings can still be seen in these places.[46]

There were other textile specializations, notably lace production in Nottingham and Newmilns, Ayrshire, but sufficient has been said to indicate the possible scope of research into the textile industries. Field surveys should again be supplemented by conventional research so as to discover more about local capitalization, mechanization, employment, and use of power resources. Regional specialization is so much a basic assumption when textile history is discussed that it seems impious to suggest that for most regions we have no entirely satisfactory explanations of the process by which it occurred.

6
Metallurgy and Engineering

Although textile production—in terms of workers and capital employed and export revenue earned—dominated the British economy for a long period, iron and steel and the engineering industries founded upon them have increasingly shaped the material basis of our society. The age of cheap iron really began with the widespread application and occasional pirating of James Beaumont Neilson's hot-blast process patented in 1828, but before that crucial invention there was a chain of technical progress leading back to charcoal smelting, a technique which had dominated metallurgy since ancient times. Steel production was gradually cheapened over the thirty years following the introduction of Bessemer's converter in 1856, but the technology of this industry also had an antique pedigree.[1] Nonetheless, whether we think of railways or ships, cars or canned goods, skyscrapers or needles, the basis of life today rests heavily upon metallurgy and engineering. Perhaps British society does not recognize this fact sufficiently, nor does it place sufficient emphasis on rewarding those—and we do not mean in terms of money alone—associated with these skills.

The charcoal iron industry had three main products—pig, cast, and bar iron. Iron ore (usually Fe_2O_3) was reduced in the blast furnace to produce pig iron, which, on account of its carbon content (3–5 per cent), was hard and brittle. Some iron was tapped direct from the furnace into moulds in the casting house, but most pig iron required further treatment in the foundry or the forge before it could be profitably used. The major cast-iron products produced in the foundry before the nineteenth century were pots and pans, firegrates and backs, some machine parts (notably for steam engines in the eighteenth century) and anchors. Quite often cannon and cannon-balls were produced in the casting house. Of the three main products, bar (or wrought) iron was unquestionably the most important, being used extensively in the production of nails, small arms, agricultural implements and horseshoes, wire, locks and bolts. This type of forge iron is distinguished from pig and cast iron by its lower carbon content (less than 1 per cent) and, therefore, it is relatively soft and malleable. A small quantity of bar iron was also used to make steel which was very expensive; in terms of carbon content this product was intermediate between bar iron and pig iron.[2]

The basic process of iron production occurred, therefore, in the blast furnace, although primitive charcoal and peat bloomeries survived in Britain, notably in Cumbria and Wales, until the seventeenth century and even later in Ireland.[3] From the fifteenth century, however, the blast furnace gradually infiltrated into Britain, displacing these earlier techniques slowly. Its country of origin is obscure, Belgium and northern Spain both being possibilities: since Spain's empire for a long period embraced the Netherlands (including modern Belgium), it seems reasonable to look to a common origin in southern Europe where the Moorish culture (and supremacy in the production of sword blades) collided with Christendom.

Whatever its origins in Europe, there can be no doubt that the charcoal blast furnace was infinitely superior to the bloomery in terms of output and speed of production. The typical blast furnace (c. 1720) was 20 to 25 feet (6.1–7.6 m) high, usually of square section and built of rubble stone blocks with a smoother interior stone lining which sloped both to the furnace bosh and to its hearth. Usually erected in a well-wooded area against a convenient hillside (to assist gravity feeding of raw materials from a bridgehouse), the furnace had also to be located near a suitable stream, pond or river, for an alternating pair of bellows commonly driven by a water wheel supplied the blast. The charge of raw materials was reduced into molten metal as it moved down the structure towards the hearth, where a temperature of about 1200°C was achieved. Periodically, liquid iron was run out of the furnace into a hollowed bed of sand known as the pig bed, the main depression being called the sow and its branches the pigs; hence pig iron received its name. The slag (impurities and unreduced ore) was lighter than the molten pig iron and was, therefore, drawn off last.

Elaborate preparations had to be made before putting a furnace into blast or, following the military metaphor employed by contemporary ironmasters, 'the campaign' began. Adequate supplies of charcoal had to be prepared; ironmasters found that the best charcoal came from young trees rather than from well-established forests, and they therefore came to practise coppicing, i.e. planting and cutting trees according to a rotation. Landowners leased their woods and either made arrangements themselves for reafforestation or insisted that ironmasters accept clauses within contracts specifying that replanting should be undertaken. Thus, it is mistaken to ascribe the wholesale decline of medieval forests solely to the activities of ironmasters or to place too much emphasis on the thesis that a scarcity of timber led inexorably to a coal/coke technology in iron smelting. Recently, Flinn, Hammersley and Phillips have demonstrated that there was no such fuel scarcity in most ironworking districts.[4]

Great attention was also paid to the iron ore. This was cleaned in water, calcined or roasted in heaps to rid it of moisture and sulphur, and, finally, crushed into small pieces. To complete the charge a flux, usually of limestone, was added to the charcoal and ore, its purpose being to encourage the slag to separate from the molten metal during combustion. Pieces of cold blast slag, with their characteristic green, smooth, glassy texture, are often the first clue in once wooded areas to the presence of a bloomery or charcoal-furnace site.

Once the blast furnace began its 'campaign', the process was continuous, recharging taking place from the 'bridge' which led from the hilltop to the mouth of the furnace. To maximize output and to maintain quality control, the furnace had to be regularly checked by experienced smelters ('furnace-keepers') who often served under contract and sometimes, as subcontractors, supplied their own teams of labourers. Smelters were often paid a tonnage bonus as well as a fixed wage; such incentive payments, together with company housing, were designed to stimulate efficiency and to retain skilled men. The opening up of new ironworking districts placed a scarcity value upon such labour, but ironmasters' associations evolved in the eighteenth century and among their objects were the prevention of labour 'poaching' and the fixing of wages and prices.[5]

According to Schubert—and there is much supporting evidence for his view—a furnace's 'campaign' lasted for about thirty weeks in the year during which an average output of slightly over ten tons per week was achieved.[6] Rule of thumb dominated furnace practice, and an output variable in quantity and quality was more normal than not! Production was restricted by the size and capacity of the furnace, and this was largely determined by the nature of the fuel. Charcoal, being friable, would be reduced to dust in the furnace stack if the furnace was built too high or too wide, rendering the unit inoperable. The cold-blast process was relatively slow, since temperatures of about 1200°C were difficult to maintain. Another constraint was the short duration of the annual 'campaign'. The furnace would normally operate from the late autumn, probably beginning in October, until early summer—to May or exceptionally early June—the following year. During warm weather cold-blast furnaces produced smaller quantities of poorer quality iron because of increased humidity; moreover, water supplies, essential for the blast and for ore-cleaning, were commonly deficient in the summer months. The repair and maintenance of the furnace and the accumulation of fresh stocks of raw materials occupied the ironmaster and his labour force when smelting ceased for the summer.[7]

From the evidence provided by the publications of the Historical Metallurgy Group and by individual historians and industrial archaeologists, it seems that the diffusion of charcoal blast furnaces from Kent and Sussex—the Weald—to the Midlands and Wales became significant after 1560, and that Cumbria and northeast England were abandoning bloomery techniques by c. 1690 and the Scots in the 1720s.[8]

In Kent and Sussex further progress in our knowledge depends indubitably upon excavation which has been enthusiastically directed in recent years, notably by Dr Crossley. In other counties, too, industrial archaeologists, often aided by the support provided by the Department of the Environment and its highly skilled staff, have increasingly turned to excavation.[9] For instance, Allensford, Northumberland, a blast furnace and forge site, which Atkinson estimates was founded between 1670 and 1710, is being excavated under the direction of Dr S. M. Linsley.

Davies-Shiel has provided the most recent (1971) and best general archaeological survey of sites in Cumbria, and other published work corroborates the impression that landowners actively participated in the expansion of the industry, not only by leading mineral rights and timber but also by providing entrepreneurial leadership. From the Furness district English ironmasters, after dallying with the idea of migration to Galloway, moved to the Western Highlands of Scotland, to places like Abernethy, Invergarry, Furnace and Bonawe.

The 'hammer pond'—for water power was used to drive tilt hammers as well as bellows in many ironworks—is often the most obvious surface indication of ironmaking in Sussex today, and Cossons has noted a few of these in St Leonard's Forest.[10] More tangible evidence exists elsewhere. Ironmasters moved from Sussex to Glamorgan, beginning with Sir Henry Sidney and his associates who moved to Tongwynlais just north of Cardiff in 1564. Morgan Rees has mapped development over the next century and indicates that remains of sixteenth-century furnaces can be found at Blaencannaid (SO035042), Cwmaman (ST004992), Angleton (SS905821), and Trosnant (SO268003), their original heights being estimated as within the range of 12 to 18 feet (3.6–5.5 m).[11] The Coed Ithel furnace in the Wye valley near

Llandogo (SO527026) dates from 1651 or before, and although it has lost much of its outer structure the lining is open to view, thus providing the student with an excellent opportunity to assess early furnace design and layout. A vertical half-section allows one to see not merely the square section and circular hearth but also the inward slope both to the bosh and the hearth. Vitrification in the lining is obvious; behind the furnace a wheel pit can easily be detected, and the watercourse to it apparently ran first to the west and then northwards.[12]

Although Cumbria and Scotland were relatively insignificant producers in the early eighteenth century, according to Hyde's estimates, some of the best remains are to be found there, one suspects because of their late date and the safety which their relative isolation provides.[13] At Duddon Bridge in the Lake District (SD197884), the furnace, begun in 1736, was only finally damped in 1867 (Plate 26).[14] It is in a ruinous state as are the

Plate 26   Duddon furnace, West Cumbria, one of the best examples of a charcoal iron furnace (1726–1867) surviving in the north of England.

associated buildings. Other remains exist at Newland (SD299798), where the casting house is virtually intact,[15] Nibthwaite (SD295883),[16] and Leighton near Arnside (SD485778), where the charcoal store has survived.[17]

At Glen Kinglass (NN082371), Bonawe (NN009318), and Furnace (NN027001) in Argyll there are good sites in various stages of decay. The West Highlands, with their abundant timber supplies, occasional deposits of bog ore, streams, rivers and sea lochs providing water power and often navigable access (thus reducing transport costs) were an obvious location, once Scotland and England were in a common free-trade market and charcoal prices in Cumbria were driven up either by competition among ironmasters for wood leases or by monopolistic agreements between landowners. In periods when iron prices moved significantly upward—for instance in the 1750s—it was profitable to move haematite from Furness by sea to Scotland, simply because the latter had such an overwhelming comparative advantage in terms of charcoal costs.[18] The York Buildings Company established the furnace at Glen Kinglass c. 1725 as part of its programme of exploitation of the resources of the estates forfeited after the Jacobite Rising of 1715, probably to supply castings for its lead-smelting mills and pigs for further refining into bar iron. By the end of 1731 this furnace had evidently ceased to operate.[19] There are remains of associated buildings as well as the base of the furnace.[20]

The most significant relic of the early Scottish iron industry is Bonawe ironworks, founded in 1752 when Richard Ford and Company—sometimes known as the Lorn Furnace Company—took leases of Sir Duncan Campbell's woods. Iron smelting continued here till 1866, and the site has been taken into care as a Guardianship Monument and restored by the Department of the Environment (Plate 27). The furnace is square in plan and apart from its scale shows little difference in design from the Wye valley furnace at Coed Ithel which was built at least a hundred years earlier. Like Coed Ithel, Bonawe is rubble built but has a brick stack (Plate 28). The lower part of the lining has been removed, but there are cast-iron lintels above the tuyere's arch and tap hole, one giving a cryptic indication of the foundation—'Bunaw F 1753'. The bridgehouse, parts of the walls of the blowing engine house and of the casting house, together with three sheds behind the furnace, make up the group of industrial buildings. Two larger sheds housed charcoal stocks, and the third, partitioned inside, held ore supplies. There are two ranges of workers' housing of great historic interest and a

Plate 27 A general view of Bonawe ironworks, Taynuilt, Argyll, showing the reconstructed furnace and storage sheds.

rubble pier on a 'T' plan.[21] An excavation took place in 1978 under the direction of C. J. Tabraham.

Not far from Inveraray is Craleckan ironworks at Furnace. Built in 1755 by the Argyll Furnace Company—Jonathan Kendall and Company from Duddon—the furnace is in excellent condition; erected on the usual square plan, it was constructed of drystone rubble tapering to the bosh. There is a single-storey casting house, now with a corrugated iron roof and the remains of the blowing engine house below the bridgehouse. The stone lining of the furnace appears to be completely intact and would be worthy of further study. The tuyere arch has two cast-iron lintels, one bearing an indistinct inscription, 'C [or G] F 1755 [or 3]'. A large building, probably a charcoal shed, also now re-roofed in corrugated iron, is located above and sufficiently close to the furnace as to allow the easy transfer of fuel to the bridgehouse, and there is the site of a reservoir to the south with a small three-bay 'waterhouse', a clear indication of an attempt to extend water supplies.[22]

Plate 28   The charcoal furnace at Bonawe, undoubtedly the best
example in the British Isles.

The West Midlands assumed the technical leadership of the
iron industry by the early eighteenth century. Bloomeries had
existed in this region for centuries, but the blast furnace came
first to Cannock Chase (SK009138) in 1561–3 as a result of the
enterprise of William, Lord Paget.[23] Dud Dudley (1599–1684),
author of *Metallum Martus* (1665), began experimenting *c.* 1620
at Pensnett with coal as the furnace fuel instead of charcoal, but
despite his claims to have been successful, he left no permanent
technique.[24]

Abraham Darby I (1667–1717) perfected coke-smelting technology in the first decade of the eighteenth century at Coalbrook-

Plate 29   The furnace bank at Coalbrookdale where Abraham
Darby first used coke instead of charcoal for smelting iron.

dale (Plate 29). There were many small furnaces in this area
within easy reach of the Severn, the best preserved being Charl-
cotte (SO638861) which dates from *c*. 1670. Darby came to Coalbrookdale from Bristol and leased in 1708 a furnace which had
been built by Sir Basil Brooke in 1638; three lintels at the old
furnace, now restored, carry the dates 1638 and 1777. Darby's
interest in coke smelting was primarily conditioned by his inten-
tion of casting iron hollow-ware cooking pots for which he had
taken a patent in 1707.[25] The Coalbrookdale Company's trade in
fine-quality castings expanded as the century proceeded, but the
process of coke smelting did not spread rapidly until the 1750s.

The explanations of the failure of other ironmasters to take up Darby's technique have varied. Some historians have argued that Darby successfully guarded his trade secret; others that Coalbrookdale coals were particularly suitable for the coking process and other coals unsuitable; yet others have suggested that coke pig was inferior to charcoal pig iron.[26] Recently, Charles Hyde has persuasively argued that other ironmasters knew of the process almost from its inception, that the quality of coal was no great constraint since low sulphur coals were both accessible and in abundant supply, especially in South Staffordshire; that coke pig iron could be converted in the forge into bar iron by the early 1730s and was certainly used earlier by Abraham Darby II at Middle Forge, Coalbrookdale. Although there were certainly differences in the quality of charcoal pig and coke pig iron, the real issue was the price differential between them; it was not till the 1750s that the production costs of coke pig showed a clear advantage over those for charcoal pig iron. As time passed, the old process was generally displaced because of the relative cheapness of coke metallurgy.[27] It is clearly a mistake, judged from the evidence presented by Professor Hyde, to imagine that coke smelting was initially much cheaper than charcoal smelting.

Coalbrookdale Old Furnace (SJ667047) is thus an exceptionally important site: many technical innovations were associated with it. In the 1720s Newcomen steam engine cylinders were first cast in iron there instead of in brass, and sent via the Severn and Bristol to the mines of Cornwall; iron rails were cast there in 1767 and later iron-wheeled vehicles were made to run on them; Abraham Darby III (1750–89), with whom the two lintels of 1777 are associated, supervised the casting of the components for the first iron bridge in 1779.[28] Much has been written about Coalbrookdale, and a visit to Ironbridge Gorge Museum should be regarded as essential by serious students of the history of the iron industry (Plate 30).

Although the industrialization of Britain gradually increased the market for cast iron, the principal market was for bars, and so pig iron was converted into bar iron at the forge. First, the pig iron was put into a charcoal-fired hearth known as a finery where it was stirred under a blast of air. Carbon and silicon impurities were thereby driven off; as the iron was purified, its melting temperature rose (to c. 1500°C), and in consequence it formed a spongy mass in the finery, ready for the hammer. After being hammered into a block weighing about 56 lb (25 kgm), it was transferred to the chafery. Here the purified iron was simply reheated—there was no air blast—and shaped under the hammer

Plate 30   The warehouse and erecting shop for cast-iron goods at
Coalbrookdale built by the Coalbrookdale Company in the 1830s.
The clock was added in 1843.

for the market. No fundamental change in its charcoal compo-
sition occurred; hence coal-firing in the chafery was generally
adopted from *c.* 1750. A typical forge contained two or three
finery fires and one chafery fire[29] and, according to Hulme,[30] on
average produced in 1717 115 tons of bar iron per annum. But
iron then went either to the blacksmith or to the slitting mill,
where it would be cut into nailrods for the nailers. Increasing
quantities of bar iron, the main raw material of the hardware
trades, were imported from Sweden and Russia in the eighteenth
century, and growing British metallurgical proficiency excited
much interest in northern Europe and led to a few attempts at
industrial espionage by Swedish 'visitors'.[31]

However, British producers presented no real threat to foreign
bar-iron suppliers before 1750; indeed, in the preceding half-
century foreigners enjoyed a growing share of the British market.

The pressure of rising charcoal prices—and to a lesser extent the increase in pig-iron prices—in the last half of the eighteenth century encouraged experimentation in the forge. The alternative was to surrender the British market completely to Sweden and Russia.[32] First, forgemasters adopted coal in the chafery, beginning in the 1730s; this change was commonplace by the 1760s.[33] There were also many attempts to use coal in the finery, but the first real success was achieved by the Wood brothers in the early 1760s. Their potting process involved heating the pig iron in the finery with coal, thereby contaminating the iron with sulphur but removing silicon. This brittle iron was then broken into small pieces and put into covered clay pots with a flux such as lime. When twenty or so of these pots were heated in a coal-fired reverberatory furnace, the flux absorbed the sulphur and the high temperature drove off the carbon. Meanwhile, the iron was protected from further impurities by the pots. However, these would eventually break, and the iron had then to be quickly removed and cooled ready for the chafery. This process was sometimes known as 'the Shropshire process', yet another sign of the supremacy in iron metallurgy of the West Midlands.[34]

The potting process was further improved and by 1780 was widespread, well before Henry Cort's puddling process was developed in 1783–4.[35] Cort's well-known process thus completed rather than began a phase of technical change. The late Dr Diane Freeman and Dr R. Riley have both contributed to our understanding of the Funtley forge site (SU550082) in Hampshire, where Henry Cort (1740–1800) operated his first puddling furnace.[36]

Cort's process had one major disadvantage: it tended to waste iron, some of which mixed with the sand in the furnace bed. A most significant improvement was made in the early 1830s by Joseph Hall (1769–1862), a Black Country ironmaster, in the process known as wet puddling or pig boiling. Instead of using sand as the bed in the puddling furnace, Hall used roasted slag. When the pig iron went into the puddling furnace, the molten oxidized slag combined with the carbon in the pig, forming bubbles of carbon monoxide—a boiling effect—which made their way to the surface, there bursting into blue flames, commonly called 'puddlers' candles'. Hall's process was adopted everywhere puddling was practised, and Thomas Walmsley and Son of Atlas Forge (SD713084), Bolton, was the last firm in Britain to operate wet puddling (Plate 31).[37]

It is thus clear that a series of technical improvements, generally inspired by economic stimuli, freed the iron industry from its

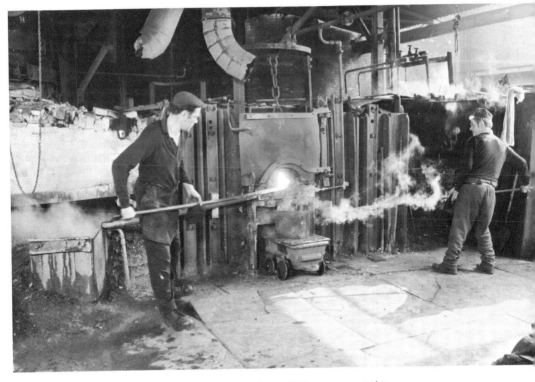

Plate 31 Changing rabbles during the puddling process at the
Atlas works of Thomas Walmsley and Sons, Bolton.

dependence on charcoal. Furthermore, the industry lost the constraints imposed by water power and by transport costs, because
steam was applied to the blowing engine, while canals and
railways improved distribution. After 1750 concentration on the
coalfields became increasingly the new logic of location, a stage
of development virtually complete by 1800 when the contribution
of charcoal furnaces to output had become marginal.

Good examples of coke furnaces of this phase are becoming
fewer. Bedlam furnaces (SJ677034) on the east side of Ironbridge
date from 1757 and 1788 and have recently been restored; this
site was one of the earliest selected for the exploitation of coke-
smelting techniques.[38] A short-lived venture at Moira has left a
substantial set of remains (Plate 32),[39] but Neath Abbey ironworks
(SS738977), Glamorgan, is the outstanding group in an area rich
in remains of the metallurgical industries (Plate 33).[40] South
Wales up to 1830 enjoyed outstanding economic advantages, once
the primacy of Coalbrookdale had been broken, and these two

Plate 32 The Moira furnace from the west. This Leicestershire iron furnace, built 1800–4, was named after Lord Moira, who promoted the venture.

very large furnaces dating from the late eighteenth century ought to be considered for preservation.

James Beaumont Neilson (1792–1865) in 1828 began to redress the economic balance in favour of the Scottish Lowlands and particularly the Glasgow–Coatbridge axis where blackband ironstone, coal, metalworking and engineering skills existed in abundance.[11] Neilson's hot-blast process (pre-heating the blast before it went into the furnace) was widely applied in Scotland but also in the Black Country. However, the price of Scottish No. 1 pig iron was the basis upon which iron prices everywhere were calculated for about fifty years.[12] Clyde ironworks, where Neilson tried his invention, and Muirkirk, where he began, as a consultant, to think about the problems of the cold-blast process, no longer provide the archaeologist with any guidance as to what a hot-blast ironworks really looked like. The remains of the blowing engine house at Shotts (NS879598), Lanarkshire, probably dating from c. 1835, is a forlorn survivor of a once-great regional industry.[13] However, near Ironbridge the Blists Hill open-air museum has remains of three furnaces (SJ695033) built in 1832, 1840 and 1844 and blown out in 1912.[14]

Plate 33 Neath Abbey ironworks, founded by the Cornish Quaker family of Fox who moved to South Wales and leased the land for this works in 1792. The furnaces were constructed in 1793.

Forge and foundry remains are very much more abundant. Iron rolling, which Cort in 1784 had established on a modern footing, was greatly improved in the middle decades of the nineteenth century as the demands of the railway age made themselves evident. At Wortley (SK294998), the Top Forge which is being restored by Sheffield Trades Historical Society dates from the seventeenth century but enjoyed a glorious heyday in the 1840s and 1850s when it was a substantial producer of wrought-iron railway axles. The helve hammers here, as so often, were water-driven, and a rolling mill dates from the 1780s.[45]

Numerous foundries and their cupolas (devised by John Wilkinson in the 1790s) existed in almost every large industrial town as well as at the ironworks, and it is still possible to detect their products even if the foundries have disappeared (Plate 34). At Coalbrookdale the museum has on display samples of local work, and a history of founding is available for visitors to consult.

Plate 34   Interior of a typical, wholly traditional, small iron
foundry in King Street, Aberdeen, showing wooden foundry
cranes. Now demolished.

The age of steel was slow in dawning. Quantities produced
before 1860 were relatively small and sparsely used for edging
tools and weapons; generally the quality was poor and incon-
sistent. Swedish bar iron was often used in the conversion process
which took place in a cementation furnace, a technique introduced from the Continent in the late seventeenth century. In the
furnace sealed earthenware or stone vessels containing iron bars
packed in charcoal were heated for five days; this process raised
the quantity of carbon in the metal sufficiently to produce 'blister'
steel. Better steel was produced by binding the bars into a 'faggot',
which was treated, forged and welded.[46]

Ambrose Crowley (1657–1713) in 1691 had taken a lease of
land at Winlaton and then gravitated to the Derwent valley on
Tyneside; this was the beginning of north-east England's interest
and specialization in steel production. Crowley hoped to take
advantage of cheaper labour and raw materials and, in particular,

he was well placed to exploit imported Swedish bar iron and had at his command foreign skilled workers, probably Belgians or Germans.[17] One of the few surviving stone cementation furnaces, the Derwentcote furnace (NZ131565) in County Durham, dating from c. 1740, is in excellent condition. This building is being preserved by the Regional Open Air Museum based at Beamish.[48]

The cementation technique was also introduced into South Yorkshire where it was improved by Benjamin Huntsman (1704–76), a Doncaster clockmaker who eventually moved to Handsworth, now a district of Sheffield. Huntsman's crucible process (c. 1742) was designed to provide better quality steel for clock springs and pendulums, and depended upon using coke to heat two closed clay crucibles containing bar iron with fluxes in a brick-lined chamber. Sheffield City Museums have established at Abbeydale Forge (SK326820) a display centre dedicated to the history of the steel industry, beginning with Huntsman's crucible steel furnace.[49]

Huntsman's process reigned supreme until the 1850s when Sir Henry Bessemer (1813–98) introduced the converter. This was simply a trunnion-mounted container into which a charge of molten pig was first poured; the converter was then turned upright and air blown through the iron. This oxidized the carbon, silicon and manganese in a fairly spectacular display; indeed, the first hand smelter judged the progress of the process by the character and colour of the flames pouring from the converter. When the metal was ready for pouring, the blast was turned off and the steel was tipped into a ladle and thence into ingot moulds. Once cold, the ingots went to the steel foundry for turning into goods. The last Bessemer plant to work in Britain was at Workington and it closed on 28 July 1974; thus a process pioneered in Britain and used almost everywhere that steel was made came to an end.[50]

Robert Mushet (1811–91), the father of alloy steels, improved Bessemer's process in 1868 by adding tungsten so as to remove any excess oxygen and thus making the steel self-hardening. Bessemer's acid process, apart from teething troubles, had the cardinal disadvantage that it could be used only with non-phosphoric ores when phosphoric ores were relatively abundant in Britain.[51] Sidney Gilchrist Thomas (1850–85) and his cousin, Percy Gilchrist (1851–1913), solved this problem in 1879 with their basic refractory lining for the converter consisting of calcined dolomite and fireclay.[52] C. W. Siemens (1823–83) introduced the open-hearth process in 1863 for converting pig iron into steel and since it was more flexible than the Bessemer converter process, it was very widely applied.[53] Clydebridge Steelworks (NS631618), Lanarkshire, founded in 1887, has six open-hearth furnaces whose future is very much in the balance.[54] In places like Middlesbrough where steel furnaces were once commonplace, closure and then demolition has removed almost every significant trace.

The changes briefly outlined here were really responses to a changing market. Markets were at first local or formed by the economic radius of water-borne transport conveying goods with a relatively high value to volume ratio. Needles made in Redditch, nails made in Stourbridge, scissors made in Sheffield, and steel made at Derwentcote could find markets at greater distance than pig iron. Specialization in heavy products such as Carron Company's production of short-barrelled cannon (carronades) could ensure business success in an age of war or cold war, particularly as the naval dockyards could be supplid by coastal shipments. Regional specialization, as for instance in Coalbrookdale's hollow-ware, produced lower costing iron goods but depended upon the exploitation of comparative advantages and overcoming any inter-regional competition.

Industrialization and its twin, urbanization, took the form, initially, of regional specialization, but to traditional markets the economic growth process added over time fresh sources of demand—for machinery and machine tools, pipes and retorts for gas and water supply, rails, boilers, locomotives, ships, structural iron and steelwork, tinplate, cans, more sophisticated armaments, and strip steel. As the international economy emerged in the late nineteenth century, comparative advantage transcended national boundaries, enforcing further technical changes in the British iron and steel industry but rarely leaving an industrial archaeology for long.

The engineering industries depended for their progress on the development of machine tools for lifting, moving and shaping substantial pieces of iron and steel. John Wilkinson's boring mill (1774) was the first significant invention. Used initially for boring cannon, it was applied to the production of steam engine cylinders, an early indication of mechanical versatility among the first generation of machine tools.[55] The bow drill and lathe had an ancient pedigree but were given fresh uses by men like Henry Maudslay (1771–1831) and his employer, Joseph Bramah (1748–1814), both of whom could reasonably be regarded as the fathers of the modern machine tool industry. Richard Roberts (1789–1864), James Nasmyth (1808–90), and Joseph Whitworth (1803–87), all engineers who worked for Maudslay, continued the tradition of invention and improvement of machine tools.[56] Although there is a developing legend that British machine tool makers failed the British economy after 1870, Hume's work on machine tools for shipbuilding points to the conclusion that this is too superficial an analysis.[57] Lancashire sent machines abroad, and so did Birmingham and Clydeside, and imports of American and German machine tools were relatively insignificant compared with the volume of British machine production.

Because of their scrap value many machine tools received short shrift when firms decided to re-equip or wind up, and museums have been relatively slow—naturally enough, considering the size of some tools—to adopt a rational conservation policy. Often the industrial archaeologist is forced back upon the documentary

Plate 35 An elegant example of the founder's art, a cast-iron bridge over the River Liffy in Dublin.

evidence provided by trade catalogues or general technical drawings.[58]

Engineering products have received better treatment. There are specialist vintage car and aircraft collections, railway museums, and surviving artefacts still in use—for instance, bridges of all sorts (Plate 35); street furniture such as manhole covers and lamp standards; iron and steel canopies and structural columns and beams, particularly at railway stations. A number of authors[59] of local and regional studies have placed on record the state of this component of the industrial heritage, but more inevitably remains to be done.

7
Mining and Quarrying

Winning coal, iron ore and non-ferrous materials, including tin, lead, copper, building stone and slate, has absorbed man's attention and ingenuity in many different parts of the British Isles for centuries. Until the emergence of a coal-based technology during the two centuries following 1550,[1] however, coal and iron ore were very much the poor relations of the non-ferrous metals, tin, copper, zinc and lead, not to mention the precious metals, silver and gold. But from the beginning of the eighteenth century coal became king.

Coal and iron

Output of this commodity was not officially measured until 1854, when production was about 64.5 million tons; a century before British pits had possibly produced about 5 million tons. In the sixty years after 1854, technical change and economic development combined to stimulate a fourfold increase in production. On the outbreak of the First World War output had reached 287 million tons.[2] These figures indicate the broad sweep of the industry's progress but they conceal much more than they reveal: they tell nothing of the social groups or regions involved in this achievement; markets, technology and methods of production could not be static during such changes in output; employment and social organization were subjects of momentous change.

Landowners in many different areas of Britain made the investment decisions which initiated substantial changes in output, and where their story has been told, they evidently regarded the exploitation of coal seams as a way to wealth and as an aid to continued conspicuous consumption.[3] Their influence was only slightly diminished by mercantile partnerships which had developed early in the Northumberland–Durham coalfield and were increasingly common in Wales, Scotland, Lancashire and the Midlands after 1780 (Plate 36).[4]

Labour supply in the eighteenth century was a fundamental problem, only solved at first by extreme measures such as binding vagrants and paupers to coalmasters—and in Scotland, by serf-

Plate 36   The coal port *par excellence,* with staithes, basin and locks!
Seaham Harbour, County Durham (NZ433495) designed by John
Dobson, architect, for the Marquess of Londonderry, who intended
to supply coal to the London market.

dom—until migration and Irish immigration began to equate
supply with demand in the nineteenth century. By 1900 mining
employed nearly one million people compared with about 200,000
in 1841.[5]

In South Wales the sinking of new pits in the 1860s and 1870s
pulled labour like a magnet, often with dramatic social conse-
quences. A most remarkable example is provided by the Rhondda
which in 1861 had only 4,000 inhabitants; in 1891 the population
was 127,980, and a peak of 163,000 was reached in 1921. Cardiff,
from which much coal was exported, increased its population in
the same period from 41,422 to 220,827.[6]

Markets changed substantially over the same period, according
to most experts. Professor Duckham, in analysing demand for
Scottish coal, for instance, noted the growing significance of
industrial consumers after 1760, particularly the ironworks.[7]
Deane and Cole remark that the principal market *c.* 1800 was the
household market and associated manufacture, with the ironmasters, brickmakers, distillers, brewers, bakers, potters and glass-

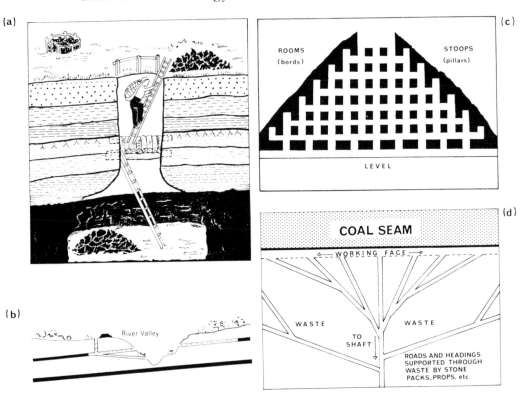

Fig. 4   Types of mine shaft and underground working
   (a) A bell-pit (after N.C.B., 1958)
   (b) Pit-and-adit system (after N.C.B., 1958)
   (c) Room and stoop working (after Duckham, 1970)
   (d) Longwall extraction (after Duckham, 1970).

makers leading the van of industrial customers. The development
of the railways and steam navigation, the growth of the gas and
electricity industries, the expansion of the chemical industry and
of the export trade greatly altered this simple pattern in the
following century. Exports, for instance, possibly accounted for
2 per cent of output in 1800, 5 per cent in 1840, 15 per cent in
1887 and 32½ per cent in 1913.[8]

Even in the eighteenth century the variety of technical practice
was very marked (Fig. 4). Some miners used the age-old practice
of following the outcrops and making drifts into the coal seam;
others sank a shallow shaft and worked bell pits. Many examples
of these primitive forms can still be detected. Drift mines or day
levels (or holes in Durham) were commonplace in the Forest of

Dean for instance, but the National Coal Board has now given this technique a greater sophistication in South Yorkshire where pits like Riddings Drift are highly productive. Bell pits collapsed toward their shaft after a time, and in most of the older coal-mining regions examples can be found: in Derbyshire at Wingerworth;[9] north of Bolton on the moors;[10] in the Thornton district of Fife; in Staffordshire at Beaudesert;[11] and in Pembrokeshire, where aerial photography has been an aid to detection.[12]

Stall and pillar working—in some places known as bord and pillar, post and stall or room and stoop—was general to most coal-mining districts by the eighteenth century and had been operated in some areas from the fifteenth century. From the pit bottom miners drove headings into the coal seams in a radius, rather like spokes in a wheel, and then they joined these headings together by making other tunnels, thus improving ventilation. The principle of working was to cut out a stall of coal, leaving pillars (commonly robbed by miners seeking easy pickings) to support the roof. This method continued, for instance in Northumberland and Durham, well into this century.[13]

However, the longwall system of mining, thought to have been developed in Shropshire in the early seventeenth century, gradually spread to other mining districts, becoming very common after 1850. This method was essential to deeper mining operations, for below about 1,000 ft there was the likelihood that the overlying rock would crush the pillars of coal to dust. Longwall mining involved removing all the coal at the coalface and supporting the roof with timber props and carefully packed rock debris. The diffusion of this technique is difficult to chart except in Scotland where Duckham has been able to associate its initial use with Carron Company (c. 1760), one of whose partners, Samuel Garbett (1717–1803), was probably well aware of Shropshire mining practices.[14]

Deep mining was, of necessity, dependent on more scientific prospecting for coal; capital investment became more significant and more speculative. In most coalfields, for example the Northumberland–Durham where deep mining was the most widespread by 1700, outcrop mining in ravines or steep river valleys had been replaced by shaft mining without real risk of missing coal. However, the use of boring rods, usually first associated with Huntingdon Beaumont in 1606, became the normal cheap alternative to sinking trial shafts during the late seventeenth century, when many patents were taken for boring equipment.[15] In 1804 James Ryan invented a boring technique (patented in 1805) which allowed the extraction of cores, and Richard

Trevithick later applied steam power to boring, saving both time and money.[16]

The shape and dimensions of shafts varied markedly between regions. In most English coalfields, while a few shafts were square, rectangular or even elliptical, most were circular.[17] For instance, in north-east England the standard shape was circular with diameters varying from 8 to 12 ft (2.4–3.6 m).[18] In Scotland shafts were usually square, an arrangement possibly associated with the long survival of stair pits and relatively shallow working.[19] Sinking shafts was a labour-intensive, back-breaking exercise; gunpowder was relatively little used until the 1770s, not so much on account of expense but because of the difficulty in devising adequate fuses.[20] Shafts of the eighteenth century were commonly lined with cheap timber and later with brick, sometimes laid without mortar for easy removal and later re-use. In the Wigan coalfield, where the strata were hard, lining was only used near the surface.[21] As cheaper iron became available from the 1790s, cast-iron tubbing, made in sections, was used, beginning on Tyneside.[22] Thus, the industrial archaeologist exploring coalfield areas has to exercise considerable care especially in dating workings.

As the Lofthouse colliery disaster demonstrated recently, water has been, and is, the miner's main enemy in many coalfields, for deep mining usually implied breaching the natural water table. In bell pits and many stall and pillar workings of no real depth, the water either drained towards the dip of the coal or naturally disappeared into lower strata. Where water did collect, the coal was often abandoned in favour of a new winning close at hand, or a drainage level driven below the seam to allow water to escape. Local terminology varies greatly to describe drainage levels: water level, adit, gate or sough are merely four among many.[23] In the Orrell district of Lancashire they were called soughs and were rarely more than 4 ft (1.2 m) wide and about as high.[24] These dimensions seem to have been fairly general, for such narrow passages served the purpose, cost less to construct than bigger levels and were less likely to collapse. Driving levels required considerable care so that dewatering one seam should not add to the problems of working another; litigation was a common result where miners, in the eighteenth century, deviated from the proper line 'as a Traveller may doe in a dark night.'[25] Examples of drainage levels can be detected in most coalfields,[26] although too often ignored by local fieldworkers.

Free-course drainage was often of little use for deep mines, and although longwall mining saved coal formerly left as pillars, it accentuated problems caused by underground water. Moreover, even where stall and pillar working accompanied deep mining, as, for instance, in most parts of the great northern coalfield of Northumberland and Durham, ancient adits were gradually proved inadequate, and new methods of drainage introduced. In some districts a windmill was used to drain a sump, and a few hours pumping sufficed: Fife in the eighteenth century possessed a number of wind pumps mostly representing a deliberate attempt to apply Dutch and fen-drainage techniques to a new problem.[27] Ingenious use was also made of water wheels to drive rag-and-chain pumps in Lancashire and north-east England; the barrel of one of these primitive devices is now in Blackburn Museum.[28] James Brindley in the period 1752–6 devised an elaborate water-power system to drain Wet Earth colliery, Clifton, Lancashire (SD774042). He constructed a weir across the River Irwell at Ringley and led the water through a rock-cut tunnel about half a mile long crossing a meander in the river. Then he made a pit on each side of the Irwell, and a syphon carried the water under the river to a leat feeding a water wheel which operated several pumps.[29]

Water 'bob' engines were found in many coalfields during the eighteenth century because they were relatively cheap, not because steam power was not considered. Duckham relates how the 10th Earl of Rothes engaged Stephen Row in 1738 or 1739 to build a 'bob' engine with twin beams in Strathore near Clunie in Fife at a cost of £200, roughly 25 per cent of the cost of a Newcomen engine. Yet Strathore 'bob' could pump at nine strokes a minute and raise over 185 hogsheads of water per hour.[30]

Although installation costs were clearly important, other economic factors retarded the application of steam power. Many coalmasters were operating on too small a scale to justify the initial capital investment and they feared that fluctuations in coal prices would further reduce potential returns. Steam engines needed a good 'wright', an engineer sufficiently skilled to deal with repairs and maintenance, for early models were often relatively inefficient and subject to breakdown. In these circumstances, water engines or horse-gins turning endless bucket-and-chain drainage systems augmented free-course drainage and seemed preferable.

Nonetheless, where large-scale deep coal mining was established and water was a problem not easily solved, the steam engine gradually took root. Although doubts are now being expressed about the practicability of his steam pump, Thomas Savery (c. 1650–1715), a prolific inventor, was granted a patent in 1698 for 'Raising water by the impellent force of fire'.[31] About Thomas Newcomen's engine and its general application to coal-mining ventures in the eighteenth century there can be no doubt. Newcomen (1663–1729), an ironmonger from Dartmouth, became familiar with the drainage problems encountered in the Cornish tin mines and produced an atmospheric steam engine which, after many years of experiment, was first installed in 1712 to pump water from Coneygre [or Coneygree] colliery near Tipton, Staffordshire.[32] The site (SO958907) on the west side of Burnt Tree has now been redeveloped for housing.[33]

Early Newcomen engines were possibly tried in Devon and Cornwall, but it was in coal-mining districts that their reputation was made. After Coneygre, Newcomen and his partner, John Calley, built engines for coal mines at Griff, Warwickshire (1714), Hawarden, Flintshire (c. 1715), Leeds, Yorkshire (1714–15), and Whitehaven, Cumbria (1715).[34] Other engineers joined the construction boom, and by 1720 as a consequence of their efforts, the Newcomen engine had spread to Wales, Tyneside, Lancashire, East Lothian and Ayrshire.[35] By 1769 John Smeaton (1724–92) calculated that about one hundred engines had been built in Northumberland and Durham alone, often erected to raise water from existing levels.[36]

Drainage engines of the Newcomen type and engine houses have survived, but not always in their native habitat. 'Fairbottom Bobs', an engine used at Fairbottom pits near Ashton-under-Lyne between c. 1760 and 1830, was taken by Henry Ford to America in 1930 for his Dearborn Museum.[37] The Science Museum has an engine built by Francis Thompson in 1791 at Oakerthorpe colliery and re-erected in 1841 at Pentrich colliery, Derbyshire.[38] An engine house in ruinous state exists at Saltcoats (NS257414), Ayrshire, and reputedly housed a Newcomen engine installed in 1719, the second in Scotland.[39] At Garrowtree colliery, South Yorkshire, the engine house of a Newcomen engine of 1777 is now converted into a private house.

At Elsecar, South Yorkshire (SE390003), the National Coal Board has preserved the Newcomen-type engine in its original engine house, a solidly built three-storey stone structure, with the beam protruding, as usual, through a wall in the top storey. From the end of the beam, part of the first section of the pump rod can be seen hanging down towards the now disused shaft. There have clearly been modifications to the original engine which was erected in 1795 not in 1787 as given on a lintel on the engine house. The original wooden beam was replaced in cast iron in 1836, and parallel motion was fitted on both the cylinder and pump ends of the beam at the same time; the first cylinder was 42 inches (106 cm) and was replaced in 1801 by one of 48 inches, (122 cm) diameter. The engine worked regularly until 1923 (when electric pumps were installed) and then intermittently till the 1930s, latterly as part of a concerted effort to keep the Fitzwilliam seam of the Barnsley Bed coal free of water.[10]

If the drainage of seams was one important priority, the ventilation of workings was another. In shallow workings blackdamp or chokedamp was commonly a problem; a mixture, mainly of carbon dioxide and nitrogen, accumulated in sufficient quantities to suffocate miners so swiftly that they had hardly time 'to cry but once God's mercy'.[11] Tests using lighted candles or burning coals (both soon extinguished) lowered in an iron basket down the shaft were developed, but where drainage was easy and no adits necessary, pockets of chokedamp awaited the unwary. Air sinks into shallow drifts were commonly driven to ventilate the seams; wooden pipes connected to a pair of bellows at the mine entrance served the same purpose; and in Wales and Lancashire a coal-fired furnace was commonly placed in the underground roadway leading up to a second shaft, the air passing over it creating an upward draught and constant circulation.[12]

Firedamp, or 'wild fire', a mixture of methane and air, was produced as a consequence of the formation of coal from decaying vegetable matter. It lingers within the cleavage places of the coal and in the surrounding strata, being released in the process of mining. Little known in Scotland before the twentieth century, it was a scourge in the great northern coalfield and in South Wales, where violent explosions, often accompanied by a great loss of life, occurred. Sir Humphrey Davy (1778–1829) devised a safety lamp which was merely one design in a series intended to deal with the menace arising from firedamp.[13] That explosions continued to occur simply demonstrates that the safety lamp could not provide a comprehensive answer to them, for the ignition of fine coal dust concentrated in the air could and did happen. Collections of miners' lamps can be seen in museums in many districts where mining is or was important. There is a particularly good collection in the Buile Hill Park Museum in Salford, and the N.C.B. mining museum at Lound Hall, near Retford, Nottinghamshire (SK701731), also has about fifty.

Remains of primitive ventilation systems are now apparently few. Blists Hill Open Air Museum at Ironbridge possesses a reconstruction of a surface ventilation furnace and chimney, and at Trehafod in the Rhondda (ST036910) a similar group can be seen. Steam-driven and then electrically powered fans were introduced from the 1870s, and there are plans to preserve a few of these. The Open Air Museum at Beamish, for instance, has a Waddle fan taken from Ryhope colliery, County Durham.

Most coal was hewn by hand until the twentieth century, and extensive collections of miners' tools have been preserved. Lound Hall Museum has tools dating from c. 1700 when wooden implements were most common, since iron was too expensive for such rough everyday use. Hamilton Burgh Museum has also made a speciality of collecting tools used in Scottish pits. Coal-cutting machinery, now so commonplace in the modern industry, requires similar attention, for otherwise early models will be available for study only by means of trade catalogues.

The N.C.B., through the initiative of Dr Alan R. Griffin, has made an excellent start at Lound Hall, and this museum should be on the itinerary of any serious student of the coal industry. Among the exhibits are a starvationer coal boat (so called because of their narrowness and prominent ribs) from the Duke of Bridgewater's Worsley mine (Plate 37), a tramway wagon from the Derby to Little Eaton (Derbyshire) horse-drawn tramroad, winding equipment, pit-pony harness, headstocks from Brinsley colliery (Nottinghamshire), and underground galleries almost two miles in length.

Underground haulage and winding to the surface were effectively the main constraints on coal production in many early collieries, for unless the output could be raised to the bank there was little incentive to improve methods of hewing. Consequently, much attention was paid to improving haulage and winding in the eighteenth century. As legislation to protect child and female workers—the main labour force employed in 'drawing' or 'bearing', i.e. haulage—increased from the 1840s, an alternative technology had to be adopted.[14] It was already foreshadowed by earlier technical developments.

Horses were substituted for human labour, and underground haulageways, usually made of wood, were laid for longer distances. Iron rails were then substituted for wood, beginning at the Duke of Norfolk's collieries in Sheffield, where John Curr (1756–1823) pioneered their use c. 1790.[15] The price of horse feed and iron were clearly determinants of social progress for the cost structure of a colliery concern would be changed only when these elements allowed.

As shafts were deepened, horses replaced the simple windlass. From the seventeenth century the horse-drawn cog and rung gin was increasingly used, but it was in its turn gradually replaced by the whim-gin, or horse-whim, whose cheapness, relative

Plate 37 A 'starvationer' boat used underground in James
Brindley's colliery canals at Worsley, Lancashire, which were built
for the Duke of Bridgewater, promoter of the celebrated canal to
Manchester. This example survived as a maintenance boat when the
underground canals were used for mine drainage, and can be seen
at Worsley.

simplicity, and smoothness of operation, a cog system could not
match. In Wales and north-east England much experimentation
with water power occurred, and colliery water-balance headgear
from the Forest of Dean has been preserved in the National
Museum of Wales. Only one such winding device remains *in situ*,
at Cumbyrgwm (SO320622) near Abersychan, and is rightly
scheduled as an industrial monument.[16]

Steam winding engines were applied in the large Midlands
and north-east coalfields from the 1780s at the deeper and larger
collieries. By the 1840s and 1850s they were commonplace everywhere deep mining was practised. Many early winders were
adapted Newcomen engines, since the fuel cost savings allowed
by Watt engines were not really significant at collieries, but from
1784, when the first Watt steam engine began winding at Walker
colliery, Tyneside, until the 1950s, steam winding dominated this

Plate 38   The Bowes Railway: winding engine house at Blackin's Hill (NZ282581), County Durham, built in 1915 for a winding engine by Andrew Barclay, Sons and Co. Ltd of Kilmarnock but now housing a 300 hp electric hauling drum by Metropolitan-Vickers Ltd, installed in 1950. A substantial part of this mineral railway is being preserved by the Tyne and Wear Industrial Monuments Trust.

branch of technology. In the first decade of this century electric winding was introduced but only made rapid headway in the 1950s and 1960s (Plate 38).

Most surviving steam winders are twin cylinder horizontal engines. Preserved at Washington F pit, County Durham (NZ302575) there is a good example with Cornish drop valves which was built in 1888 by the Grange Iron Company (Plates 39 and 40). In South Yorkshire there are still a number working, for instance at Markham Main colliery, Armthorpe (SE617046), Dinnington (SK518867), and Edlington (SK544992). Twin compound engines were also extensively used for winding, and there is an

Plate 39   The preserved winding engine house and head stocks, built 1926 at Washington F pit, County Durham.

excellent example at Astley Green Colliery, Lancashire (SJ705999), built by Yates and Thom in 1908, with Corliss valve gear operated from a return-crank-actuated eccentric shaft. Vertical winding engines were most commonly operated in north-east England, although at Pontypool (ST265999) there was a derelict single cylinder vertical winding engine dating from the early 1840s. However, an excellent preserved example may be seen at the North of England Open Air Museum taken from the nearby Beamish colliery (NZ220537).

Non-ferrous mining

Mining for other metals was also a very significant industrial activity, as was quarrying. In the 1850s the pithead value of metal ores mined was about one-third that of coal, while building stone,

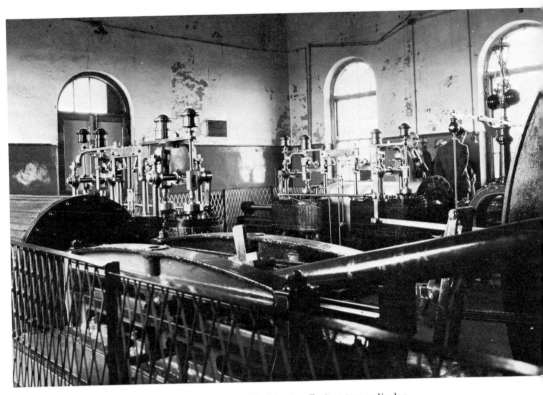

Plate 40   The winding engine at Washington F pit, a two cylinder,
horizontal engine with Cornish drop valves, probably older than its
engine house.

road metal, clays, slates, and limestone must have been fairly
close to another third. The most significant developments in
eighteenth-century non-ferrous metal-mining occurred in south-
west England, but there are less substantial parallels elsewhere.
Newcomen's engine was intended for pumping in the Cornish
tin and copper mines, but it was expensive on coal and was,
accordingly, at first limited in local application. In 1720 the first
certain Newcomen engine was built at Wheal Fortune, Ludgvan,
Penzance, and Joseph Hornblower erected another at Wheal Rose
near Truro in 1725.[48] The widespread local application of the
atmospheric engine coincided with the expansion of the domestic
market for tin in the 1740s and with the growth of tinplate
manufacture, centred on Swansea and Llanelly, Pontypool, and
Cydweli, as an exporting industry.[49] The principal earlier uses
for tin had been to form alloys (with copper for bronze and with
lead for pewter), but these Bristol and London trades had much

more limited potential than tinplate manufacture. Of the tinplate sites Cydweli (SN421079) is of most interest, much of the works dating from the early nineteenth century.

The tin-mining relics of Cornwall are more spectacular. Commonly, copper was also mixed with tin, but there was some specialization, notably at South Crofty mine, Camborne (SW669409), and Geevor (SW378342) at Pendeen, St Just, where a small mining museum has recently been opened. The principal tin areas were west of Truro, around Wendron, St Just-in-Penwith, Breage and St Ives, and Penzance became an obvious coinage and exporting point. Much of the old housing in these areas, notably the granite terraces in St Just, had been built for tinminers' families. Boulton and Watt engines were extensively used in Cornwall for pumping, but fuel costs stimulated further improvements, in particular the 'Cornish engine' developed by Richard Trevithick (1771–1833). Throughout the Duchy there are engine houses, built by mine captains exploiting copper and tin, to accommodate these pumping engines (Plate 41a and b). A number of these engines have been preserved as a result of the efforts of the Cornish Engines Preservation Society, established in 1935 and now part of the Trevithick Society. The National Trust has taken responsibility for two beam engines at East Pool, Redruth (SW675 416), which the Cornish Engine Preservation Society had taken into its care.

Cornish tin oxides required crushing and stamping before smelting. Stamps consisted of vertical iron-shod wooden beams which were lifted by cams on a water-powered (or less often, steam-powered) shaft and fell on to the ore slowly being fed into a box below. Water-powered stamps or remains of them can be seen in a number of places and remind one forcibly of their similarity with fulling stocks. Nancledra (SW500355) has a set of eight stamps, which were in use until 1948; they were driven by a water wheel 18 ft (5.5 m) in diameter and 29 inches (73.7 cm) wide, made by E. T. Sara of Camborne.[50] The Tolgus Tin Company's works (SW690438) near Redruth was until 1968 tin streaming (Plate 42) from water raised from deep mines at South Crofty and Geevor. Now it extracts tin from the waste tips of earlier mining ventures in the area. Owned by Madame Tussauds, the site is today exploited as a tourist attraction, and has its water-drawn stamps in regular operation during the summer season.

Copper mining and smelting was also an ancient activity in Cornwall. An increasing demand for brass, an alloy of copper and zinc, and the use of copper for sheathing the hulls of naval vessels were the bases for the expansion of copper and zinc

Plate 41 (*a*) East Pool. Whim or winding engine on the road
between Camborne and Redruth, now preserved by the National
Trust.

mining. Although some copper was mined in Wales, Staffordshire, Perthshire, and the Lake District, before 1770 Cornwall
dominated production. After 1770 Anglesey became a significant
producer so that by the mid 1780s Cornish and Welsh output
amounted to over 8,000 tons, at least eight times as great as
production in the 1740s. Cornish output continued to rise but
that of Anglesey began to decline after 1800. However, it is
important to know that in terms of value copper mining and
smelting was Britain's major metal industry in the late 1780s;
according to Deane and Cole, output at current prices in 1788
was worth about £600,000 or roughtly twice the value of pig-
iron production. No doubt, the developing brass manufactures

Plate 41 (*b*) The engine house chimney at the Tregurtha Downs Mines, Marazion.

Plate 42 Tin-streaming equipment at Tolgus Tin (Cornwall) Ltd, Redruth.

of Birmingham, Bristol and London represented a growth in demand for both consumer and capital goods.[51]

The archaeology of the processes of extraction and smelting is exceedingly rich. The Swansea valley and St Helens show less now then even ten years ago of the processes of roasting and smelting the copper ores, but there are mining remains in Anglesey at Parys Mountain (SH440900), in the Lake District in the valley of the Red Dell Beck (SD289986) where the Coniston mines were worked from the sixteenth century, and particularly in Cornwall and Devon. The Cornish engine houses and surface remains at Botallack (SW362333), Levant mine (SW369345), Bassett mines (SW689397), St Agnes Head (SW720516), Trewavas mine (SW600265) and Tregurtha Downs (SW537311) are merely some among the most spectacular. In general, they are the remains from the heyday of the Cornish copper industry, when output rose from about 35,500 tons per annum in the period 1785–90 to 154,000 tons in the peak between 1840 and 1845.[52]

Zinc ores occur, usually with lead, in many districts, notably in North Wales, Cumberland, Somerset and Derbyshire. Apart from its use with copper as an alloy to make brass, from the 1840s it was applied to sheet iron or steel as a galvanizing agent. In the Mendips near Shipham and Rowberrow (ST4457) there are remains of zinc ore calcining.

Leadmining was much more widespread—in north-east England, Wales, Devon and Cornwall, Scotland, the Lake District, the Isle of Man, Pennine Yorkshire, Shropshire, and Derbyshire. Operations were mainly concerned with working 'galena' or lead sulphide and were often many centuries old; as might, therefore, be expected, technology varied from the very primitive to the exceedingly advanced. Moreover, the sale of economic activity varied greatly, but the lead industry was increasingly characterized by the evolution of chartered companies and capital-intensive mercantile partnerships, intent also on retrieving the silver often found in lead ore.

Nonetheless, leadmining also provided opportunities for landowners and independent miners. In Derbyshire the Duke of Rutland had ore royalties in six High Peak liberties; at Leadhills the Earl of Hopetoun owned the leadmines, while his neighbour at Wanlockhead was the Duke of Buccleuch.[53] A greater tonnage of lead was mined than of any other base metal: between 1850 and 1949, a government report estimated that 4.5 million tons of lead concentrates were produced, a figure which would reach about 7 million tons, if the chronology of the industry was extended back to 1700.[54]

The archaeology of the lead industry is a very rewarding study. One of the finest examples of Cornish mining architecture is the engine house and chimney stack at West Chiverton lead mine (SW793509); from 1869 to 1882 a pumping engine made by Harvey and Company dewatered the mine from which tons of lead, 1.25 million ounces of silver and much zinc were raised.[55] In the Tamar valley Bere Alston silver-lead lodes near Morwellham were worked from medieval times, and remains of the Tamar smelting works (c. 1820) adjoining Weir Quay can still be detected.[56]

Wales was always a substantial contributor to total British lead output. The most important mine in Carmarthenshire, for instance, was Nantymwyn, worked in the eighteenth century as Cerrigmwyn (SN785445) by the Earl of Cawdor, and still being operated in the 1930s. This mine had extensive drainage adits, but in c. 1880 a Cornish pumping engine was erected to dewater the lowest working levels. Ore sales from this mine amounted to about 80,000 tons, according to existing records, but these are incomplete. The mine engine house and stack, and a profusion of shafts and drainage adits, remain to provide the industrial archaeologist with existing field evidence of great industrial activity.[57] In Cardiganshire Esgair Hir mine (SN737787), first surveyed c. 1700, was worked by the Welsh Potosi Lead and Copper Mining Company from 1852, and 15,000 tons of 'galena' and zinc blende with considerable quantities of pyrites were produced here. Remains survive of elaborate drainage levels and an intricate pumping system which dewatered the lodes.[58] One of the richest Welsh lead mines from 1862 to 1892 was the Van in Montgomeryshire (SN942876); 96,739 tons of lead ore were produced and 771,557 ounces of silver separated from it. Furthermore, about 25,000 tons of zinc blende were raised. There are remains of three ore-dressing floors, an inclined tramway and two chimney stacks.[59] Bryntail lead mine (SN918869) in West Montgomeryshire was the first site in Wales to be taken into care as an industrial monument. Although worked intermittently from 1770, its most profitable period was from 1845 to 1867; this small mine produced nearly 2,000 tons of lead ore and is now being restored by the Department of the Environment.[60]

In Shropshire, Allbutt and Brook have documented the exploitation of the county's lead ores in a recent careful study.[61] Adits, Cornish engine houses and dressing floors are visible remains of the regional industry which produced about 10 per cent of Britain's lead ore in the 1870s. Snailbeach (SJ375022), once reputedly the richest lead mine in Europe, was worked from Roman times and is now one of the best sites for the serious student to study, for there are very extended remains of timber headgear, ore-dressing floors, engine houses, mine buildings and shafts. Tankerville (SO355955), Bog mine (SO356978), Roman Gravels (SJ334000), and East Roman Gravels (SJ336003) are simply examples of operations which have left remains.[62]

Spectacular relics also exist on the Isle of Man. Lead and zinc mines here were particularly prolific, and none more so than the Great Laxey and the Foxdale groups. Outcrops were worked from medieval times at least, but the nineteenth-century entrepreneurs reached lodes previously unattainable. Shafts were driven at Great Laxey, for instance, to depths approaching 2,000 ft (609 m), and extensive use of water power was made for pumping, winding (known here as hoisting) and ore-dressing. Now a tourist attraction, the Lady Isabella water wheel (SC432852) with its pump rods drained the deep mines in Glen Mooar (Plate 43). Great Laxey closed in 1919, but the site is well worth visiting.

Much clearance has been undertaken in other lead-working areas on the Isle of Man, but the Foxdale–Glen Rushen area (SC2678), where much use was made of Cornish engines because good water supplies were lacking, has substantial remains. Cross's mine (SC263780) has an engine house, erected c. 1840, which is an obvious landmark for miles around. Beckwith's mine (SC253778) at the western edge of the Foxdale group had grave drainage problems, and its shafts have now collapsed. However, apart from an engine house and stack, there is a washing floor and crusher house (Plate 44)[63].

Derbyshire has remains of extensive leadmining, including open-cast operations at Dirtlow Rake near Castleton (SK154821), and museums at Derby and Buxton have good collections of lead-miners' tools and equipment. The Magpie mine at Sheldon (SK173682) is the headquarters of the Peak District Mines Historical Society and is the best site to visit, not merely for its collections but also because of its extensive surface remains. Stone Edge smelt mill (SK334670), high on the moors between Chesterfield and Ashover, ceased operations c. 1850 and was operating, purifying the crushed lead ore, from the 1770s. Its stack is now an industrial monument.[64]

Arthur Raistrick, Bernard Jennings and Robin Clough have recorded for us lead mining and smelting activities in Yorkshire, and C. J. Hunt has written the social history of mining in the northern Pennines.[65] Their classic studies make it a relatively easy task to select sites of particular significance. The Craven museum in Skipton has a large collection of mining tools mainly

Plate 43 Lady Isabella, the Great Laxey mine wheel opened in 1854 and named after Lady Isabella Hope, wife of the Governor, was designed by a Manxman, Robert Casement. A pitch back-shot wheel, 72 ft 6 in (22.1 m) in diameter and 6 ft (1.8 m) broad, once producing an estimated 200 hp for lead-mine pumping, it was acquired in 1965 by the Isle of Man government and extensively restored.

Plate 44   Beckwith's lead mine (SC253778), at the western end of
the Foxdale group of mines, was worked by the Isle of Man Mining
Company from *c.* 1831 and was always faced with grave drainage
problems until its closure *c.* 1870. The engine house and main stack
are in the background and the crusher house in the foreground.

from mines in Wharfedale and Airedale and ore-crushers from
Providence mine, Kettlewell. Moreover, its documentary collections are sufficiently rich to make it an important starting point
for the student. Grassington Moor (SE0367) was extensively
worked for centuries, and there are numerous bell pits, remains
of dressing floors, water wheel pits and smelt mill remains. The
Earby Mines Research Group has repaired the smelt mill stack
and has placed conservationists everywhere greatly in its debt
because of its general restoration efforts. Long flues led to such
chimneys in order to aid precipitation of valuable refined metal
from the fumes given off in smelting, and at Keld Heads Mill
(SE077910) in Wensleydale there is a particularly long example.
Similar specimens could be examined at Woodhead (NX5293),
Galloway, Charterhouse-on-Mendip, Somerset (ST504556), and

Lintzgarth mill, Durham (NY925430). One of the finest lead-mill sites is Killhope ore-crushing plant in Weardale (NY927429), where a water wheel over 33 ft (10 m) in diameter provided the power.

In Scotland, the best sites are Leadhills, Lanarkshire (NS8815), and Wanlockhead, Dumfriesshire (NS8713).[66] Though, as in most leadmining districts, complete structures, apart from housing, are few, these two villages have interesting remains. At Leadhills there is the Miners' Library and the warning bell used to call the community to any accident, while at Straitsteps mine, Wanlockhead, the Department of the Environment has taken into care the water-bucket pumping engine (NS873125). Some demolition, under army auspices, has been mistakenly undertaken in the area.

Mining for other metals—ironstone, arsenic, antimony, barytes, fluorspar, graphite, plumbago, oil-shale, manganese and gold—has left remains scattered from Merioneth to Sutherland, and local studies, listed in the Bibliography and Notes, should be studied by those particularly interested in these more esoteric aspects.[67]

Quarrying

Quarrying (Plate 45) for building stone, road metal, limestone, gravestone, paving stone, slate, brick and fireclay, and china clay were common activities where local resources allowed their exploitation, but increasingly as transport improved, regional specialization occurred where comparative advantages existed. Caithness paving stone and Aberdeen granite made their way coastwise to London;[68] Galloway granite built Liverpool docks, beginning in the period 1826–32, and sandstone from south-west Scotland the New York State Capitol at Albany.[69] Rapid urban growth, in the late nineteenth century especially, increased the demand for all forms of building stone and slate and, therefore, many parts of Britain far from the madding crowd were drawn into the cyclical booms associated with the construction industries.

The archaeology of quarrying is generally less exciting than its business history, but even the latter has been strangely neglected. We have no good account of the Leicestershire road-metal industry for instance, although historians are beginning to take more interest in granite, china clay and slate.[70]

Plate 45 Monumental sculptor's yard, Keith (NJ432509), Banffshire.
Note the blocks of stone and wooden derrick crane of a type once
standard in stone quarries and yards.

Clay and china clay quarries were significant employers in
only a very few counties, Cornwall and Devon being quite
unusual in this respect. St Austell was the centre of an area
extending over 45 square miles, in which the best remains of the
china clay industry are concentrated. At Parkandillack (SX945568)
what is generally believed to be the remains of the first coal kiln
in Britain, built c. 1848 by Charles Truscott for drying about 8
tons per week, is preserved by the Goonvean and Rostowrack
China Clay Company. The water wheel was used extensively to
pump clay slurry from considerable depths to the surface, and
there were also a number of beam engines applied to the same

Plate 46 Dinorwic Quarry workshops, Gilfach Dhu, Llanberis, Caernarvon (SH586603), now preserved and part used as a depot of the Llanberis Lake Railway Co. Ltd.

purpose. At Wheal Martyn, Carthew, St Austell (SX005554) there is an interesting china clay industry open-air museum showing operations at a works *c.* 1880 with working water wheels and much other machinery.

There are many building-stone quarries worth visiting and recording, but we have to be very selective and trust that our readers will perhaps assist in filling gaps in existing knowledge. Quarries often contain powder houses, remains of cranes or tramways and sometimes rock-sawing equipment. David Viner has recently recorded the marble quarry on Iona and found a Fielding and Platt (Gloucester) gas engine installed there in 1911 and a most interesting cutting frame made by Anderson of Arbroath.[71] Welsh slate quarries dominated this sector of the building supplies industry from the 1850s, although local quarries occasionally survived, especially in Westmorland and Argyll.[72] In North Wales quarries at Penrhyn (SH6265), Blaenau Ffestiniog (SH7046), Dinorwic near Llanberis (SH5960) were very considerable employers of labour.[73] Dinorwic, for instance, employed nearly 3,000 men *c.* 1900, and its workshop buildings erected in 1870 are among the most impressive in the industry (Plate 46). These now form the North Wales Quarrying Museum, demonstrating all the stages in the production and transportation of slate. The machines were originally driven by a 80 hp water

Plate 47   A typical rural small circular single-draw lime-kiln at
Appersett, Wensleydale, North Yorkshire.

wheel, and four blacksmiths' hearths were the central production
point for the metal parts of tools and machinery used within the
quarry. Equally massive slate quarries can be seen at Easdale
(NM735173), and at East and West Laroch, Ballachulish. Terraced
workings (NN085583 and NN073584) similar to those in North
Wales were first begun in the late seventeenth century, and the
tenements of Glasgow and Edinburgh were, and often still are,
roofed with this material.

Limestone quarrying was subject to many demands. Agricultural improvement led to a multiplication of simple, small kilns
in limestone country, but many are in ruins or have disappeared
altogether (Plate 47).[74] Lime was used in mortar from quite early
times and thus the largest complexes commonly occur near
quarries on the edges of large towns, not far from cheap coal. An
illustration of these favourable circumstances is provided by the
two large three-draw kilns at Middleton, Midlothian (NT357584),
not far from Edinburgh (Plate 48). Ironworks demanded lime as
a flux, and thus ironworking districts often possessed kilns. Brook
(1977) provides a number of examples from the West
Midlands—near Consall Forge (SJ999491), the large complex at

Plate 48   Lime-kilns at Middleton, Midlothian (NT357584). Two large three-draw kilns, one of the largest pairs in Scotland, now disused. Their size is an indication of the importance of the local Edinburgh market for lime as well as of demand from farmers.

Froghall (SK027476), and at the Black Country Museum in Dudley (SO948917).[75] Equally, Lanarkshire, Ayrshire, Dumfriesshire, Yorkshire, Glamorgan and Carmarthenshire had large numbers of kilns situated in their extensive limestone districts. Devon and Somerset commonly had kilns near the shore facing South Wales from which much of the coal used in them came. The use of limestone with clay, sand and gypsum in cement-making led to the foundation of many Thames-side works from the 1870s onwards, and the development of concrete building techniques gave further impetus to the Portland cement industry. Charles Dodsworth has examined the Kirklington site (SP493200) in the Cherwell valley beside the Oxford canal, which dates from 1906, and this plant seems to have been relatively small by modern standards and ceased production in the late 1920s.[76]

Whether one thinks of the urban skyline or the country landscape, the mining and quarrying industries have moulded the shapes and colours of what can be seen. Whether it be the great Delabole slate quarry of Cornwall or Rubislaw granite quarry in Aberdeen, their depth is an indication not merely of commercial exploitation but also a symbol of the colour and texture of concentrated social organization elsewhere. Stone, clay, slate, coal and steel remain fundamental materials to urban society. The archaeology of these underlying industries deserves more attention from local societies and individuals.

8
Chemicals, Ceramics and Glass

The historical origins of this group of industries, despite much research, are still shrouded in mystery. Relatively complex processes require careful unravelling, and generally industrial archaeologists can add little to the information derived from documentary sources. The reasons for this limitation are fairly numerous. First and foremost, plant and machinery have been destroyed very rapidly and for perfectly good reasons. These industries occupied valuable space, often in urban areas such as St Helens, Newcastle, Glasgow, London, Birmingham, Bristol, Widnes, Leith, and 'the Potteries' of North Staffordshire. Clearance and demolition, therefore, commonly released valuable land for further development. Tips and wastelands in places like Widnes and St Helens were removed because they were unsightly and occasionally dangerous. Potbanks and glass cones, on account of their design, posed problems of public safety once they became unstable. Subject to constant technical change in the twentieth century, these industries rarely attracted the attention of historians until too late—and then when they did become the subject of academic investigation, the physical evidence had become much less useful.

Chemicals

The chemical industry, in particular, presents the industrial archaeologist with special problems. Its creation, rooted in a craft tradition, is so ancient as to tax the energies of prehistorians; its surviving structures are generally relatively modern; it encompassed a wide range of processes; it supplied a massive clientele, varying from meat-curers to glassmakers, and in consequence, grew in response to economic developments in other sectors; it depended for its raw materials on a variety of organic and inorganic substances. Systematic classification and study is likely to be, therefore, a major problem.

It is easy for the historian of glass or ceramics production to become obsessed with products and museum specimens. This temptation should be resisted by the industrial archaeologist, although it would obviously be a mistake to avoid one good source for assessing the nature, scope and quality of production. Even allowing for the fact that what products survive may not be entirely representative of output, there are many other questions which should excite attention. For instance, where did raw materials originate? How were they supplied? What markets were served? What scale—in terms of labour and capital—of operations was being conducted? What business problems were encountered? What were the conditions of workers—in terms of hours, pay, unionization, grades of skill, family life and leisure?

Rule of thumb fused with chemical science in techniques employed in food preservation, brewing, distilling, tanning, soap-making, candle-moulding, cloth bleaching and dyeing, activities which occupied considerable time in most agricultural and many urban households in pre-industrial Britain. Industrialization allowed free rein for the law of comparative advantage, and gradually local or regional self-sufficiency collapsed, as the modern chemical industry evolved.[1]

Salt (sodium chloride), a basic raw material for many other products and processes, was at first produced primarily for the preservation of fish and meat. Although extraction by evaporation from sea-water was widely practised, South Shields was by the seventeenth century the principal centre in the British Isles. Along this north-east coast, Blyth and Seaton Sluice were also important salt-producers, and Atkinson estimates that the regional salt industry c. 1780 consumed a quarter of a million tons of small coal per annum.[2] The Firth of Forth, as Dr Adams has demonstrated, was dotted with saltpans, and in coastal areas where cheap coal was available temporary opportunities existed for an industry which enjoyed its heyday in the eighteenth century.[3] In southern England, Lymington, Hampshire (SZ326934), linked as it certainly was with naval demand for salt beef and pork, was the regional centre for an industry producing 50,000 tons of salt per annum c. 1750. The salterns of this area were used in the summer months to concentrate the brine before transfer to saltpans in the autumn prior to the autumnal slaughter of cattle and pigs. Woodside Salterns still has three buildings once associated with the salt industry, and the Chequers Inn (SZ323936) was the headquarters of the excisemen who collected the local salt tax.[4] Natural brine wells were exploited in Worcestershire and Cheshire, and rock-salt mining in Cheshire (c. 1690) and Teesside (1863) gradually destroyed the sea-salt industry.[5]

The expansion of the textile industries increased the demand for bleaching agents, mordants and dyes, and together with

Plate 49   Mock Tudor housing at Port Sunlight, the model factory
community built by Lever Brothers (1892).

demographic changes raised profitability for soap producers.
London, Bristol, Liverpool, Warrington, St Helens, Bradford,
Newcastle, and Glasgow became important centres for the pro-
duction of some or all of these products. The soap industry on
Merseyside—in Widnes, Warrington and Liverpool—has been
the subject of study on account of the entrepreneurship of William
Lever (1851–1925) and the multinational conglomerate, Unilever,
which he founded. Soap-boiling in this region was based upon
South Lancashire coal, Cheshire salt, and kelp (alkaline seaweed
ash), imported coastwise from western Scotland and Ireland.
Imported barilla from the Mediterranean, and tallow and palm-
oil extended this region's control over British soap output. By
1835 Liverpool exported four-fifths of all British soap exports,
and Merseyside was the most important centre of production for
soft and hard soaps, far surpassing London.[6] Lever, therefore,
joined an established success story and then in 1888 founded Port
Sunlight (SJ3484), a model factory village on the Cheshire side
of the Mersey estuary (Plate 49). Remains of soapworks are now,
apparently, according to Dr Gittins, few and far between.[7] Fortunately, the Black Country Museum has taken into care the soap-
making plant from the Borax 'Californian' Works, Tipton
(SO955924).[8]

Bleaching was the first of the textile processes in the eighteenth century to succumb to science. Previously cloth had been treated with a mild alkali solution (kelp or extract of wood ashes), followed by an acid, normally sour milk. Oily impurities and common dirt were removed by the alkali while the acid disposed of earthy substances which prevented even dyeing. Sulphuric acid was imported from the Low Countries in the early eighteenth century and replaced sour milk in the process; gradually, from the 1740s, chemical plants were established in Birmingham, Prestonpans and Bradford to supply the finishing trades, and imported sulphur from Sicily replaced acid imports.[9]

The growth of the fine linen trade and its successor, the cotton industry, stimulated further developments in bleaching, notably the use of chlorine discovered by Berthollet in France and pioneered by Charles Tennant (1768–1838) at St Rollox chemical works, Glasgow. Bleaching powder was widely produced, despite Tennant's attempts to use his patent to restrict competition.[10] Although many bleachers preferred to continue with older techniques, especially when the price of bleaching powder remained high, Tennant had, in fact, paved the way for a revolution in textile printing and dyeing.

Before this stage had been reached, other economic considerations had begun to affect the location of the calico printing and fine cloth finishing trades. London, which had been the most important centre for many centuries, succumbed, principally on account of high wage levels, to competition from the West Country but particularly from Lancashire and Scotland.[11] Moreover, where fine linen production survived competition from cotton, as in Ulster and in Dunfermline and parts of eastern Scotland, local printing and dyeing replaced external facilities. Thus, it is to Lancashire and Ulster (Plate 50) that the industrial archaeologist needs to turn for the best remains of this phase of industrial change. Professor Ashmore has carefully charted what survives in Lancashire, assisted by a number of local historians;[12] Professor Green has performed a similar service for County Down.[13]

Dyeing remained the province of the practical man rather than the domain of the laboratory scientist for much longer than bleaching, although from the late eighteenth century progress was being made in this branch of textile technology.[14] Natural dyestuffs and their qualities have recently been thoroughly revealed to us by Kenneth Ponting;[15] at Keynsham in Somerset (ST656679) Albert Mill remains to remind us that logwood was the basis of dyeing for centuries; it was merely one logwood mill

Plate 50   Castlewellan flax-spinning mill and bleachworks,
Annsborough, County Down (OS4/3537) built between *c.* 1818 and
1863 and belonging to James Muirland Ltd, a family firm dating
from the eighteenth century.

of many in textile finishing districts ranging from the West
Country to the Vale of Leven.

Artificial dyestuffs production took root principally in the
Manchester and Glasgow areas. Turkey red dyeing was pioneered
in the 1780s by French immigrants, notably Borelle and Papillon,
and aniline dyes were produced from the early 1860s in both
these districts after W. H. Perkin's initial discovery of 'mauve' in
1857. Prussian blue and a range of yellows and greens were
produced from chemical agents, but dyestuffs technology based
upon coal tars became a German preserve until the First World
War arrested official opinion to this state of affairs.[16] A few calico
printing works survive in Lancashire, and Ulster has a small
number of dyeworks attached to textile complexes.[17]

To fix dyes, the cloth was first treated with a mordant. Alum
shales were mined and formed the basic raw materials for the
chief mordant, copperas. In England the principal source of
supply was in North Yorkshire at Ravenscar, (NZ9701), Boulby
(NZ7519) and Kettleness (NZ8415), but mining and quarrying
took place also at Pleasington, Lancashire (SD635281), and at
Hurlet, Renfrewshire, and at Campsie, Stirlingshire.[18] Acetates
were also used, the acetic acid mainly arising from the destructive
distillation of wood; output of acetates was, therefore, linked to

Plate 51   Chart gunpowder mills at Faversham, Kent (TR009613),
the major munitions centre in south-east England for nearly three
centuries. Closed in 1934 and now being restored by the Faversham
Society.

the production of charcoal and pyroligneous acid. These activities
occurred in many parts of Britain, notably in the Forest of Dean,
the Lake counties and in Western Scotland.[19]

Charcoal-based technology was, in consequence, the goad to
chemical production in many woodland areas. Oak bark was
stripped from the trees and used by the tanners as a source of
tannic acid. Charcoal itself was a principal ingredient in gunpowder, and the Weald provided supplies for the Chart mills at
Faversham, Kent (TR009613), the major munitions centre in England for centuries and now, fortunately, a preservation project of
outstanding importance (Plate 51).[20] Powder mills were found in
many areas, particularly in the Lake District, Argyll, Arran, Dean
and Dartmoor (Plate 52).[21]

Coal-based technology did not entirely destroy these chemical
activities. Moreover, it unleashed, as already indicated, new forces
for change. Distillation of coal for oil, tar and pitch was of
strategic significance, particularly to the Admiralty in days of

Plate 52   Packing canisters at Oare gunpowder mill *c.* 1925.

wooden men-of-war. The production of coke and the development of the gas industry added further opportunities for chemists
to exploit. The days of the town gasworks are now certainly
numbered, and at Biggar, Lanarkshire (NT040378), a small hori-
zontal-retort works is being preserved.[22] Many holders still survive, but their numbers are likely to be greatly diminished (Plate
53). In these circumstances, local industrial archaeological societies ought to make recording them a priority.

The oil refinery at Milford Haven might not seem an obvious
candidate for attention from the industrial archaeologist, but it
seems likely that as a consequence of off-shore exploration in the
North Sea existing oil installations may now be rendered obsolete.
Beyond dispute are the oil-shale industry's relics, notably the
great red bings of the Lothians near Broxburn (NT0873), Pum-
pherston (NT0769) and Tarbrax (NT0255). This industry
pioneered by James Young (1811–83) provided the technical base
for the modern petroleum industry, but no refinery survives from
this early phase of the oil industry.[23] The tar tunnel at Coalport,
Shropshire (SJ694025), driven in 1787 as an underground canal,
according to Mr Trinder, to allow the easy transport of coal from

Plate 53 An historic gasworks! Muirkirk (NS695270), Ayrshire, closed in September 1977, was the last in Britain to be replaced by a connection to the gas grid. Note the traditional air condenser in the foreground, with the retort house behind and to the right.

Blists Hill pits, is a spectacular relic of a natural bitumen spring, occasionally found in British coal measures.[24] This tunnel is now one of the Ironbridge Gorge Museum's exhibits and is accessible to visitors.

Thus, the chemical industry has historic origins which it has long outgrown. Only occasionally is it possible to examine physical remains of that past, yet the fragments remaining to us have a significance which cannot be ignored.

Ceramics

Just as so many of the activities associated with the chemical industry were widely dispersed, so was ceramics production. The most sophisticated, pottery and porcelain, have received much attention recently. Yet it was the more commonplace—brick and tile works—that were most commonly encountered. Brickmaking, in particular, was highly localized wherever good clay deposits coincided with a lack of cheap building stone. Clean-air legislation and modernization have greatly reduced the number of brick and tile works in recent years, but sufficient survives of this industry to indicate the main characteristics of its history.

Claypits in many districts, but especially in the London area, and in the South Midlands, are one indication of the significance of bricks and tiles to the building industry and to the process of urbanization. In coal-mining districts clays were often encountered during initial shaft sinking and exploited, even when—as, for instance, in parts of South Yorkshire and Lancashire—there was good local stone.

The most primitive form of brick production occurred in clamps or piles: the hand-moulded 'green' bricks were stacked with layers of small coal under a covering of turves and earth. This method was gradually abandoned from the late eighteenth century in favour of kilns which are classified according to the direction of the draught and the method of working. Initially, intermittent updraught kilns known in many places as Scotch kilns, were tried.[25] They were once very widely used throughout Britain but are mostly now derelict. Usually between 20 and 50 feet (6–15 m) long and rectangular in section, kilns of this type are commonly about twelve feet wide and about the same high. At Ashburnham in Sussex such a kiln built in 1844 remained in use till 1961 and probably fired not more than 20,000 bricks at a time.[26] Mr Hammond has recently provided an illustrated survey of the main types now likely to be encountered, and there can be little doubt that this category of kiln was relatively adaptable and met most contingencies.[27]

However, despite its advantages, this type of kiln was not so efficient as the downdraught kiln. Where bricks were required to be fired to higher temperatures and given, thereby, with more even heating, a better finish, downdraught intermittent kilns were commonly used. Surviving specimens of this type are often circular and between 20 and 30 feet (6–9 m) in diameter (Plate 54).

These batch processes by their nature were likely to be replaced by continuous methods of firing, simply because they were expensive on fuel and labour. Friedrich Hoffmann (1818–1900) patented a circular kiln in 1858 which was continuous in operation, and Humphrey Chamberlain brought the idea from Germany to Britain. This kiln has a central chimney and consists of

Plate 54   Tile-kilns at Ochiltree, Ayrshire (NS517206). Both beehive
and rectangular kilns are of the downdraught type and are still
coal-fired. The kilns produce field drains.

twelve or more radiating chambers which could be successively
charged with 'green' bricks, fired and emptied. Fuel consumption
was reduced to about 6 cwt (304.8 kgm) of slack coal per 1,000
bricks at a firing temperature of about 1,000°C, the main saving
occurring as a consequence of using the previously wasted heat
to preheat the fresh bricks. Many refinements to this design
further reduced costs. The most important was probably the
Staffordshire kiln, patented in 1904 by Dean and Hetherington,
kiln builders of Accrington, and so called because it was designed
originally to fire Staffordshire blue bricks, cheap and mass-pro-
duced, often for urban buildings of no great distinction. Even
these kilns are now giving way to oil- or gas-fired tunnel kilns,
particularly in the area between Peterborough and the northern
suburbs of London.

Major makers of decorative tiles for floors or walls have also
abandoned time-honoured methods. Fortunately, two of the largest nineteenth-century firms, Maw and Company (1840) and
Craven Dunnill (1875), were based in the Ironbridge Gorge and,
in consequence of this, the local museum has several thousand
tiles from the works that supplied the Mysore Palace, the University of Toronto, more humble Birmingham 'pubs' and butch-
ers' shops, and the London Underground.[28]

A major yardstick for archaeologists of all periods has been a society's ability to produce pottery. Clay suitable for this activity is found in many parts of the British Isles, but the variations in quality of output partly arise from the variability of this basic raw material. According to methods of production, raw materials and finishes, it is possible to classify pottery into three categories—earthenware, stoneware and porcelain. The glaze finish has been widely used from ancient times to make pots impermeable and more decorative but was produced with a range of materials: salt, sand, lead or copper ores. Flint, calcined and then ground into white powder, was used both in the pottery (to give its paleness and hardness) and in some glazes.[29]

From the Continent a high-domed furnace was introduced into Britain before 1600, but this was replaced in the eighteenth century by the potbank, a bottle-shaped kiln which had a firing place separate from the pots, rather in the style of the reverberatory furnace. The pots were packed in 'seggars' or 'saggars', small clay boxes stacked one upon another, to keep the smoke away from the product, and the dome of the kiln reflected the heat back down among the 'saggars'.[30] Large bottle kilns are now disappearing with the advent of the horizontal tunnel kiln (first introduced c. 1912), but fortunately there are at least two ambitious preservation projects—Gladstone Pottery Museum, Longton in Stoke-on-Trent (SJ914432), and Portobello Pottery near Edinburgh (NT304742).

Inevitably much enlightened interest has developed in Staffordshire, the principal area of pottery production in Britain since the eighteenth century. The Stoke-on-Trent Museum Archaeological Society has undertaken useful investigations, including excavations, at Burslem and Longton Hall. However, the Gladstone Pottery Museum is a major achievement of the charitable trust which now administers it. A working museum where the visitor can see a typical Victorian potbank (1857) in operation (Plate 55), it has the equipment for milling clay, throwing it on the wheel, glazing, moulding and decorating. Moreover, apart from the bottle kilns and workshops there are galleries illustrating the history of the industry, the making of sanitary ware, decorative tiles and fancy ware.

Stoneware was probably the most common variety of pottery in use from c. 1700. This was made from a mixture of clay and 20 per cent ground flint, with a salt glaze. Imitation of porcelain was consciously attempted as a substitute for very expensive East India Company imports from China which the Dutch first pioneered in Delft. Imitation of Delft ware, in turn, was wide-

Plate 55   A typical Victorian pot bank in the Potteries! Gladstone
Pottery Museum, Longton, one of the most imaginative
conservation efforts in the British Isles.

Plate 56   Cheddleton Flint Mills (SJ972525), now restored. The flint was calcined and ground before use in the local potteries.

spread in Britain, especially after 1740, in Glasgow, Bristol, Liverpool, and Lambeth. Gradually, however, Europe and Britain transformed—and perhaps vulgarized—the qualities of Chinese porcelain in indigenous products which conquered quality markets for china throughout the world. Following Meissen and Sèvres products, British potters came to use china clay (kaolin) as a basic ingredient in production, once William Cookworthy (1705–80), a Plymouth chemist, had demonstrated in 1768 that Cornish and Dartmoor mineral kaolin was the 'Petunz' of China. This 'new' industry concentrated on Staffordshire, and one of the best potters was Josiah Wedgwood (1730–95), whose Etruria works became world-famous.[31]

Essential to this industrial concentration was the existence of cheap coal and equally important an abundance of local skilled labour. For the Staffordshire potters had been attempting to improve their wares for at least a century before Wedgwood changed to hard-paste porcelain; one indication of this was the proliferation of flint mills in the area along the River Churnet and the River Trent and in the Moddershall Valley.[32] Near the old Sandon-Leek turnpike on the River Churnet are the flint mills of Cheddleton (SJ972525), now belonging to a preservation trust and in working condition, yet another example of enlightened local endeavour (Plate 56).[33]

Plate 57   Etruscan bone mill, Etruria (SJ872468), built by Jesse Shirley in 1851 and located just south of the summit of the Trent and Mersey Canal (right). The kiln (left) was used for calcining bones, and the little Dutch-gabled engine house (right) houses a beam engine called *Princess* to drive the mill. Preserved.

Traces of earlier bone-china production, particularly the bone-grinding mill at Etruria (SJ872468) which dates from 1857 (Plate 57), can be seen throughout the 'Potteries', but a major project is under way at Coalport in Shropshire (SJ695024) where the Iron-bridge Gorge Museum Trust intend to create a museum devoted to all branches of the history of the pottery industry. Certainly, it is likely that Stoke-on-Trent and the surrounding pottery districts may soon have lost all physical traces of their distinguished past, for most bottle kilns have already disappeared.

Glass

If pottery was one sign of a developed culture and society, glass production represented an even higher phase of civilization. Despite the antiquity of its technology, glass had uses confined mainly to a relatively affluent group in society before the nine-teenth century. The materials and methods were simple enough. Glass was made from sand, soda or potash, and lime in a charcoal-fired furnace. These raw materials were placed in a simple clay crucible and fused at high temperatures in the furnace. Archae-ological excavations at Eccleshall and Bagot's Park, Staffordshire, and at Rosedale, North Yorkshire, have provided good evidence of the characteristics of Elizabethan glass furnaces. At Eccleshall (SJ759312) Pape in 1931 excavated a simple rectangular glass furnace built of sandstone blocks. The interior base was relatively small—4 ft 5 in by 2 ft 10 in (137×86 cm)—and had sloping sides. The flue was central with two firing holes and on either side of it there was a platform on which the fire-clay crucible containing the molten glass stood.[34] The Rosedale furnace has been partially reconstructed at the Rydedale Folk Museum, Hutton-le-Hole near Helmsley, Yorkshire (SE705900), and like the Eccleshall furnace it can be seen by visitors.

These furnaces, prodigal in their use of timber for fuel and alkali, very likely represent the flight of the glass industry from the Weald and other parts of southern England where defores-tation posed problems for Tudor and Stuart governments.[35] Flem-ish and Huguenot refugee families—the Tyzacks, Henzeys and Titterys—seem to have given the industry a considerable boost by introducing continental technology from Lorraine and Flan-ders, and although Italian merchants still brought glass vessels from Venice to England, simple green bottles and window glass were increasingly produced in this country.

Stourbridge became a principal centre of the industry in the seventeenth century; in 1621 two of the four glasshouses in England had been erected there. Coal-firing in a reverberatory furnace was pioneered in this town, and the characteristic British glass cone with a base of up to 50 ft (15 m) and a tapering height of about 80 ft (24 m) had been developed from the early eight-eenth century. The industry took root in a number of other places where raw materials were abundant, coal was cheap, urban demand strong, and waterborne transport available; in London, South Yorkshire, north-east England, south Lancashire, Bristol, Glasgow, Dumbarton, Leith, and Alloa (Plate 58).[36]

By the eighteenth century the industry was dominated by the glassmakers of the north-east. Centred on South Shields and Newcastle itself, this region's glass industry produced more bottles and window glass than any other area. Sole survivor of this period is the Lemington glass cone (NZ184646) near New-castle. Founded in 1787 by the Northumberland Glass Company,

Plate 58   Glass cone at Alloa glassworks (NS881923),
Clackmannanshire, which was founded *c.* 1750. The last surviving
cone in Scotland dates from *c.* 1825.

the Lemington glassworks once had four cones; the survivor was
originally 130 ft (39.6 m) high but the top 20 ft (6 m) has been
taken down for safety reasons.[37]

In the mid seventeenth century the industry became established in South Yorkshire, and Dr Hey has recently demonstrated
how local probate inventories can not merely help to untangle
the economic condition of glassmakers but also assist in explain-
ing the technology they employed.[38] Catcliffe (SE425887), near
Sheffield, has possibly the oldest glass cone in Europe. Built in
1740 by William Fenny, formerly manager at Bolsterstone glassworks, it is 68 ft high (20.7 m) and 40 ft 6 in (12.3 m) inside

diameter at the base. Excavated by G. D. Lewis of Sheffield City Museums, it has now been restored and scheduled as an industrial monument.[39]

There is an excellent cone at Alloa (NS881924), although the most significant Scottish glassworks at Dumbarton was demolished to make way for Denny's shipbuilding yard. Mr Logan has given an admirable account, however, of working conditions at Dumbarton glassworks, and industrial archaeologists should refer to his article for a detailed treatment of a relatively neglected aspect.[40] Pilkingtons of St Helens are now the pre-eminent firm in the British glass industry and they have established a comprehensive museum (SJ498946) and associated research services to which researchers can turn. In the Midlands Red House glassworks belonging to Stuart Crystal at Wordsley, Stourbridge (SO894865) is the best site. The cone here was erected c. 1780 and is about 87 ft (26.5 m) high; tours of this works can be arranged. At the Dudley Glass Museum at Brierly Hill (SO916870) and in the Birmingham Museum of Science and Industry there are many examples of products of this region's still flourishing but ancient glass industry.[41]

Visitors to the Science Museum, South Kensington, should take the opportunity to see the gallery devoted to glass technology, since this provides perhaps the best introduction to glassmaking techniques and changes in them over the years. The effects of these changes are so commonplace in our lives that it is usually the case that we take them for granted. Sheet glass, windscreens, jam jars, bottles, food-processing jars, beads, drinking vessels, and ornaments are so much part of our lives that we may not take proper account of the history of the industry which produces them.

9
Transport: Roads and Canals

In the first stage of industrialization roads and canals provided the two main arteries of inland communication. Between 1750 and 1850 a widespread network of canals and turnpike roads was created. It transformed the landscape as railways were later to do, creating a heritage of unparalleled interest and importance to the industrial archaeologist. Before the middle of the eighteenth century improvements were made to river navigations, particularly in Ulster, the Midlands, East Anglia and the southeast. Roads and bridges were also constructed, usually on local initiative rather than as part of a national network. Few canals were built or extended after 1850: by that time the initiative lay with the railways. The only notable exception was the Manchester Ship Canal constructed between 1887 and 1894. In the latter half of the nineteenth century there was a hiatus in road development, except in the cities where urban expansion often involved large-scale construction of both roads and bridges.

Roadside archaeology of the turnpike age is characterized by features which include cambered and formally engineered roadways, bridges, toll-bars and toll-houses, smithies, change-houses, inns, milestones and wayside markers of every description. Despite the road and motorway construction of the past few decades, thousands of miles of turnpike still carry present-day traffic and many of the wayside features mentioned have escaped removal or vandalism. The era of the early motor-car has also contributed some fast-disappearing relics: vintage petrol pumps, road signs and other ephemera, now mainly found on country roads. In town too an ornate Edwardian façade can indicate the origins of a garage-cum-showroom established in the early days of motoring. These and many other related features command the attention of those interested in the history and industrial archaeology of road transport.

The industrial archaeology of canals presents a similarly cohesive and linear pattern of survivals. The evidence of the earliest river navigations and canals is more extensive than might be imagined. The flashlocks and man-made weirs which made it possible to bypass natural falls survive in considerable numbers, especially in eastern England. Many of the pre-industrial navigations, such as the Thames, Exe, Severn and Trent, underwent substantial subsequent change, though much of interest still remains. Canalside archaeology proper incorporates settlements, locks and reservoirs, passing-places, wharfs, warehouses and cranes. Major engineering works necessary to maintain the canal as much on the level as possible include embankments, cuttings, aqueducts and tunnels. By the towpath edge are milestones and markers, while a variety of bridges allows roads to pass over the canal without interrupting navigation. Apart from stone or brick-built structures, swing and draw bridges in wood and iron are also common. Most canals had inns for the refreshment of bargees and travellers: some were modest affairs providing only drink, others were more ostentatious with facilities for overnight accommodation. Many canalside inns and pubs survive, revitalized by the increasing use of waterways for recreation. Since the 1950s, indeed, there has been a growing interest in the restoration of abandoned canals. Much has been done to restore life to old waterways which had gradually ceased to be navigable.

Roads

The pre-turnpike road network, though far from comprehensive, was locally of great significance in many parts of Britain. Everywhere there were age-old tracks, pack-horse routes, smugglers' trails, cattle-droving roads (often called 'greenways') and military roads. In some instances these routeways were maintained in some form well into the nineteenth century, and can still be followed on the ground. In the most fortunate circumstances, associated bridges, fords and causeways have been preserved. As with early turnpike roads, the evidence of many old routeways has been wholly or partly obliterated by subsequent development, but much of interest can be found. Features associated with early roads, such as bridges, change-houses and distance markers where they survive, are commonly of great antiquity. Many parts of the country are rich in old pack-horse routes, particularly the Peakland and West Riding.[1] The more formal pack-horse routes of stone cobbles had great commercial significance in these and other nascent industrial districts isolated from river navigation.

Two other types of routeway which have survived the turnpike age are cattle-droving and military roads. The former are to be found in most pastoral districts; the longest and most interesting stretches probably occur in the Scottish Borders, Northumberland and Cumbria. The drove road can be readily identified by the broad swath it cuts across country and by the high drystone walling by which it is enclosed. Cattle-droving on long cross-country routes of this kind remained common until the mid nineteenth century.[2] The military roads, found mainly in the Scottish Highlands, are significant for their wealth of interesting and often well-preserved features, particularly bridges. One of the best sections in the central Highlands is that linking Braemar and Spittal of Glenshee (1748–50), while further south in Galloway another military road from Dumfries to Portpatrick (c. 1760) can be followed along some of its length.[3]

The turnpike trust movement of the eighteenth century had its origins in the first turnpike act of 1663. Parliamentary sanction was granted for the turnpiking of sections of the Great North Road in the counties of Hertford, Cambridge and Huntingdon. There, as elsewhere, the growing volume of traffic made it increasingly difficult for parishes, especially on main routes, to repair their roads. Throughout the eighteenth century the number of English turnpike acts receiving parliamentary sanction grew considerably, the peak being reached between 1761 and 1772:

	No. of Acts
1663–1719	37
1720–29	46
1730–39	24
1740–50	39
1751–60	184
1761–72	205
1773–91	65
1792–1815	173
1816–39	139
Total	912

Between 1663 and 1839 no fewer than 912 acts were passed. Among those who promoted turnpikes were town councils, landowners, farmers, merchants and manufacturers.[4] Similar developments took place elsewhere in Britain, though generally at a later date; the peak of turnpike activity in Scotland, for example, came in the 1780s and 1790s.[5] In Ireland turnpike road construction was concentrated in the period 1730–60, the great bulk of building thereafter being financed by the levying of a county rate.[6] Depending on the financial resources available, turnpike trustees employed a wide range of expertise in the construction of their roads, from local masons and surveyors to prominent civil engineers of the day like Thomas Telford and John Loudon Macadam. The roadmakers of the eighteenth century—humble or famous—created a legacy of outstanding importance to the industrial archaeologist: the roads themselves and diverse road-side archaeology, of which we count bridges, toll-houses and milestones, the most important features.

Prior to the turnpike age there were few formal roadways outside towns. Even there cobbled streets for horse and wheeled traffic separated by kerbs from pavements for pedestrians were the exception rather than the rule. Nevertheless plenty of examples of original cobbled roadway or street survive, and much has been done to restore old surfaces, especially in the pedestrian precincts of older towns like York or Norwich. As previously indicated, some stretches of cobbled pack-horse road still survive in the north of England. More is hidden under subsequent road surfaces and holds considerable potential for future research through excavation. Such work could also contribute greatly to our understanding of the improvements brought about by revolutionary changes in road engineering in the latter half of the eighteenth century, achieved mainly by greater attention to careful surveying of the line of the road, ditching and drainage, and the materials used in construction.[7]

Turnpike roads can be identified by several features including the line of the road, especially gradients and corners, and cuttings, embankments and bridges. The turnpike surveyors and engineers often followed existing roads and improved the line by straightening out corners and wherever possible avoiding the steep gradients which might present problems to horse-drawn vehicles. New, and generally much wider and stronger, bridges were built alongside earlier ones. Where the turnpike trustees ran into trouble with landowners over the route, the road might suddenly take an L-bend to right or left: sometimes this occurred when the turnpike route followed the line of field enclosures between adjoining estates. Many such acute bends survive on country roads following turnpikes.[8]

The main technical developments, apart from bridge building, were in road construction, and essentially sprang from the work of the two Scotsmen, Telford and Macadam, who were almost exact contemporaries. A cross-section of a typical Telford road is identified by a carefully laid and packed foundation of large stones, covered with a relatively thin layer of small stones consolidated by wheeled traffic. Telford paid considerable attention to drainage, constructing stone-lined drains and culverts both under and at the edges of the roadway where required. Improved drainage was also the basis of Macadam's technique and he too constructed cambered roads with surfaces designed to shed excess water. In cross-section his road consisted of compacted yet properly graded small stones, six to ten inches (15.3–25.4 cm) in depth on a natural foundation or built over existing roadway. The economy of the Macadam system had much to commend it, and it was widely adopted by turnpike trustees in the south of England and elsewhere. Both Telford and Macadam realigned and resurfaced existing roads as well as constructing new ones. Telford's most important works were the Highlands roads and bridges, the Carlisle and Glasgow road in the Lowlands, and the Holyhead road in North Wales. Macadam was associated with many major turnpike developments and improvements all over the country, but particularly in the west of Scotland and around Bristol and Bath.[9]

Apart from the roadway itself, the largest and most significant features associated with the industrial archaeology of roads are bridges. Many bridges of the turnpike period (and especially of the period 1780–1830) still carry modern-day traffic, notably on secondary routes relatively unaffected by road-widening or motorway development. Pre-eighteenth-century structures can still be found in considerable numbers (often side by side with a later replacement). These range from small single-span to larger multi-arch bridges set near or immediately above water level, incorporating traditional cut waters and passing-places on the roadway. Bridges with low parapets, or none at all, were built primarily for the passage of pack-horses, heavily laden with side-saddle packs. Northumberland and Durham, in common with most north-country districts, preserve excellent examples of every type: the seventeenth-century Old Berwick Bridge (NT995526) spanning the River Tweed and constructed in red sandstone is an outstanding survival from the pre-turnpike era.[10] Like others of the period it was built as a result of civic initiative.

Undoubtedly the greatest legacy of the turnpike age is the great number of solidly engineered bridges which have survived regular use for upwards of two hundred years. Turnpike trusts, in accordance with parliamentary requirements, sought to maintain and construct bridges on the roads for which they were responsible. Other agencies and individuals also built bridges, notably civic authorities and landed proprietors. Government finance was generally forthcoming for bridge-building along routes used by the mails or by troops, for example, the London to Holyhead road. Even at the end of the eighteenth century a great many bridges were built by public subscriptions, the most generous contributors being gentry, merchants or businessmen with an interest in improving local communications and economic developments in land or industry.

The bridges themselves, like the roads, reflect both the physical requirements of their local environments and the finances available for their construction. Hence a country trust responsible for a long stretch of rural turnpike was likely to build as cheaply as possible and probably employ local masons working to traditional designs. More affluent trusts, or those subsidized by government or civic authority, could call upon the services of the great engineers and bridge-builders of the day, men like John Smeaton, John Rennie, Robert Mylne and Thomas Telford. The great men applied new techniques to traditional materials, often to designs reflecting contemporary architectural taste. Mylne was perhaps the greatest exponent of this genre, working almost wholly in stone. Rennie and Telford were at home with both traditional stone and the new material for bridge-building, iron. Following the success of the first cast-iron bridge at Coalbrookdale (1779–81), iron was increasingly adopted by bridge-builders (Plate 59).[11] The most revolutionary exponent in bridge engineering was undoubtedly Telford, whose work is readily appreciated in his many bridges (Plate 60), two examples being the Menai Straits (1819–26) and Conway (1826) suspension bridges.[12] His genius is almost matched by the brilliant Isambard Kingdom Brunel, who in 1829 designed the Clifton suspension bridge at Bristol. Perhaps the oldest surviving suspension bridge in Britain is the Union Bridge over the River Tweed near Paxton (NT934511), which dates from 1820 and has a 316 ft (96 m) span.[13] Few districts in Britain and Ireland do not preserve the whole range of bridges from pre-turnpike through to those of the present century and the scope for investigation and recording is considerable.[14]

The toll-house may not be the most common feature (Plate 61) found by the wayside along former turnpikes, but next to the bridge it is certainly the most readily recognized. Toll-bars with associated toll-houses were built at regular intervals along the turnpikes—sometimes as frequently as every couple of miles, but more often five miles apart. Some toll-houses have been victims of road widening, but many survive in something like original condition. A few still display outward signs of their former function, such as the old toll-bar or a board detailing toll schedules (Plate 62). Like bridges, toll-houses come in all shapes and sizes. The early ones and those built by trusts in districts provid-

Plate 59   Ironbridge in Coalbrookdale bridging the Severn. Cast in
1779, the ribs and deck members were erected under the
supervision of Abraham Darby III, and the completed bridge was
opened on New Year's Day, 1781.

ing limited revenue are generally very simple in construction.
Conversely those built toward the end of the eighteenth or
beginning of the nineteenth centuries in more remunerative
districts tend to be more lavish or ornamented. Toll-houses have
attracted considerable attention from industrial archaeologists
interested in turnpike studies. It is therefore possible to compile
a basic typography of the most common toll-house designs: local
examples can readily be checked in the many regional industrial
archaeology studies to be found in the chapter references and
Bibliography.

Plate 60   Tongland bridge (NX692533), Kirkcudbright, built by
Thomas Telford (1804–8). An exceedingly interesting structure, its
segmental arch is 112 ft (34 m) flanked by a semicircular 'cutwater'
on either side. There are also three flood-relief arches and a
corbelled parapet.

Plate 61   Mossat Toll-house, Tullynessle and Forbes (NJ477195),
Aberdeenshire. A small, single-storey, harled rubble dwelling
house with the typical semicircular bay window.

161

Plate 62   Toll-board, Ironbridge Museum.

Nationally it is possible to identify five main types of toll-house: rectangular, round-ended, half-hexagonal, octagonal and circular. Easily the commonest type of toll-house is the simple rectangular type, or basic variants on the rectangular pattern. Out of the 37 survivals in the greater Fife area 26 are of this type, while in Sussex no fewer than 25 of the 27 extant toll-houses are rectangular in plan.[15] Rectangular houses often have large windows and a porch fronting the road, or perhaps windows well forward in the gable walls. The second and third types are essentially variants of the rectangular layout, with doors giving on to the road and observation windows on either side. All three rectangular types were generally divided into two rooms, the collector's room being located at the front and the living room to the rear. The octagonal and round types may look more ornamental but were just as functional and tended to be built by more affluent trusts. All five types can be found in a variety of combinations, both single- and two-storey. Cupar East

(NO378147) and Cupar South (NO376139) in Fife are variations on the rectangular pattern and are interesting in that they cover Y-junctions (Fig. 5). Cupar East has a heated collection room, with a main door flanked by Doric columns and surmounted by an entablature. Cupar South has three rooms and a door at one side, which could not have been very convenient for the toll-keeper. Botley (SU509137) on the A.3051 in Hampshire is a good example of the half-hexagonal type. It is of two storeys built in red brick with yellow-brick quoins and window surrounds. The doorway to the road survives, its round-headed light matching the first-floor windows. Above the door is a recess for a toll-board, embellished with an attractive lamp.[16] The octagonal toll-houses are perhaps the most attractive, a good example being at Butterrow, Stroud (SO865042) in Gloucestershire. Built of local stone and roofed in slate it dates from 1825. Of two storeys, it has four pairs of Gothic windows and a detailed toll-board still in position over the main door.[17] Circular houses are less common. One at Ashcombe (TO389093) in Sussex, probably dated from c. 1810, is of brick and has a domed roof. It was probably one of a pair. The best surviving toll-houses in Staffordshire provide good examples of layouts combining those of the basic types. Those at Ipstones (SK024502) and Mobberley (SK006405) are basically rectangular in shape but have hexagonal projections to the road in one corner. They both have large observation windows on ground and first floors.[18]

The most frequently found features of roadside archaeology along the turnpikes are milestones and other wayside markers. Milestones came into general use in England after the Turnpike Act of 1766 made them compulsory on turnpike roads. Before this act milestones were placed by the roadside occasionally, often as charitable acts and commemorations. The 1,760 yard mile was fixed in 1593 but much longer customary miles remained common in various parts of the country until the nineteenth century. Several milestones measuring customary miles survive in Yorkshire, the distance being anything from 2,200 to 3,300 yards. Similar milestones and wayside markers can still be found in Ireland in some numbers, both on roads and navigations.[19] Like bridges and toll-houses milestones come in many shapes and sizes, and an increasing number of detailed local studies has already shown the wide variety that can be found along the turnpikes (Plate 63).

One of the major surveys of turnpikes and their wayside markers has been undertaken in the Bristol area, which has a notable turnpike history. The Bristol Trust was one of the largest

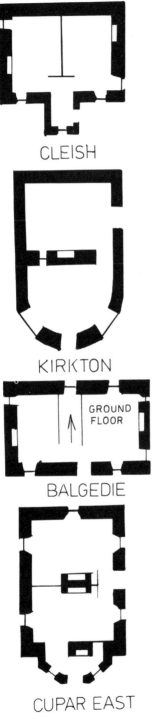

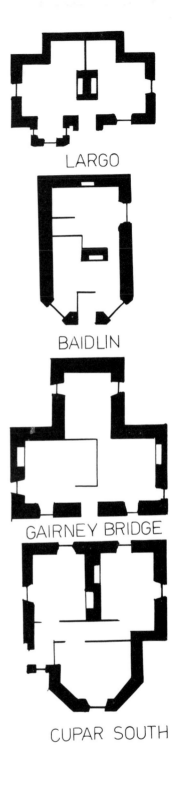

CLEISH

LARGO

KIRKTON

BAIDLIN

ft
30

15

0

GROUND
FLOOR

BALGEDIE

GAIRNEY BRIDGE

CUPAR EAST

CUPAR SOUTH

Fig. 5   Ground plans of Fife toll-houses.

in Britain with 180 miles of road under its control, and the celebrated John Loudon Macadam as its General Surveyor. In an area covering North Somerset and South Gloucestershire no fewer than 350 milestones and 50 toll-houses were recorded. The survey identified boundary stones and posts (marking the boundary between one parish and another), milestones and mileposts, terminus posts and stones, as well as toll-houses. The wayside markers are generally of simple design, mainly rectangular or rectangular with a curved top. The majority had cast-iron plates affixed, bearing the legend. Cast-iron markers and posts—generally 'V'-shaped—occurred in significant numbers. Some have been lost through removal for scrap, a perennial cause of frustration for the industrial archaeologist.[20] The Fife survey—covering an area of essentially early-nineteenth-century turnpiking—revealed 148 complete milestones, 28 stones without their cast-iron tops or plates, and 11 wayside markers at road junctions. Stephen identified twelve main types (classified A–L), the commonest being Type A, which consists of a 'V'-shaped stone surmounted by a cast-iron top. Place names are abbreviated and distances given in miles and eighths. Some fine cast-iron milestones were found, particularly those of Stephen's Type G on the main turnpike through Fife linking Pettycur, New Inn, Cupar and Newport, the first and last being the ferry ports for passages over the Firths of Forth and Tay respectively.[21] Another study by Cox is concerned with the dating of milestones of differing types and construction, mainly in Gloucestershire where a previous survey had identified large numbers of survivals.[22]

A great deal more roadside ephemera of the turnpike era is of interest to the industrial archaeologist, notably smithies, stage-coach inns and change-houses, where they have survived in anything like original condition. The need for wayside smithies where horses could be shod, and coaches, wagons and carts repaired, meant a proliferation of such facilities along the length of the turnpike. Smithies are often found in wayside villages or at country crossroads—commonly simple, single-storey buildings of rectangular plan (Fig. 6). The blacksmith's hearth is sometimes located centrally, seen through a large door which allows ease of access for beasts, vehicles or machinery. Others have the hearth located in one of the gables. Smithies did not rely solely on road traffic for business, but also served the surrounding countryside, repairing and building iron implements and farm machinery. Many smithies survived on such business during the remainder of the horse age. With the development of the motor-car some

Plate 63   A selection of West Country milestones and wayside markers.

Plate 63 (*continued*).

of the surviving smithies were converted into repair shops and garages.[23]

The requirement of accommodation for both passengers and animals was readily met by a network of inns and change-houses of every description and level of comfort. Former stage-coach inns serving turnpike travellers can be found in most towns and villages as well as by the roadside in more isolated country districts. As examples of good town-centre inns are so numerous, let us cite just two, in Barnstaple, Devon, the Royal and Fortescue Hotel and the adjacent building of the former Golden Lion (SS559331), both serving the London and Exeter roads. Like other former coaching inns they had extensive stabling and outhouses, built around courtyards to the rear.[24] Distance stones giving mileages to towns along the turnpike were generally displayed outside coaching inns: a good example survives at the Douglas Arms in Castle Douglas, Dumfries and Galloway.[25]

The change-house, incorporating stables and limited accommodation for travellers, was found at regular intervals along the turnpikes, especially in the country where coaching inns were less frequent. In Ireland and Scotland change-houses had a reputation as dens of drunkenness and ill-repute, but probably nevertheless served a useful function, providing tipples of

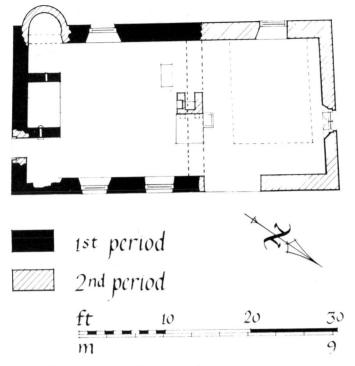

1st period

2nd period

ft   10   20   30

m   9

Fig. 6   Kirkton Manor Smithy, Peebleshire.

whisky or pots of ale to tired stage-coach travellers while the horses were changed. Drink was also sold illegally at toll-bars and smithies adjacent to change-houses.

The early motor age has left a fast-disappearing legacy which has attracted the attention of both industrial archaeologists and enthusiasts of the history of motoring.[26] Donald Cross, a notable pioneer in this field, has indicated the considerable scope which exists for research into early motoring relics, such as road signs, distance indicators and old petrol pumps.[27] Early hand-cranked petrol pumps can be found in country districts, outside smithies-cum-garages. The garage itself began to appear in the Edwardian period, mainly highly ornamented structures, incorporating forecourts and showrooms, being built in the 1900s. On close examination the original façade can be seen, lurking behind modern trappings.[28]

Most of the regional studies so far undertaken have examined roadside archaeology in greater or lesser detail depending on the extent and nature of local survivals. These and other more specific studies already cited provide an indication of the enormous possibilities which still remain in many parts of the British Isles for further research in this fascinating branch of industrial archaeology.

River navigations and canals

River navigation provided perhaps the most reliable means of inland transport in a great many parts of the country prior to the Industrial Revolution. There is plenty of surviving evidence of waterway improvement before the mid eighteenth century, particularly in central and southern England, which had overwhelming natural advantages for the development of waterborne transport. Ireland shared some of these advantages, while Scotland had few waterways suitable for navigation. In central and southern England the improvement of river navigation was being undertaken as early as the seventeenth century, often in association with drainage schemes such as those in the Fens. The flashlock—a single gate used to pass boats from one level of the waterway to another—was of considerable antiquity but became increasingly common despite its relative inefficiency and wastage of water. Flashlocks were used in three main areas of the country, the Thames basin, some tributaries of the Severn, and rivers bordering the Fens. Other rivers with flashlocks included the Stour, Medway, Itchen, and two Trent tributaries, the Soar and Derwent. A recent survey indicated traces of no fewer than fifty flashlocks, having remains of considerable interest to the industrial archaeologist. Two basic types of flashlocks have been identified: the beam and paddle type, which was usually kept closed; and the staunch, which normally stood open and embraced three different varieties of gate. The best example of the beam and paddle type survives on a small tributary of the Thames, the Eynsham Wharf Stream (SP446089), a shallow, half-mile navigation up to Eynsham wharf. Staunches exist in larger numbers, particularly good examples being found on the Nene, Great Ouse, Little Ouse, Warwickshire, Avon, Thames and Parrett. The gate staunch is well represented by Tuddenham Mill Stream staunch (TL732729) on the River Lark, while the guillotine type, once common throughout East Anglia, can be seen at Bottisham Lode (TL516651), a small tributary of the Cam, formerly used for both drainage and navigation. The simplest type of staunch, consisting of a stop-plank arrangement slotted into wooden or masonry supports on either bank, was not common. Later adaptations of such types survive on the River Lark; an example at Bury St Edmunds (TL849665) dates from the late nineteenth century. Therefore despite their primitive design flashlocks and staunches were useful features on river navigations well beyond the Canal Age, and some at least survive as relics of early waterway improvement.[29]

Pound locks which originated in Italy in the first half of the fifteenth century, were developed in England from the sixteenth century onwards, first on river navigations and then on canals. Perhaps the best example is the well-known Exeter Canal. Constructed by John Trewe of Glamorgan (whose name is commemorated in Trewe's Weir) in the 1560s, the Exeter Canal was improved in the 1670s, again about 1700, and by James Green in 1824. Of particular interest is the basin with its warehouses (SX921918) which Green built at the Exeter end to relieve congestion. He also extended the canal to Turf Inn about a mile below Topsham. The tow path can be followed for the whole length of the canal and many interesting features survive.[30] Elsewhere in the south and east, river navigations were improved by the construction of locks and the straightening of watercourses by cuts. Two good Hampshire examples are the Avon and Itchen Navigations. In the former case various cuts were made in the late seventeenth century, to make navigation possible between Christchurch and Salisbury. The remains of the artificial cuts on the river in Hampshire can be traced at Fordingbridge (SU157144 to 148141) and at Sopley (SZ159973 to 156964).[31] The Itchen Navigation was more ambitious, and although certain parts of the river itself were used, there were some long stretches of canal proper. By 1710 the river was navigable from Woodmill to Winchester and a horse towing path was provided. Later seventeen locks and two half-locks were constructed, remains of which can still be seen. There are also a number of bridges, and in Winchester, Blackbridge Wharf (SU485288) still marks the terminus of the navigation.[32]

The subsequent development of canals, mainly in the latter half of the eighteenth century, created in retrospect both a heritage of outstanding interest to the industrial archaeologist and a facility of great recreational and environmental potential. Canals, however, were first and foremost of considerable economic importance to the development of agriculture and industry. Together with turnpike roads, canals brought about a transport revolution which pre-dates the Railway Age by many decades. The canal system opened up new opportunities in agriculture, mining, quarrying, metallurgy, and in manufacturing

Plate 64   The Newry Canal at Newry, County Down. Note the
substantial warehouses on the left, mostly built after the
completion of the Ship Canal in 1765.

industries like pottery, because the waterways essentially provided a cheap means of transport in bulk. In many instances the
entire industrial history and industrial archaeology of an area
was conditioned by canal development, and many of the surviving features can be most readily appreciated from the canal bank.

The first major canal in the British Isles was the Newry Navigation in County Down, an impressive engineering achievement
for its time, which still preserves many features of interest (Plate
64). It was originally constructed between 1730 and 1744, eighteen
miles long with fifteen locks, linking Newry with the Upper
Bann and hence to Lough Neagh. Thomas Steers, who was the
engineer chiefly responsible for building the canal, is well known
for his work on Liverpool's first dock and on the Sankey Brook
Canal (later the St Helens Canal). Subsequently a ship canal was
made down the west side of the estuary, terminating in a lock
120 ft (36.5 m) long and 22 ft (6.8 m) wide. The work, under the
direction of Thomas Omer and Christopher Myers, was completed
in 1765. Many improvements were made to the Newry Canal
during the following century, notably those undertaken by Sir
John Rennie between 1830 and 1850. A new entrance lock and

harbour basin were appropriately named Victoria Lock and Albert Basin, and Rennie himself proudly proclaimed that this was 'the largest canal in Great Britain, or in any other country, with the exception of the great canal from Amsterdam to the Helder'. Little physical alteration has been made to the canal since the completion of Rennie's work, and the whole length preserves many interesting features, including the locks, lock houses, bridges, quays and canalside buildings. With the exception of outer-gates constructed in the 1930s, Victoria Lock (J109207) survives in virtually original condition. At the old harbour in Newry, Butter Crane Quay, Merchant Quay and Canal Quay are lined by former warehouses with gablets and loading hoists. The Albert Basin has been modernized, but much else on the inland canal proper remains unchanged since the early-nineteenth-century reconstruction.[33]

The Newry Canal was the first of many more important waterways in England, Wales and Scotland created during the late eighteenth and early nineteenth centuries. While previous schemes had concentrated on river improvement, the Canal Age really began with the opening of the Duke of Bridgewater's famous canal near Manchester in 1761. The canal was the work of the Duke himself, his land agent John Gilbert, and James Brindley, the millwright turned civil engineer who pioneered canal building in England. Notable engineering and architectural features included the Barton Aqueduct, which carried the canal over the River Irwell, major lengths of tunnel at either end, and extensive use of embankments to maintain the waterway at the right level. The Bridgewater Canal was designed for coal carrying. At Worsley a basin was built, and from this tunnels ran into the mine so that coal could be loaded directly into the boats. Coal could be sold in Manchester at less than half its previous price, and the price fall therefore emphasized the great potential of canals as a means of bulk transport.

Construction in the years 1780 to 1820 created a widespread network of canals—both broad and narrow—serving many parts of the rapidly industrializing countryside. Major waterways were provided by the Trent and Mersey (Plate 65), the Leeds and Liverpool, the Shropshire Union, the Birmingham Canal Navigation, the Staffordshire and Worcester, the Grand Union, and the Kennet and Avon Canals. Apart from the trunk routes there were dozens of other canals and branches, some of considerable local significance. These can best be listed briefly on a regional basis, describing in turn the West Country, Wales, southern and central England, the Midlands, Yorkshire and Lancashire, Scot-

Plate 65   Narrow boat and covered dry-dock on the Trent and
Mersey Canal near Preston Brook, Lancashire (SJ568806).

land and Ireland. These areas preserve remains of considerable
interest to the canal enthusiast and industrial archaeologist.

Practically all of the canals in the West Country (including the
Exeter Canal, previously described) were essentially designed to
improve and extend river navigations. With the exception of the
Grand Western Canal and the Bude Canal, most were short canals
built to carry minerals, fertilizer, agricultural and general produce. The Grand Western Canal, an 11-mile level waterway
running between Tiverton and Lowdwells, was constructed
between 1810 and 1814. It was originally intended to link the
English Channel and the Bristol Channel with terminals at Topsham and Taunton, but the scheme was never completed. The
canal was mainly used to transport limestone, coal and building
stone. Despite its lack of locks (like the Edinburgh and Glasgow
Union Canal in Scotland) the Grand Western Canal is of consid-

erable interest, and is presently being restored as an amenity by Devon County Council.[35] The Bude Canal, with a total length including its branches of 35½ miles, was the longest tub-boat canal in England. Built by James Green and opened in 1825, it once had no fewer than six inclined planes. The basin at Bude (SS204065) with wharf buildings and a warehouse can still be seen, and the three branches to Alfardisworthy, Holsworthy and Launcester, though long-abandoned, are traceable along some of their length.[36] Other lesser canals of interest to the industrial archaeologist in this area include the Tavistock Canal, the Torrington (or Rolle) Canal, the Bridgewater and Taunton Canal, the Chard Canal, and the Somersetshire Coal Canal, all of which have been the subject of detailed study, though not always from the point of view of surviving relics.[37]

The canals of South Wales follow the valleys inland from the ports of Swansea, Neath, Cardiff and Newport, and were built mainly for the carriage of coal. A notable feature of the canals there is the large number of tramway feeders designed to augment traffic (see Chapter 10). The major valley canals are the Swansea Canal, a 16-mile navigation from Swansea harbour to Ystradgynlais, near the head of the Swansea Valley; the Neath Canal, 13 miles in length; the Glamorganshire Canal (and its feeder the Aberdare Canal), 25 miles long, linking Cardiff with Merthyr Tydfil; and the Monmouthshire and Brecon Canal (the collective name now used to identify the former Brecon and Abergavenny Canal, and the Monmouthshire Canal, including the Crumlin Arm), which runs from Newport in the south to Brecon in the north—a distance of 42 miles. The Tennant Canal was designed to bypass Neath, giving the Vale of Neath a direct link with the River Tawe below Swansea (Plate 66).[38] There are remains of interest on all of these navigations, including numerous sets of locks built to lift the canals into the valleys. The industrial archaeology has been admirably described by Morgan Rees.[39] The Monmouthshire and Brecon Canal represents a major achievement in restoration. The remaining portion of the canal between Pontypool and Brecon plays a key recreational role within the Brecon Beacons National Park. Discussions began in the early 1960s between the British Waterways Board, the former National Parks Commission, the Welsh Office and the Breconshire and Monmouthshire County Councils and ultimately restoration was undertaken by the British Waterways Board. Considerable engineering difficulties were encountered owing to the decayed state and difficulties of terrain. The canal is now fully restored as a cruising waterway, offering a scenic panorama over the Usk

Plate 66   Aqueduct at Aberdulais (SS774993), South Wales, on the
Tennant Canal near the junction with the Neath canal.

Valley.[10] The canals of north-east Wales, the Ellesmere and Llangollen Canal and the Montgomeryshire Canal (both essentially
branches of the Shropshire Union), offer the industrial archaeologist features of outstanding interest, notably the famous Pont-
cysyllte aqueduct designed and built by Thomas Telford between
1795 and 1805.[11]

Excepting the lesser canals and river navigations, those of
central and southern England were built to link together the
Thames, Severn and Midland waterways. The major canals
include the Grand Union, Basingstoke, Kennet and Avon, Wiltshire and Berkshire, Oxford (Plate 67), Thames and Severn,
Stroudwater, and Gloucester and Sharpness. All have their historians and have been examined, at least in part by industrial
archaeologists.[12] The Grand Union, with the associated Paddington and Regent's Canals, is substantially intact and preserves

Plate 67   Iron bridges over the Oxford Canal and the Thames near Oxford.

much of interest. In Ealing, for example, there is a good section of canal containing eight locks, some with side ponds, and lock-keepers' cottages, where the navigation descends to the valley of the River Brent. Paddington Basin (TQ267815) contrasts considerably with the better known stretches of the Regent's Canal, famous for its boat trips between London Zoo and the basin at Little Venice.[43] The Basingstoke Canal was opened in 1794, linking Basingstoke with the River Wey and hence London. Although the canal was closed to commercial traffic at the turn of the century, part still holds water and some restoration work is being undertaken. The Basingstoke end has been obliterated, but there is still much of interest to be seen elsewhere along the canal, especially Greywell Tunnel (SU708518–719515) near North Warnborough and Ash Lock (SU881518) near Aldershot.[44] Perhaps the most ambitious restoration scheme has been undertaken on the Kennet and Avon Canal, with the aim of eventual opening to through-navigation in the 1980s. Major features here include the Dundas Aqueduct (ST786626), Avoncliffe Aqueduct (ST805600), the Devizes locks (ST976614–995615), and Crofton Pumping Station (SU264624), built to supply water to the summit level, and now completely restored.[45] It is possible to trace the Wiltshire and Berkshire Canal along most of its length, although careful map-reading will be required. Further west in Gloucestershire, there are many old canals; the Stroudwater, Thames and Severn, and Gloucester and Sharpness Canals, each of which offer considerable potential.[46]

Few areas offer such an opportunity for the study of canals and canalside industrial archaeology as the Midlands. The major canals here include the Staffordshire and Worcester, Birmingham Canal Navigations, Shropshire Union, Trent and Mersey (Plate 68), Coventry, Caldon, and Cromford, as well as many minor waterways and branches. River navigations are also of great importance, notably on the Trent, Severn and Weaver. The history of canals in this area is well documented though undoubtedly much remains to be discovered on the ground.[47] Happily the increased amount of attention paid to waterways here is opening them up to recreational and educational interests. Major rehabilitation schemes have been undertaken on several stretches of canal, notably on the Birmingham Canal Navigations (Plate 69), the Caldon Canal and the Erewash Canal.[48] No single study could possibly describe the richness of interest that exists along the banks of the Midlands canals, though a number of regional studies have been undertaken in the specific field of industrial archaeology.[49] There seems little doubt that industrial archaeology can do much in this area—as elsewhere—to draw attention to the value of both the canals and their riparian heritage.

Like those of the Midlands, the canals of Yorkshire, Lancashire and the north of England have been well researched by transport historians, but to date few detailed studies in industrial archaeology have been undertaken.[50] The principal canals are the Sheffield and South Yorkshire, Chesterfield, Rochdale, Huddersfield Narrow, Peak Forest, Macclesfield, Leeds and Liverpool, and Lancaster. Important waterways systems still preserve much of interest, especially the Ouse, Aire and Calder, Don, Mersey and Irwell Navigations. There are many lesser canals and branches throughout the area: two contrasting examples are the Pocklington Canal in Yorkshire, and the Ulverston Canal in the Furness district of Lancashire. All of the major canal features can be found in abundance. Three outstanding examples are Bingley Five-Rise

Plate 68   The Anderton boat lift, near Northwich, Cheshire
(SJ647753) is the only one in Britain still in use. Completed in 1875,
this lift allows boats to pass between the Trent and Mersey Canal
and the River Weaver Navigation, about 50 ft (15 m) below.

Plate 69   The metropolis of the Midland canal network was
Birmingham. Here is a canal basin in the city, with warehouses, a
typical canal bridge of the region, and a narrow boat under steam.

locks (Plate 70) on the Leeds and Liverpool Canal (SE108400),
Standedge Tunnel on the Huddersfield Canal (SE030100), and
the historic Worsley Canal Basin on the Bridgewater Canal
(SD749005). The Lancaster Canal preserves John Rennie's superb
aqueduct carrying the navigation over the River Lune (SD484639);
the Kendal end has been the subject of an interesting study using
industrial archaeology.[51] In Cumbria canals were never of great
importance, though remains can still be traced at Ulverston and
Carlisle. The former is still intact, with a sea-lock, pier and inn
at Canal Foot (SD313777).[52] At Carlisle the infilled canal basin
with associated warehousing is just one of many survivals of the
long-abandoned waterway which linked the city with the Solway
Firth.[53].

    In Scotland the generally sad state of decay in which the
Lowland canals survive contrasts greatly with the health and
vigour of the two great Highland waterways, the Crinan and

Plate 70   Bingley 'Five-Rise' locks on the Leeds and Liverpool Canal near Bradford (SE108400), a staircase of wide locks to the summit level.

Caledonian Canals (Plate 71). The Lowland system consists of the Forth and Clyde, the Monkland, and the Edinburgh and Glasgow Union, all three preserving features of considerable interest despite the fact that through navigation has long been abandoned. A fourth canal, the Glasgow, Paisley and Johnstone, has all but disappeared, though riparian buildings still exist. Lesser canals with interesting remains include the Aberdeenshire Canal (which once linked Aberdeen with Port Ephinstone, near Inverurie), and the Fleet Canal at the industrial village of Gatehouse-of-Fleet in Galloway.[55] Belated interest is now being shown in the restoration of the Lowland waterways, and much has already been achieved through the co-operative efforts of waterway interests and local authorities. Canal archaeology on the Forth and Clyde and Union Canals has been recorded in some detail. Many remains may be found on the Forth and Clyde, including locks, aqueducts, basins, stables and a wide variety of bridges. The Union Canal has three fine aqueducts surviving at Slateford (NT220727) over the Water of Leith, Almond (NT1057606), and Avon (NS967758) near Linlithgow.[55]

Plate 71 Bridge and keeper's cottage on the Crinan Canal (built by Rennie 1794–1809) at Ardrishaig (NR854853), Argyll.

The canals of Ireland, in common with those elsewhere, have experienced mixed fortunes over the years. Their history is now well documented, though the scope for on-the-ground investigation is clearly considerable.[56] The Newry Canal, previously discussed, was the forerunner of several more ambitious schemes, notably the Royal, Grand, Ulster, Lagan, and Ballinamore and Ballyconnel Canals. River navigations were of great importance in Ireland, the best known being those of the Lower Bann in Ulster, the Shannon, linking the loughs of the Central Plain, and the Barrow and Suir in Leinster. These and other canals preserve much of interest to the industrial archaeologist. The two major canals begin in Dublin. The Royal Canal (90 miles long) terminates at Cloondara on the River Shannon, while the shorter Grand Canal (79 miles) also joins the waterway at Shannon Harbour. Much has been done to rehabilitate these waterways and there is a growing awareness among national and local authorities of the importance the canals and canalside buildings have in environmental and recreational planning in the Republic.[57]

From this cursory survey of the main canals it will be clear that opportunities for fieldwork exist in many parts of the country. The industrial archaeologist with an interest in canals has not only to look out for a whole range of typical canal features and architecture, but also for related industrial buildings, social archaeology and transport installations. Several useful general studies now exist on canal architecture. These examine engineering features and canalside structures, and provide a clear indication of the range of features which can be recorded in more localized surveys.[58] Fortunately, the growing enthusiasm for canal rehabilitation—albeit belated in many instances—has saved some of the waterway heritage for posterity. Yet many of the lesser canals remain neglected and ought to command the attention of the industrial archaeologist if they are not to escape record altogether.

Road and canalside archaeology are without question two of the most attractive and interesting fields open to the industrial archaeologist. A study of such features often holds the key to an understanding of the impact industrialization had on a locality, particularly in the pre-Railway Age. At the same time old roads and tracks, as well as canals, offer linear features of enormous environmental significance, which is only now being realized. The sterling efforts which have gone into the creation of long-distance footpaths and bridleways (such as the Pennine and Cleveland Ways) and the canal restoration schemes in many parts of the country point the way forward. The industrial archaeologist can undoubtedly do much both to record these features and to heighten awareness of their importance to the national heritage.

10
Transport: Railways and Shipping

Railways played a critical role in the second stage of the Transport Revolution during much of the nineteenth century, while shipping was of great importance at almost every stage of industrialization. Both sectors have left a legacy of considerable value to the industrial archaeologist and although much has gone unrecorded, railways and ships—like canals—have been fortunate enough to attract the enthusiastic interest of historians and preservationists at least a generation before the birth and early infancy of industrial archaeology. Railways, or rather the prototype wagonways and tramroads, first seen as extensions of waterways and later of canals, were constructed to carry off the output of collieries, quarries and ironworks. But the first major developments came during the later stages of the Industrial Revolution when horse traction started to give way to steam power. The rest of the nineteenth century saw first the creation of essentially local lines (such as the Stockton and Darlington or the Liverpool and Manchester) followed successively by the development of a national network and then an infilling of branch lines. Finally, toward the end of the Victorian era many light railways to link country districts into the existing network were constructed. Other developments included some now-famous narrow gauge lines—seen at their best in North Wales—and many thousands of miles of mineral railways serving industrial plant, mines and quarries. Virtually all stages of development are represented in the surviving heritage and despite subsequent developments many interesting artefacts of the earliest stages have endured to the present day. The history of railways has been extensively documented and there is hardly a branch line anywhere in the British Isles about which something has not been written. Until recently much railway history was overtly technical, mainly concerned with engines and engineers, with little or no attention devoted to general economic and social aspects. The balance is now beginning to be redressed. Preservation is naturally a major interest for those active in this field, and in a sense the success of railway preservation is an example to others interested in industrial archaeology and the preservation of industrial monuments. Railway museums and working lines in many parts of the country show what can be done by enthusiastic amateurs prepared to sacrifice time and effort.

Shipping provided one of the most important means of communication until the beginning of the present century. In a sense we tend to exaggerate the role of canals, turnpike roads and railways at different points in the Transport Revolution, and hence overlook the continuous importance of shipping. Coastal shipping was vital to the development of agriculture, mining and industry during the eighteenth and most of the nineteenth centuries, and this led to the redevelopment of older harbours and the construction of many more new ones around the coasts of Britain. Foreign trade also contributed enormously to the expansion of shipping, particularly from the larger ports like London, Bristol, Liverpool and Glasgow. Whaling and the subsequent development of fishing fostered further harbour building. There is therefore enormous scope for the examination and recording of ports, harbours and a variety of dockside features, crafts and industries of many periods. Like railways, shipping and ships have attracted enthusiastic historians and preservationists. There is a growing number of maritime museums, museums of shipping, and preserved ships of all shapes and sizes. Most major museums in coastal towns and cities have a maritime section, for example, those in Bristol, Cardiff, Liverpool and Glasgow—all of outstanding interest. Artefacts of the fishing industry in days gone by have been preserved in many places, notably at Whitby, Yarmouth, Anstruther and Aberdeen. The industrial archaeological picture is less happy, for the problems of recording harbours and harbourside features are not without parallels in the field of workers' housing described in Chapter 12. A great deal has been lost through demolition or infilling, clearly illustrated for instance in London, Liverpool, Cardiff or Leith, but common enough everywhere to make the point that docks have been progressively abandoned over the past few decades. The need for recording lesser harbours is just as acute, despite the revival that some have enjoyed since their development for recreational functions like yachting and pleasure boating. Considerable conservation work has been undertaken at a few harbour sites. The development of the open-air industrial museum and outdoor centre at Morwellham (Devon) is perhaps best known, but there are other equally commendable schemes on a more modest scale, such as the landscaping and improvement of the old coal harbour at Seaton Sluice, Northumberland (see p. 208). Even these two examples from opposite ends of the preservation spectrum provide an excellent indication of what can be achieved when new life is brought back to abandoned harbours.

Railways

Railways offer a range of features interesting to the industrial archaeologist and well worth recording. Many of the railway buildings conform to a distinctive company style, or perhaps to the vernacular architecture of the district. These include railway settlements, stations and platforms, station buildings, goods sheds, warehouses, engine sheds—and a plethora of lineside features, such as engine turntables, signal boxes, level crossings, and crossing-keepers' houses. The major engineering features of interest are cuttings, embankments, bridges, viaducts, and tunnels. Railway engineering and architecture have been the subjects of several studies, the most popular being railway station architecture which has attracted a lot of attention from those interested both in Victorian architecture and in the large-scale use of materials like cast iron and glass in nineteenth-century buildings. Much has already been done to record railway archaeology but the coverage varies greatly from one part of the country to another. There are some excellent regional and local studies which provide good examples of what can be achieved even on long-abandoned tramroads or railways.

The early development of wagonways or tramroads has been exhaustively treated and the surviving relics throughout Britain recorded in some detail.[1] We have space here to indicate only something of the enormous scope which still exists for the industrial archaeologist to chart and to record these interesting and often early features. Later mineral and other goods lines abound and should be seen essentially as extensions of the contemporary railway system, though many such lines followed the routes of earlier installations. The best examples of old wagonways and tramroads can still be found in former colliery or metalworking districts such as Cornwall, Devon, Wales, the Pennines, Cumbria and the north-east. Many others elsewhere were built to extend the canal-carrying trade, for example in Shropshire and the West Midlands.[2]

Turning first to South Wales we find that many outstanding early tramroads have been recorded by both Baxter and Rees. There, the building of tramroads, as Rees has indicated, was an integral part of the programme of canal construction which began

Plate 72   Parson's Folly, a dramatic incline on Parson's Tramroad, Glamorgan, which connected Blaen-Cregan collieries circuitously with the Neath Canal (SN7989), a distance of 5¾ miles. The track, 3 ft 3 in (1 m) gauge, was abandoned in 1867.

in the 1790s to link the waterways with ironworks and collieries (Plates 72 and 73).[3] The earliest tramroads served the Montgomeryshire Canal and the Brecon and Abergavenny Canal. They include the famous Brinore tramroad which brought limestone from the quarries around Trefil (SO122126) to Tal-y-bent on Usk. Other local tramroads served ironworks at Rhymney, Tredegar and Ebbw Vale, including Hill's Tramroad from Blaenavon and Bailey's Tramroad from Nant-y-glo. Sections of the Pen-y-darran tramroad which ran from Merthyr to Abercynon are particularly well preserved, especially to the north and south of Pontygwaith Bridge (ST081978), mid-Glamorgan, which shows much of its original engineering including stone blocks and 3 ft (91.5 cm) long cast-iron rails.[4] There are many other interesting survivals elsewhere in Wales, mainly associated with the metalworking

Plate 73   Pantycafnau Bridge (late eighteenth century?), the
survivor of two cast-iron bridges in Merthyr Tydfil (SO038072),
Glamorgan, which carried a tramroad into the north end of
Crawshay's Cyfarthfa ironworks. The iron channel carries a leet in
its centre and on top of this ran the tramroad.

and quarrying districts of the north. The major sites are described
in Rees' Welsh volume cited previously.

The north-east coalfield was one of the earliest districts to see
the development of wagonways and tramroads which were constructed in considerable numbers after the middle of the seventeenth century. As Lewis has indicated, an extensive network
had been created by the 1780s, although construction continued
until the 1800s.[5] Much of interest remains on the ground and has
been charted in some detail in Atkinson's regional study. The
earliest wagonways were built within easy reach of the Tyne,
Wear or other tidewaters but rapidly extended over the whole
coalfield. One of the best-known wagon routes, the Tanfield Way
(County Durham) was begun in the mid 1720s and involved the
construction of a large earth embankment and a magnificent

stone arched bridge over a gorge. The Causey Arch (NZ201559) or Tanfield Arch was constructed in 1727 with a single span of 105 ft (32 m), and is a scheduled monument, recently restored. An even earlier wagonway can be traced from Plessey Checks to the quayside at Blyth (Northumberland). A particularly interesting section can be seen at NZ245791. The Plessey collieries were first sunk about 1660 but the wagonway is later and dates from 1709.[6] Like wagonways elsewhere, most of those in the northeast began with wooden rails which were later converted to iron, mounted on stone blocks or sleepers. Wrought-iron rails were first used about 1808 on another northern tramroad, the Tindale Fell Waggonway, which was built some time after 1797 by the Earl of Carlisle to open up his isolated east Cumbria coalfield. Originally about six miles in length the wagonway was designed to link two collieries at Tindale (NY616594) with a staith or depot situated on the eastern outskirts of Brampton. It also served limestone quarries and kilns at Clowsgill (NY590592). The line used natural features to ease the passage of loaded wagons but nevertheless had some formidable gradients, including two steeper than 1 in 30, the gauge being about 4 ft 8 in. (1.4 m). Later extensions served further collieries and lime works.[7]

In north Staffordshire—as elsewhere in nearby Shropshire and the West Midlands—tramroads were built to link limestone quarries, collieries, ironworks and potteries to the canals, in this case the Trent and Mersey Canal and its feeders. The most important tramway system was that connecting the limestone quarries at Caldon Low (SK075485) with the Caldon Canal at Froghall (SK030478). The line had an unfortunate if interesting history: it had to be reconstructed twice, on the last occasion in 1803 by John Rennie. Ultimately a whole network of tramways in the pottery towns connected the centres of Burslem, Hanley and Longton with the Trent and Mersey Canal. The pottery tramways were built from the 1770s onwards, but most had fallen into disuse by the middle of the nineteenth century or had been replaced by standard gauge mineral lines. The rapid growth of the pottery towns resulted in the disappearance of survivals, but in the Froghall and Caldon areas there are remains of considerable interest. Another wagonway in the Churnet Valley was the Consall Plateway. As its name implies this ran from Consall Forge (SJ997497) on the banks of the River Churnet to Weston Coyney, a distance of seven miles. It can still be traced in parts, particularly in the neighbourhood of Consall Forge.[8] The scope for local studies on early wagonways is considerable. The monographs of Baxter and Lewis, previously cited, provide compre-

Plate 74 Building *c.* 1825 apparently used as a booking-office or weigh-house for keeping records of wagons that passed along the Stockton–Darlington Railway.

hensive guides to survivals which can be followed up by enthusiasts.

Remains of early railways have inevitably become confused with those of later developments. Yet there is still much to be seen along routes built before the great railway booms of the early Victorian period, when essentially local lines were extended and railway companies amalgamated to create a national network. The birth of the modern railway system lay in the north-east of England, for the Stockton and Darlington, if not the first public railway in any formal sense, was certainly the most famous (Plate 74). Much of the original line built between 1823 and 1825 can still be traced along its western section from Wilton Park near Bishop Auckland to Darlington itself (where part of the route near the modern railway line is marked). Major features include the remains of Gaunless Bridge, West Auckland (NZ186265), the world's first iron railway bridge, a farm access bridge at the foot of Brusselton West incline near Shildon (NZ211256), and at Darlington Station, George Stephenson's famous 'Locomotion No. 1' stands at the southern end of Platform 1.[9] Another early railway in the area preserving much of interest to the industrial archaeologist is the Stanhope and Tyne Railway. Built in 1834 to the design of Robert Stephenson it was 33¾ miles long and combined every form of motive power then known. Ten and a half miles were worked by horses, nine stationary steam engines hauled traffic on a total of 11 miles, there were five self-acting inclines for 3 miles, and the remaining 9¼ miles were worked by locomotives. Some of the route can still be traversed and original buildings and lineside installations still survive. At Stanhope itself are the lime-kilns (NY989401) which the line was built to serve, while at Consett the industrial archaeologist can see Hownsgill Viaduct (NZ095490), designed by Sir Thomas Bouch in 1857 to replace a double incline worked by a steam haulage engine originally constructed by Robert Stephenson. Further east at Annfield Plan is the Stanhope and Tyne public house (NZ169515), near a point where the railway ran.[10] The majority of other early public lines in north-eastern England were built to link existing collieries with shipping ports. Lines were later extended into the hinterland to serve newly-opened pits. These developments are well illustrated by the cases of the Durham and Sunderland Railway (1836) and the Hartlepool Railway (1835), constructed to provide outlets for coal shipments at their respective termini. Some lines used portions of earlier private wagonways, for example, the Blyth and Tyne Railway, opened in 1845.

The other district of the north which saw the development of pioneer lines was Lancashire: according to Ashmore's survey, major archaeological remains can be found on many abandoned lines, including those built between 1830 and 1850. The features included are tunnels, bridges, viaducts, stations, warehouses, and railway workshops.[11] On Merseyside there is much of interest including a whole series of remains associated with the Liverpool and Manchester Railway between Lime Street Station, Liverpool, and Manchester Victoria, via Earlestown. The famous railway opened on 15 September 1830. In August 1836 Lime Street Station was opened to accommodate ever-increasing passenger traffic, including the Grand Junction trains from Birmingham which began in the following year. The Liverpool and Manchester was amalgamated in 1845 into the Grand Junction Railway and by further amalgamations in the following year became part of the London and North Western. Lime Street Station (SJ350905) mainly dates from 1860s and 70s, while the Edge Hill Station (SJ371899) preserves much of the early date. The original station of 1830 is off Chatsworth Street (SJ367898) north of Spekeland Street. It is to be found deep in a cutting at the mouths of Wapping and Crown Street tunnels, though it is not easily visible owing to high walls. It includes on the north side former porters' and waiting rooms cut out of rock, and on the west end part of

Plate 75 The North Yorkshire Moors Railway at Goathland station,
showing a fine range of railway features, including a water tower
on the right.

an embattled tunnel portico, including the base of chimneys
associated with former rope haulage engines. To the west on
Crown Street was the original passenger terminus (SJ364398)
which was superseded by Lime Street. The site became a coalyard
(itself now disused), though a sandstone tunnel portal beneath
Smithdown Lane is still visible. The present station includes the
original offices of 1836, probably the oldest working station
building in Britain.[12]

The archaeology of the Cumbrian railways has been described
in some detail by Davies-Shiel and Marshall. There are many
parallels between developments there and those of Wales, Devon
and Cornwall, where the development of mines and related
industrial enterprise was facilitated by rail transport. In west
Cumbria the nineteenth-century expansion of coal-mining and
iron-making—both long-established in the area—was partly due
to the opening of railways from north and south. The first line
to reach the coast was the important Maryport and Carlisle

Plate 76   Carlisle Citadel Station, a splendid exercise in neo-Gothic architecture, designed by Sir William Tite (1798–1873) and built in 1847–8.

Railway, opened in 1845, and still preserving features of that date (Plate 76). The vital link skirting the Lake District between Lancaster and Carlisle followed in 1846, while later railways reaching the industrial districts of the coast included the Furness Railway and the Whitehaven and Furness Railway (both of 1850) and the Ulverston and Lancaster Railway (1857). Numerous branches to collieries and ironstone mines were later constructed, and these have left substantial remains.[13] The building of the Carlisle and Silloth Railway in 1853—partly in the drained bed of the Carlisle Canal—led to the ultimate development of the port of Silloth in which the North British Railway had a substantial interest. A short distance along the estuary from Port Carlisle at Bowness-on-Solway on the English side of the firth is the station house and stone-faced embankment of the Solway Viaduct (NY212625) erected in 1869 to carry Cumbrian iron ore to the Lanarkshire district. Nearly a mile and a half long, including approaches, the viaduct was a monumental piece of cast- and wrought-iron engineering. Regarded as unsafe by 1921—it was breached on two occasions by iceflows—the Solway Viaduct was finally dismantled in 1934–5, leaving the truncated embankments on either side of the Solway.[14]

The Welsh railways have a great fascination for enthusiasts because of the famous narrow gauge lines which have been rescued, preserved and put to work again. The local amenity value of these railways is considerable, as is the impact on tourism. There is much else besides to interest the industrial archaeologist, as Rees indicates in his survey of survivals in the Principality. Most of the key routes were constructed by the 1850s and in South Wales there was a great deal of branch line building to meet the transport needs of collieries and ironworks which had previously been served by tramroads. The pressures on the valleys were released by the building of such railways as the Rhymney, the Brecon and Merthyr, the South Wales Mineral, the Neath and Brecon, the Swansea Vale, London and North Western into Swansea, and extensions to such existing lines as the Taff Vale. During the last two decades of the nineteenth century six new lines were built in South Wales, four of which served the Rhondda valleys. Their construction meant ready access to the ports at Newport, Cardiff, Penarth, Barry, Port Talbot and Swansea. The widespread network which was ultimately created has almost completely disintegrated, but a great deal has been done to record and photograph what survived before the wholesale closures of the 1960s. Many items of railway interest are preserved in the National Museum of Wales, and record offices also hold more local railway archives and photographic collections. Much of interest survives elsewhere in Mid and North Wales and has been studied in detail by railway historians and other enthusiasts. Tramways and narrow-gauge lines, built to serve metal mines and quarries, carried ore and slate to the nearest shipping point, invariably through difficult terrain.[15]

Two other areas which have lost many of their railways are Devon and Cornwall, which had early associations with the Great Western Railway and the railway engineering genius, Brunel, whose broad gauge line from London via Bristol reached Exeter in 1844 and Plymouth in 1848. The section between Exeter and Newton Abbot was the scene of his experiment with atmospheric traction; two fairly complete pumping engine houses survive, the Starcross engine house (SX977817) and the Torre engine house (SX898663). The broad gauge system of the Great Western and associated railways was finally converted to standard gauge in 1892. On Sutton Wharf, Plymouth (SX483543), there survives what is reputed to be the last length of broad-gauge rail still *in situ*. The great Royal Albert Bridge at Saltash linking the two counties was opened in 1859. Engineering problems were formidable, though the lines of Devon and Cornwall provide excellent examples of Victorian ingenuity in the construction of viaducts, embankments and tunnels. Much of interest is to be found on abandoned branch lines, which, as Minchinton suggests, offer considerable scope for detailed investigation. These include the Exe Valley Railway, the Kingsbridge Railway, and the Moretonhampstead and Tavistock lines. The Dart Valley Railway is one of the most picturesque lines in Devon, now restored, with a historic railway collection to be seen at Buckfastleigh (SX667743).[16] There are several outstanding tramways and mineral lines in Devon, notably the Haytor Granite tramway, ten miles long linking the granite quarries with Ventiford Wharf (SX864718) on the Stover Canal.[17] Cornwall offers less opportunity to examine railway archaeology than Devon, though there are a number of interesting branch lines and mineral wagonways. Todd and Laws in their survey of the county provide some discussion of the historical background to railway development in the area and their gazetteer lists interesting survivals, especially stations.[18]

The Midlands and the English shires present widespread opportunities for the examination and recording of railway archaeology. In the former area railways played a vital part in nineteenth-century industrialization, but the complex network of lines which linked the Black Country towns has since suffered the same fate as many of the crafts on which the economy of the region was originally built. Much has been done to record abandoned features throughout the Birmingham area, where railway history is particularly well documented and an excellent museum of technology and transport has inspired similar ventures including restoration schemes.[19] The East Midlands is also fortunate in having a useful record of its railway archaeology, and as previously indicated, considerable attention has already been devoted to the development of such features for the visitor.[20] Of particular interest in the preservation field is the Crich Tramway Museum (SK355541), a collection of over forty tramcars from Britain and overseas, built between 1873 and 1953. About half are in working order and a small number are operated in the one mile of tramway. The Main Line Steam Trust operates a 5½ mile standard gauge railway worked by steam locomotives running between Loughborough Central and Rothley. Two other railway museums have been developed: the Dinting Railway Centre at Glossop (Derbyshire) which is an operational steam museum with ten locomotives; and the Shackerstone Railway Depot (Leicestershire), a comprehensive collection of railway relics, many referring to the Ashby and Nuneaton line and including seven steam locomotives and various items of rolling stock.[21] Railway museums are becoming numerous, and any visitor to York or Carnforth should not miss the collections there.

In London and the south-east of England there are ample opportunities to examine railway archaeology and relics. In London itself there are many features of interest including the outstanding group of near-original termini at King's Cross, St Pancras, Liverpool Street, Paddington, Victoria and Marylebone. The architecture of the great railway stations is discussed later but industrial archaeologists working in the London area have also recorded many important lesser features. In both Bromley and Croydon, for example, there are extensive remains of early railways. The earliest are those of the Croydon, Merstham and Godstone Railway, opened in 1805 to carry an extension of the Surrey Iron Railway to Greystone Limeworks at Merstham. The Surrey Iron Railway was the first public railway or plateway, built for horse-drawn wagons. There are several substantial earthworks, notably the Summit Cutting (TQ288555) adjacent to the Brighton Road between Hooley and Merstham, and the Cane Hill Embankment (TQ296594) at Coulsdon. Now a series of footpaths and rights of way, the route can still be traced for much of its length along the side of the valley opposite that of the main Brighton line, and three sections of track have been preserved.[22] There are also a number of interesting survivals from the Croydon Atmospheric Railway opened in 1845, including two flyovers (at TQ352708 and TQ343692) and a former engine house and chimney (TQ322654). This last was bought from the former Atmospheric Railway in 1851 by the Croydon Local Board of Health and re-erected on the present site. As with the other atmospheric lines (Dublin–Kingstown and the South Devon Railway), the Croydon Railway had been beset with mechanical problems associated with valve-sealing and with the stationary engines and pumps.[23]

Elsewhere in the south-east commuter lines and those to the Channel ports were of great importance. The Sussex field survey devoted considerable attention to railway archaeology, including engineering features and stations associated with the London, Brighton and South Coast Railway and with the South Eastern Railway. The major monument of the Brighton line is the Ouse Viaduct near Balcombe (TQ323278) built 1839–41, 1,475 ft (449.6 m) long, 96 ft (29.3 m) above the River Ouse, with 37 semicircular arches. The four stone pavilions at each end form an attractive feature. Construction materials were brought up the Ouse Navigation, although the modern visitor will find this hard to visualize! At Brighton Station (TQ310049) David Mocatta's original façade of 1840 can still be traced under the extensive additions of the late Victorian period. The massive artificial terrace built to carry the railway can be seen from the valley to the east. The present building dates substantially from 1883 when the magnificent curved overall roof was constructed. A carriage ramp, now disused, ran from Trafalgar Street up to platform level under the station building. Among many fine wayside stations in the country is that of Battle (TQ755155), designed by Willaim Tress for the South Eastern Railway and opened in 1852. Battle is widely regarded as the finest Victorian roadside station in Sussex and apart from the chimneys is externally unaltered. Sympathetic restoration has displayed well the attractive roof, baronial fireplace and Gothic doors of the booking hall.[24]

Railway relics in Hampshire have also been the subjects of detailed record, the most notable building being Southampton Terminus Station (SU426111) which survives virtually unchanged following transfer of traffic to the present station. Elsewhere in the county a wide variety of features from the early days of railways may still be seen.[25]

Finally, most parts of Ireland present tremendous opportunities to survey and record railway archaeology. Irish railway history has been extensively documented by the Irish Railway Record Society and others, but, as in Britain, there has been less attention to what survives on the ground. The development—and decline—of railways in Ireland have close parallels with the British experience in general. Although the Dublin to Kingstown line of 1834 was followed by other equally modest schemes, the railway construction boom did not get under way until the mania of the mid-forties. The Dublin to Cork line opened in 1849, and the construction of a magnificent viaduct over the Boyne at Drogheda in 1855 gave through traffic from Dublin to Belfast. By 1880 there were more than 2,300 miles of railway in Ireland, and another thousand were to be added before 1913. The total mileage of the rail system at present is approximately 1,350—some indication of the degree of rationalization and closure of branch lines which has taken place in recent years.[26]

The architecture of the great railway stations is documented in some detail, while an increasing amount of attention is being devoted by industrial archaeologists to lesser stations. The work of pioneers like I. K. Brunel, Robert Stephenson, Francis Thompson and John Dobson was followed in a spirit of eager rivalry by other eminent engineers of the period 1845–80. Brunel at Bath and at Bristol Temple Meads (1841) was the first to give serious architectural treatment to styles seen earlier in the first wooden station at Liverpool Lime Street and the iron station at Euston (1835) which were essentially rough and simple prototypes of the later structures. Despite the loss of Euston and major changes elsewhere, London is fortunate to preserve some of her splendid railway termini. The outstanding example is St Pancras, certainly the grandest exercise in Victorian railway station architecture with the former Midland Grand Hotel fronting it in neo-Gothic splendour. Much of Liverpool Street Station, built in 1875 as the terminus of the Great Eastern Railway, is original with yellow-brick Gothic main buildings and vast train sheds beyond (Plate 77).

The large provincial stations still offer much of interest, particularly at Edinburgh, Bristol, York, Newcastle, and Sunderland (Plate 78).[27] Many smaller stations retain original architectural features—for instance those along the Norwich to Peterborough section of British Rail—which ought to be recorded by the railway archaeologist. As with much else that concerns the industrial archaeologist the need for systematic survey and record is acute, for the rate of alteration and demolition over recent years has been considerable. Yet many opportunities also exist to record abandoned railways where a variety of lineside features are equally worthy of attention. The survey by Rees of the East Lancashire Railway is an excellent indication of what can be achieved in this type of exercise.[28]

Plate 77   Liverpool Street Station, London, now in danger of
demolition or substantial alteration. Note the exceedingly fine roof
structure and ironwork.

Plate 78   Monkwearmouth Station Museum, Sunderland
(NZ396577), built in fine classical style as the terminus of the
Sunderland, Newcastle and South Shields Railway to the design of
Thomas Moore of Monkwearmouth.

Ports and harbours

The study of ports and harbours offers enormous scope for the
industrial archaeologist, for there were few parts of the coastline
of the British Isles which did not experience harbour development during the eighteenth or nineteenth centuries. Harbours
were of two main types: those built on natural harbour sites and
those which were almost entirely artificial. The former were
often improved by dredging, and made safer for shipping by the
construction of piers and breakwaters; the latter, constructed on
similar principles, were often excavated from mud flats, and
incorporated docks for the use of shipping at all states of the
tide. Harbourside features include a wide range of jetties, slipways, dry docks, lock gates, sluices, and smaller items such as
dockside cranes, coal drops, and mineral lines. Harbour architecture is also of great interest, especially warehouses (often with

199

hoists) commonly found at all but the smallest ports. Fishing ports have many special features, including markets, fish stores, net stores and processing plant such as curing houses. Prior to the development of artificial refrigeration, ice-houses were widely used for preserving fish, and these can still be found at the older harbours. Finally, there are many navigational and other features, such as lighthouses, and lifeboat stations, which are worth the attention of the industrial archaeologist. The former have already been the subject of major study. So widespread are ports, docks and harbours that only a few examples can be examined here. The approach we have adopted is simply to look at what appear to be representative types from different parts of the country, though inevitably they are mostly drawn from areas already covered by regional or local surveys. Depending on the particular bias of existing surveys, harbour archaeology has received detailed or cursory treatment in different places and those familiar with particular areas will no doubt find many omissions. One glaring omission is Ireland where there is a wealth of sites worthy of examination and recording. The largest concentration of harbour and dockside installations can be found in the major ports of London (Plate 79), Southampton, Bristol (Plate 80), Cardiff, Swansea, Liverpool, Hull, Tyneside, Leith, Glasgow, Belfast and Dublin. Fortunately most of the major sites have been the subjects of detailed survey and record. All have undergone considerable alteration in recent years, some to the point of virtual abandonment and obliteration.

Just as fascinating as the larger harbours and docks are numerous smaller ports found round the coasts. They range widely in size, construction and function, from the simple landing stage or slipway for general cargo, through small fishing ports, to industrial harbours shipping coal, metal ores, building stone or slate. Many might have had all three functions, and most shipped raw materials and manufactures. Harbours had a close relationship with their hinterland and were invariably developed by local landowners, merchants, and industrialists, not only as outlets for agricultural produce or minerals, but as focal points of economic development. Planned villages and towns grew up at harbours, and industries based on locally available or imported raw materials followed. Even smaller harbours had an important range of industrial activities and crafts related to ship supply, including rope and sail making, timber and metal working. These often provided a basis for further industrial development.

Finally, there were many eighteenth- and nineteenth-century harbours with special functions, notably naval ports and packet

Plate 79 Carron Company warehouse on the River Thames in the
Port of London.

Plate 80 The port of Bristol with warehouses and bonded stores on
either side of the River Avon.

stations. The former preserve numerous features of interest, including boat-houses, slipways, dry-docks, arsenals, and warehouses. Naval dockyards were often heavily defended, and the fortifications—including look-out towers and martello towers—are of considerable architectural and historical interest. The best example by far, of course, is Portsmouth (Plate 81) where docks, arsenals and storehouses appropriate for a major naval base are preserved much as they were in Lord Nelson's day. Packet stations were vital to the fast and efficient communication of mails and passengers, particularly across the English Channel and the Irish Sea. Hence eighteenth- and nineteenth-century governments devoted considerable time and expense to the selection and construction of suitable harbours along the South Coast and the coasts of Ireland, Wales and Scotland. Since considerable strategic significance also attached to most packet stations, they were often fortified and staffed by a garrison. Impressive harbour works, constructed by eminent civil engineers, characterize many of these ports, for example, Fishguard and Holyhead in Wales, Dun Laoghaire and Donaghadee in Ireland (Plate 82), and Portpatrick in Scotland.

Turning first to the larger docks and harbours we have the benefit of a series of studies, from which London and Liverpool are typical examples. London is in a sense atypical because of the scale and extent of dock and harbour installations in the port, but developments along the Thames show a chronology common around the coasts of the British Isles. The majority of features are of eighteenth- or nineteenth-century origin and although many have been lost, there is still plenty to interest the industrial archaeologist. In the City of London there are still a number of early warehouses: the Port of London Authority warehouses in Cutler Street (TQ335815) date from *c.* 1790 and were originally built for the East India Company. This particular group of warehouses was designed by Richard Jupp and Henry Holland, the last an early pioneer in the construction of fire-proof buildings. St Katherine Docks, south of East Smithfield and downriver from the Tower (TQ339805), is now a marina and has undergone much redevelopment. The two original docks linked to an entrance basin have been retained, as well as a number of warehouses, mostly built after 1828 to the design of Thomas Telford, who was Chief Engineer to the Dock Company. The earlier London Docks (TQ3480/3580) and West India Docks (TQ3780/3779) are still of interest despite partial abandonment and infilling. The former has a swing bridge by John Rennie, Sen. (at Hermitage Cutting), while the latter, engineered by William Jessop, was the first

Plate 81 Portsmouth naval dockyard showing (*above*) No. 6
boathouse built in 1843 and (*below*) the dry-dock.

Plate 82   Donaghadee Harbour, County Down (OS2/594802), a
former packet station on the short (21 miles) sea-route between
Ireland and Scotland, constructed between 1821 and 1837 under the
direction of Sir John Rennie.

enclosed wet-dock system built for the trade in London. Typical
Thames dockside warehouses can be seen on both banks at
Wapping and Rotherhithe. Downriver the Royal Group of Docks
is on a massive scale by comparison with earlier nineteenth-
century constructions. The system comprises the Royal Victoria
Dock (opened 1855), Royal Albert Dock (1880), and the King
George V Dock (1921). Although the installations are generally
modern the docks nevertheless provide an interesting comparison with earlier ones. Elsewhere on the riverside are numerous
wharfs, smaller docks and associated warehouses, which can
readily be identified from the London survey.[29]

Liverpool's growth as a port owed more to the development
of its hinterland than did that of London, though its origins in
the early eighteenth century did arise from an extension of the
American trade. During the remainder of the century a number

Plate 83   A general view of Liverpool docks, the brainchild of Jesse
Hartley, dock engineer from 1824 to 1860.

of different industries grew up, notably pottery, sugar refining,
and port-related trades like shipbuilding and rope-making. The
Victorian era saw a rapid extension of the Mersey dock system
to cope with the constantly increasing volume of shipping. The
two oldest docks are the Salthouse Dock (ST343898) built 1734–53,
and the South Ferry Basin (SJ344885), a small tidal basin opened
in 1816. Of several major docks, the outstanding is Albert Dock
(SJ340897), one of the 'Top Ten' sites of Merseyside (Plates 83
and 84). Designed by Jesse Hartley and opened in 1846, it was
Liverpool's first enclosed dock warehouse system. It is widely
regarded as one of the finest examples of nineteenth-century
dockland architecture in Britain, and consists of a square-shaped
basin surrounded by five-storey warehouse buildings into which
merchandise could be unloaded directly from ships. Brick, cast
and wrought iron were used extensively in the structures, which
were designed to be as near fire-proof as possible. At the north-
eastern corner is the Dock Traffic Office, built 1846–7 to designs
by Philip Harwick who was co-designer of St Katherine Dock in

Plate 84 Albert Dock (SJ342897), Liverpool, Hartley's masterpiece with its massive warehouses.

London and whom Hartley had consulted about the warehouses. Alongside is the former pumping station which supplied power for the operation of dock equipment such as hoists and swing bridges. Hartley's two other docks are Stanley Dock (SJ337921) and Wapping Dock (SJ345893), similar in design to Albert Dock; while there is much else of interest in other areas of the port. North-east of the Herculaneum Dock (SJ357873), for example, is a row of about fifty cellars—excavated out of the cliff and fitted with iron safety doors—which were built at the end of the last century for the storage of petroleum. The Dock Company's workshops are located at Coburg Dockyard (SJ344885), while the nearby South Ferry Basin serves the last of Liverpool's fishing fleet.[30] A similar range of features can be found in most of the other major ports: detailed surveys have already been made of a number, notably Southampton, Bristol, Hull and Glasgow.[31]

By far the greatest number of ports found around the shores of Britain and Ireland were on a smaller scale, although, as we have seen, many had specialized functions, principally as fishing harbours or for the shipment of coal and other minerals. The fishing industry itself must of necessity receive limited coverage here, but there is much that ought to merit the attention of the industrial archaeologist in fishing ports and harbours. Of particular importance are relics associated with the storage, marketing and processing of fish. These have already undergone substantial change and many seem likely to disappear altogether in the not-distant future. Most of the features described can be found in any fishing port, though obviously the larger ports like Yarmouth, Grimsby, Fleetwood or Aberdeen have a more complex archaeology and architecture. Quayside stores and warehouses were generally multi-purpose, serving as repositories for fish, fish boxes, nets, sails, rope and other ship supplies. The preservation of raw fish in the days before the development of artificial refrigeration was made possible by the construction of ice-houses—often larger versions of those commonly found on country estates—where fish could be stored fresh, or ice could be obtained for fish packing. At Berwick-upon-Tweed there are three examples of commercial ice-houses associated with the salmon fishery in the lower reaches of the River Tweed. At Bankhill (NT997529) there is a well-preserved ice-house built into the northern river bank, which is now safeguarded by the Department of the Environment. Near by at Ravensdowne is another ice-house which, although no longer used, is at least 150 years old. Other ice-houses associated with the fishing industry can be found around the coast at old harbours.[32] There are several in Easter Ross, notably at Cromarty (NH789676) and at Fortrose (NH747557)—both on a larger scale than domestic structures of their type.

The preserving of fish by salting or curing was of great importance in former times and both crafts have left substantial remains in places where they were carried on. The most interesting buildings are former curing houses, fish stores and cooperages (see above, p. 69). The curing house is readily identified by its kiln-like appearance and ventilators, amply illustrated by survivals at Great Yarmouth and North Shields. At Great Yarmouth a survey in 1971 recorded a range of curing premises adjoining the quays by the River Yare.[33] In North Shields, where kippering is still carried on, there are good examples of curing houses at the harbour—mostly square in plan and of two storeys, the lower being of brick and the upper of slatted timbers, the whole topped with vents along the ridge of the roof. Further north in Wick's suburb of Pulteneytown many relics of the once-prosperous herring trade can be found in and around the harbour, particularly fish stores and curing sheds, some very large compared with those of Yarmouth and Shields. The typical Caithness store-cum-smokehouse is of three storeys, built of sandstone rubble and roofed with the pantiles common to most of the eastern seaboard of Britain. Examples of smokehouses can be observed in Fraserburgh, Eyemouth, Whitby, Scarborough, Lowestoft and Yarmouth. Pilchard curing is represented by similar physical remains in the small ports of south-west England. The layout is similar to that of a corn mill with the kiln at one end of the building, the rest of the space being given over to storage. There were upwards of twenty such plant in Wick before 1914, though most have since closed due to recession in the herring fishery. Finally, fish markets—where they survive in the larger ports—are of some interest to the industrial archaeologist. The older ones have glass roofs supported on cast-iron columns and are generally of Victorian vintage.

Some of the best coal ports, not surprisingly, are to be found in the north-east, including Amble, Blyth, Seaton Sluice, Shields, Sunderland and Seaham, all with remains of interest. Seaton Sluice and Seaham are both dramatic harbours largely cut out of rock, the former in the early 1760s, the latter between 1828 and 1831. Seaton Sluice (NZ339769) was built by Thomas Delavel, a typical northern landowner turned coalmaster-industrialist. A 'New Cut' was made to provide an additional entrance to the old harbour, its dimensions being 800 ft (243.8 m) long, 30 ft (9.14 m) wide and 52 ft (15.8 m) deep. Delavel also constructed a deep-water dock where vessels could be loaded at all states of the tide. The harbour was connected to nearby collieries by a network of wagonways. Although coal was the main export, Delavel established a large glassworks, brickworks, and a quarry which supplied materials for the construction of both dockside buildings and workers' housing. Further south, Seaham (NZ433495) was designed by the Marquis of Londonderry to an earlier plan of William Chapman. A large outer harbour formed by piers was built to protect a series of inner docks. Related facilities included a dry-dock, shipbuilding yard, coal drops, haulage machinery, timber yards, workshops and offices. The gates to the Northern Docks were once powered by a beam engine, parts of which are now at the North of England Open Air Museum at Beamish.

What was believed to be the last traditional coal drop in the north-east—from Seaham—is also preserved at the museum. But much of original interest still survives on site including many of the harbour installations and a tramroad which reached the quayside through a rock-cut tunnel. The town of Seaham itself was developed at the same period to the design of John Dobson, architect of some of Newcastle's finest buildings.[34] Other areas with interesting coal ports include Cumbria and South Wales.[35]

Harbours were also constructed for the shipment of other minerals, notably non-ferrous ores of lead, tin and copper, and for the shipment of building stone and slate. In Devon there are numerous harbours of this kind, the heaviest concentration being in the Tamar valley, once an important centre of metal-mining. The focal point of navigation on the Tamar was Morwellham Harbour (SX445695), until 1900 the port of the Devon Great Consols mine. A canal, opened in 1817, linked Morwellham with Tavistock. Goods from the canal and a mineral railway from the mine reached the harbour by inclined planes down a steep slope to the river. Almost all of the harbour and other installations were abandoned after the turn of the century; the harbours silted up, and the quays became overgrown and forgotten. But in 1970 the Dartington Amenity Research Trust leased the harbour area and established the Morwellham Quay Centre as an open-air industrial museum. An old dance hall behind the Ship Inn has become the Centre's museum, and long-hidden features, such as the harbours, tiled quays, inclined planes, water wheels, ore chutes and lime-kilns, are gradually being excavated. There are many other interesting features including some splendid workers' housing (SX445689) built by the Duke of Bedford for miners and dock hands.[36] Both Cornwall and Wales offer similar scope for the recording of ports formerly employed in shipping metal ores, granite and slate. Many have ancillary installations like crushing, smelting or polishing plant, as well as mineral railways, derricks and cranes.[37]

The major naval dockyards, past and present, preserve much of interest to the industrial archaeologist. These include Portsmouth, Plymouth, Sheerness, Deptford, Woolwich, Chatham, Milford Haven and Pembroke Dock. Portsmouth Naval Dockyard covers over 300 acres and has much of its eighteenth- and nineteenth-century architecture intact, including boat-houses, store houses, block mills, Great Ropery, smithies, chain-testing shop and a foundry. The docks themselves are of Portland stone, have bow recesses at their landward end, stepped sides, and, with the exception of No. 5 Dock (No. 2 Dock being permanently closed because it holds the *Victory*), have caisson gates. Among a wealth of interesting buildings are the Block Mills of 1802 (SU628008), constructed for the mass production of rigging blocks using machinery designed by Marc Isambard Brunel, the No. 6 Boat-house (SU630004) built in 1843 behind the old Mast Pickling Pond of 1666, the Fire Station (also of 1843), and the 1,095 ft (333 m) long Great Ropery, a fine Georgian building dating from 1775. A unique railway relic is the decorative train shed (SU627004) on the South Railway Jetty, built to protect royalty from inclement weather when crossing to and from the Isle of Wight. At nearby Gosport, the Royal Clarence Yard (SU617006) was the chief naval victualling centre for the Portsmouth fleet, and many interesting buildings, including cooperages, brewery, granaries, mills and bakeries, mainly of early-nineteenth-century date, can still be seen.[38] At Plymouth there is also much of note in the Royal Naval Dockyard (SX448552): the Gun Wharf, constructed 1718–25, is the work of Vanbrugh, while there are two roperies similar in scale to that at Portsmouth. The Royal William Victualling Yard (SX460535) corresponding to the Gosport yard was designed by John Rennie and built between 1826 and 1835.[39] Elsewhere there have been many changes. Sheerness Dockyard, also the work of Rennie, closed in 1957, and many of the original buildings which survived until that date have since been demolished to make way for an industrial estate and deep-water harbour with a new ferry terminal.[40]

The best surviving examples of harbours developed primarily as packet stations are to be found on either side of the North Channel at Portpatrick in Wigtownshire and Donaghadee in County Down. For over a century between 1750 and 1850 they were at the centre of a great debate about the safest Short Sea crossing between Ireland and the mainland, and consequently, both harbours attracted the attention of notable engineers like Smeaton, Telford and the Rennies. The present harbour installations, dating substantially from the beginning of the nineteenth century, include piers, breakwaters and lighthouses. At Portpatrick (NW998542) a limited natural harbour approached by a rocky and dangerous entrance was extended by the construction of two massive piers, North and South. Only a short section of the South Pier survives, though much of the inner harbour and a small lighthouse is maintained in good order. The abandoned harbour branch of the Portpatrick Railway can be traced nearby.[41]

Twenty-one miles across the North Channel the harbour of Donaghadee, in a more sheltered location, has weathered the years better than Portpatrick and shows nineteenth-century civil engineering to great advantage. The harbour again consists of two piers, the southern 900 ft (274 m) long, and the northern 820 ft (250 m) in length. The lighthouse stands 50 ft (15.2 m) high and is of limestone masonry painted white. The building was designed by Sir John Rennie and the fitments, including glazings, railings and wrought-iron door were provided by Deville of London. Despite massive expenditure on both harbours, the route was ultimately abandoned by Post Office, government and the railway companies: Larne and Stranraer became the termini of the short sea-route after 1850. Both Portpatrick and Donaghadee are still actively used by fishing boats and pleasure craft, as well as serving as lifeboat stations.[42]

Various dockside industries have left an important legacy which ought to be recorded. Port architecture includes a wide variety of interesting buildings formerly used as warehouses, granaries, mills, timber yards, cooperages, bonded warehouses, roperies, net and sail works. Most are readily identifiable by external appearance, and former functions can be checked against early Ordnance Survey maps of 6 in. scale or larger. Boat-building, shipbuilding and repairing were carried on at most larger ports, and even small harbours had a boatyard and dry-dock. Ship supply and victualling was an important function of the major ports, so warehouses for the storage of provisions can be found in considerable numbers, as can public houses for the liquid refreshment of those on ship and shore. These and a great many other harbourside features are worth recording before they decay or are demolished.

The limited space available here can do only rough justice either to the history of railway and harbour development in the British Isles or to the rich archaeology which can be found in almost every part of the country. It is worth emphasizing again that attention in the past has been neglectful of surviving relics on the ground—saving the tremendous devotion of enthusiasts for the preservation of old railway engines and ships. The environmental and recreational possibilities for abandoned railways and old harbours have only begun to be realized. More than 2,500 miles of railways have been taken out of service since the early 1960s; the track now provides a network of greenways throughout the country and many make fine walks. As with the old routeways and roads described in Chapter 9 the potential for the creation of long-distance footpaths using abandoned railway track is considerable, while the naturalist can find a wealth of wildlife and flora along old embankments and cuttings even in built-up areas. The revitalization of abandoned harbours owes much to the growing demand for water-based recreation, especially pleasure boating, yachting, sea fishing and water sports in general. Such development has an important multiplier effect in the encouragement of ancillary and service industries such as boat-building and repairing, nautical supplies and craft industries. Preservation of quayside buildings and housing for new functions is often the result. As far as the industrial archaeologist is concerned these developments can only have a positive effect. They create new interest and activity in a heritage of considerable importance which has been neglected since the decline of shipping in all but the larger harbours.

11
Public Services and Utilities

Urban growth in the nineteenth century depended upon a number of variables. Labour was attracted by a diverse range of economic opportunities; food supplies had to be reorganized and retailing improved; building land had to be developed into residential districts. The provision of public services and utilities was usually an afterthought, for towns and cities were rarely planned. Water supply, refuse and sewage disposal, lighting, fire-fighting, and urban transport, all essential services today, were created in a haphazard fashion usually on a district basis by private enterprise and then taken into municipal ownership.

Of these public utilities water supply was initially the most significant. Although a number of cities and towns, notably London and Exeter, had water companies in pre-industrial times, most places became concerned about pure water after the cholera epidemics of the 1830s. Improvement schemes often took decades to perfect and were subject to continuous improvement as urbanization proceeded. Nonetheless, slow progress brought benefits, for hydraulic engineering in its many forms and steam technology were refined in the face of new demands placed upon them.[1] Pumping water was essential not only to provide tap supplies but also for street cleansing and sewage disposal, and the ingenuity of engineers was constantly tested by local problems often of colossal dimensions.

Lowland Britain, in particular eastern and southern England, has many relics of Victorian water-supply engineering. The great industrial and commercial cities received water from hilly and mountainous terrain; lakes, lochs, dams and reservoirs were constructed in Wales, Scotland, the Pennines, and the Lake District from which Birmingham, Glasgow, Sheffield, Leeds, Manchester and Liverpool were supplied. London posed special problems, and from the early seventeenth century water companies were being floated to supplement local well supplies. Generally, the pace of metropolitan development outstripped the capacity and capital available to water companies. Intermittent pressure from the London County Council eventually led in 1902 to the formation of the Metropolitan Water Board. Kew Bridge pumping station (TQ188780) at Brentford has one Maudsley beam engine and four Cornish pumping engines, two made by Harveys at Copperhouse Foundry, Hayle and preserved by Kew Bridge Trust. This station is representative of the larger unit already arising in London well before the formation of the Metropolitan Water Board.

Waterworks engineering was undertaken by many firms, but two were outstanding for their work in improving the efficiency of steam pumping engines—Hathorn Davey of Leeds and Worthington Simpson of London.[2] Both these businesses happily survive and now manufacture *inter alia* steam turbines and electrically driven turbo-pumps which have rendered reciprocating steam engines obsolete.

Yet many of the older types, together with their splendid engine houses, still survive, especially in the Midlands. The South Staffordshire Waterworks Company and the Potteries Water Board have left an outstanding historical heritage. Cresswell pumping station (SJ974394) is not particularly impressive as a building, but inside there are two inverted vertical triple expansion Hathorn Davey engines installed in 1932 and still pumping water to the Potteries, and a horizontal single cylinder engine made by Green and Son.[3] Other interesting pumping stations are Huntington (SJ974123), Lichfield (SK112084), Milford (SJ975213), Rugeley (SK038194), and Swynnerton (SO829370).[4] The Brindley Park pumping station at Rugeley, opened in 1905, was built in the style of a Jacobean manor house and contains a Hathorn Davey tandem compound engine installed in 1907 and operating till 1968. Coal for the boilers came via the Trent and Mersey Canal, with which James Brindley was, of course, associated: hence the name of the pumping station.[5] Mill Meece pumping station (SJ830339) was designed in more orthodox style by William Campbell, architect of Hanley, in 1914 and contains two horizontal tandem compound engines, one installed in 1927 by Hathorn Davey and the other an original from 1914 by Ashton Frost of Blackburn.[6]

If Staffordshire is a particularly rich county for those interested in waterworks engineering, there are many other notable examples. Broomy Hill pumping station in Hereford (SO497393) is now owned by the Herefordshire Waterworks Museum Trust; this venture, opened in 1975, owns two engines dating from 1895 and 1906, both made by Worth Mackenzie of Stockton-on-Tees.[7] In Nottinghamshire among several interesting relics undoubtedly the outstanding monument is Papplewick (SK582522) (Plates 85 and 86), a pumping station built to supplement capacity at Basford (built *c.* 1857) and Bestwood (*c.* 1873) in 1883–5. The

Lighting
today electr
cation to hea
and machin
try is given
and less ph
exciting and
electrical re
The scientif
by Volta, Oe
generator i
dynamo, it
filament lan
in the Unit
supply was
by steam e
technical ba
electricity w
in the censu
valued at £
capacity of
steam engi
electric sch
ming, Surre
1874, varied
and Lynmo
by Professo
survivals of
Powick, Wo
ities in 1894
Largy, Lima
During th
stations wer
nies. Apart
power for s
operate an e
in 1893 it p
proved to be
The origina
Back, and r
station build
West Midla
tions still st
and are bei

Plate 87   Ry
with the eng
right. Restore

new pum
in Bristol
Hathorn I
Somerset,
at Twyford
in East Yo
Metropoli
various m
Davey and
of their sp
pany, Ashv

Plate 85   Interior of Papplewick waterworks engine house
(SK583522), showing the beautifully decorated supporting columns
and the flywheel on the left.

215

Plate 90   The City of Worcester Electricity Works at Powick (SO835525), 1894. Now used by an engineering firm but once was Britain's largest hydro-electric station used for public supply.

Plate 91   The main hydro-electric power station at Dog Leap, Largy, Limavady on Roe River, County Londonderry, dating from 1897.

power station, opened in 1902, was finished only just ahead of the demolishers.[25]

Before the evolution of the National Grid in the late 1920s, the electricity supply industry was dominated by small stations like Newton Abbot and relatively small companies. Regional groups merged, and the least efficient power stations closed. For many decades uncertainty existed about whether alternating or direct current should be generated. After the Electricity Supply Act of 1926 a.c. at 50 Hz became standard as the National Grid developed.[26] Power stations have become enormous in their capacity compared with the early days of the industry, and obsolescence is a constant feature. Efforts at preservation of small items such as early dynamos are being made; the best collection is in the Science Museum, South Kensington.

Communications including telecommunications, have also left their relics. The National Telephone Company dominated telecommunication until the General Post Office acquired all private systems except that of Kingston-upon-Hull in 1912. Urban transport systems have already been discussed, and many enthusiasts support tramway societies and visit specialist museums. Urban and rural fire-fighting services became more efficient as fire losses became more significant, and Shand Mason and Merryweather fire engines now join the ranks of exhibits in museums throughout Britain.

12
Social Archaeology

The study of industrial archaeology, while wholly valid in itself, should never be divorced from its historical and social context. Kenneth Hudson, a leading pioneer and propagandist, has consistently argued the view that the main purpose of industrial archaeology is to shed light on people's working conditions and past attitudes to them, an aim which not everyone would accept.[1] Nevertheless there is much to interest the industrial archaeologist in strictly 'non-industrial' features which shed light on industrial, economic and social changes.

'Social archaeology' can be defined here as those buildings, artefacts, and other heritage features which show something of how people lived, worked and took their leisure in past industrial society. Social archaeology covers a wide field, many of the features being of interest to architectural historians, social historians, planners and conservationists. It includes housing (particularly working-class housing) of many kinds, industrial settlements, factory villages, gaols and workhouses, buildings and other places associated with worship and entertainment in industrial communities, and a variety of other miscellaneous features, such as 'military archaeology' (which is currently attracting considerable attention). It seems only right that the social artefacts of the industrial past should receive the same attention as that so far devoted to technological monuments. Industrial archaeologists will also, like historians of the more recent past, need to learn the techniques of the oral historian.[2] The present chapter indicates something of the social archaeology that came in the wake of changing technology and economic circumstances during the past two hundred years.

Workers' housing

In no area of industrial archaeological survey is the need for recording more urgent than in that of workers' housing. By its very nature much has been lost through decay and demolition, and there is less incentive to restore and preserve housing than most other classes of industrial monument. Our knowledge of the history of working-class housing and of housing conditions in general during the past two hundred years has been greatly extended by recent studies undertaken by social historians.[3] Yet the physical dimension has largely been neglected by all but a few architectural historians and historical geographers. The architects have pioneered systematic fieldwork on housing, while the geographers have concerned themselves more with settlement forms and studies.[4] The increasing amount of attention devoted to studies in vernacular architecture has been partly responsible for a greater interest on the part of researchers in workers' housing. As we saw in Chapter 1, it is particularly heartening to find a growing enthusiasm in schools of architecture for industrial archaeology and much student-based research on industrial buildings, including housing. For their part the geographers have done much to advance the study of industrial settlements, especially within the context of the evolving historical landscape over the past two hundred years.

As far as the industrial archaeologist is concerned the architect's emphasis on the vernacular is right and proper, for traditional styles considerably influenced the development and forms of industrial housing during the latter half of the eighteenth and early part of the nineteenth centuries. One study of rural housing in and around Dartington in Devon shows the evolution of local cottage architecture since the seventeenth century and demonstrates how old-established styles continued to be used in later housing.[5] Parallel instances could no doubt be cited from most parts of Britain, for housing of the Industrial Revolution era, where it survives, generally reflects the vernacular tradition and the use of local raw materials in construction.

Industrial housing has been the subject of a number of significant studies in different parts of the country. Although the degree of attention devoted to physical remains is variable, some kind of pattern is gradually emerging. Many different types of industrial housing can be identified, but there are five principal categories: first, the group which includes a wide range of housing-cum-workplaces common in the domestic textile and iron trade; second, a variety of basically cottage-plan housing; third, the omnipresent back-to-back housing; fourth, tenement housing, common in Scotland, but also found elsewhere; fifth, terraced housing, often a variant of the cottage or back-to-back categories. One or more of these categories can be seen in the same place, and if the evidence of those surveys undertaken so far is taken as a guide, much interesting workers' housing can still be recorded even where demolition has removed whole streets.

Many excellent examples of housing-cum-workplaces—reflecting the strength of the domestic system in the early stages of industrialization—can be found throughout the country. One study, based on detailed field research, carefully relates the regional traditions of domestic building to the architecture of the domestic system in the south-east of Lancashire, particularly in and around the woollen districts of Rochdale and Saddleworth, and Middleton, where specialization in fine cottons and silk meant the survival of handloom weaving until the 1860s.[6] Smith indicates that the vernacular building traditions of the Pennines can be seen in most surviving domestic workers' housing. Many loom-shops were at first incorporated in existing farmhouses or cottages. Examples abound in the Saddleworth area, as at New Tame (SD9808) near Delph, where a mid-eighteenth-century farmhouse was rebuilt with an enlarged attic workroom lit by new windows. A house at Ballgreave (SD9905), Uppermill, was enlarged in two phases: first a new wing was added at the southern end, and later a complete upper storey was constructed running the full length of the building and with a long row of twelve lights facing west to illuminate the loom-shop. At the rear was a 'taking-in' door (now blocked up), and the sharp rise in the ground behind also allowed direct access across a flagstone bridge, since demolished.

The vernacular style was subsequently translated and developed in the construction of loom-houses in urban districts. Many were built adjoining wool-spinning mills. Chesham Fold, Bury (SD819113), is a terrace of ten loom-houses fronting Rochdale Old Road, behind which is a woollen mill. The row consists of three-storey sandstone houses, each with a loom-shop on the top floor running the full depth of the range. The workroom has mullion windows above a continuous sill and there are five lights of which the widest, in the centre, is fitted with a sash to allow control over ventilation. The workshops in Middleton showed a similar arrangement, but other local designs placed the loom-shop at the rear or in the basement area, for example the handloom weavers, housing in Dyehouse Lane, Smallbridge (SD911151) near Rochdale, where the workshops were located in semi-basements reached by stairs from the living quarters above. The nearby woollen districts of West Yorkshire also afford tremendous scope for recording the architecture of the domestic system. One particularly valuable study of Coffin Row, Linthwaite—a workshop with four underdwellings—provides an indication of the sort of feature that can still be found in large numbers.[7]

Nottingham, a major centre of cotton spinning, of domestic

hosiery and of lace manufacture, preserves good examples of workers' housing with industrial functions.[8] Some of the earliest, dating from 1785, were built back to back, often in three storeys with the workshop on the top floor. The height of these dwellings and the occupation of the top floor by stocking frames was more common in Nottingham than elsewhere, probably because land was more expensive. The expansion of lace-making was also based on the domestic system. Larger dwellings of artisans engaged in the trade were built in new suburbs at New Sneinton, Carrington, New Basford, Hyson Green, New Radford and New Lenton. The typical dwelling was of three storeys, the whole of the second floor being intended for lace machines. Large windows 10 ft (3 m) wide lit the machine room at both front and rear. An attic was probably designed for storing yarn, or might have been used as sleeping quarters for children or apprentices. Chapman's study indicates other varieties on the basic pattern in the Nottingham district, while David Smith records both framework knitters' cottages and lacemakers' workshops in many parts of the East Midlands.[9]

The domestic system was also common in the metal trades before and during the Industrial Revolution. One analysis of housing in such an area around Wolverhampton indicates the developments which took place in a typical Black Country district where housing and industry were inexorably juxtaposed. In 1750 most of the working-class housing was the first generation of brick and tiled cottage-type dwellings. Most houses constructed between then and 1800 were of similar design, the majority built in courts squeezed into gaps in the existing houses. Premises for a variety of metalworkers—mainly nailers and lockmakers—invariably included living quarters. By the 1820s standard back-to-back housing had begun to appear, though much building was still done in courts and alleys. When terraced back-to-backs were built in large numbers during the rest of the nineteenth century, the high densities which characterized the older parts of the town were maintained.[10] Although the majority of this old housing and related metalworking shops has been cleared, much of interest still remains to be recorded in Wolverhampton, and neighbouring communities like Wednesbury, Willenhall, Bentley and Darlaston.[11] Another centre of metalworking, Sheffield, still preserves considerable evidence of the domestic organization and small workshops which characterized the trade there. The rural nature of much of the metal trade before the Industrial Revolution has been the subject of detailed research by Hey. In 1972, when he undertook his researches in the country around Sheffield, he was able to find evidence of long-abandoned metal crafts, such as nailers' smithies at Staincross (SE330100), a fork-making smithy at Shiregreen, and the Nailmakers' Arms at Norton.[12] In Sheffield itself many metalworking shops—particularly cutlers' shops—can still be found in the older central parts of the city, while at Abbeydale the late-eighteenth-century scythe-works has been carefully and accurately restored. Workers were housed in simple stone-built cottages built in or near the works.[13]

By far the most common workers' housing was built to traditional cottage plan, and many examples can be found in different parts of the country. A detailed study of iron-industry housing in South Wales has revealed much about the history of the cottage style in that locality and shows how traditional forms were adapted in the construction of company and other housing. The general survey covers housing in the valleys of Gwent and Mid Glamorgan, while more detailed studies have been concerned with representative examples of standard housing types. In every sense the iron-industry housing survey is a model of practice for industrial archaeologists elsewhere. Lowe and his colleagues began by examining two 'prototype' houses, Coedpenmaen Lock Cottage (ST079907) near Pontypridd and Maes Llan Cottage (ST127996), Gelligaer. The former—since demolished—stood near the topmost lock in the flight which carried the Glamorgan Canal past Pontypridd. Built some time before 1798, Coedpenmaen had a four-room, two-storey layout, and was constructed in heavy, roughly squared, rubble. The upper floor was reached by semicircular stone stairs, built into one of the gable-ends. Maes Llan cottage is generally similar in size and plan (total floor area about 50 sq metres or 59.8 sq yards) and was probably built in the first decade of the nineteenth century. Both cottages continue the tradition of much earlier vernacular architecture once common in Monmouth and Glamorgan, examples of which can still be seen in some rural housing in the area.[14]

Subsequent fieldwork produced detailed analyses of early housing constructed in the main by local ironmasters. One survey describes standard houses built by the Blaenavon Company during the period 1817–32. The ironworks began in 1789 and was successful in its early years, expanding rapidly during the Napoleonic Wars. A major reorganization of operations was carried out during 1817–19, and this work included the building of the first houses. Further batches of housing were constructed until the early 1830s. The standard house was a single-fronted three-room dwelling two storeys high, usually laid out in long terraces of up to thirty units, but constructed in batches of five or ten. The main living room was square, with a substantial brick-built fireplace. Behind this room, and leading off it, were a pantry and a small, unheated bedroom, roughly square in plan. Over the whole upper floor there extended a large unpartitioned sleeping chamber, open to the roof for its full height. The construction was as straightforward as the layout. The roof was covered with heavy Welsh slates laid in regular courses. They were carried on softwood rafters which rested directly on the dividing walls of the houses. The stair was nearer to a ladder than a staircase, narrow and steep with shallow treads and no riser boards. It is said to have sloped backwards over the front door, climbing into an unprotected opening in the first floor. The external construction was equally basic in character. The outside walls were of stone rubble, and openings at ground level were spanned by a single-brick arch, backed inside by a rough timber lintel. The distribution of openings on the front elevation is typical of the standard house. By placing the first-floor windows alternately above door and window openings to the ground floor, the builders could obtain an equal spacing at each floor level, despite the pairing of the houses. This arrangement gives a characteristic rhythm to the terraces. Early sanitation was non-existent. One report of 1850 noted that 'the sanitary arrangements of the workmens' cottages were deplorable. There was not a single W.C. convenience to the whole of the cottages of the works'. At the same time a company agent had declared that these facilities were of no use and 'if constructed the people would not use them'. Two examples of such housing are Lower New Rank, Blaenavon (SO245095) (Fig. 2, p. 22)—since demolished—and Forge Row, Cwmavon (SO270065) (Plate 92)—a very early example of twelve terraced houses. Many more examples of such housing can still be found around Blaenavon.[15]

Back-to-back housing probably came in for more criticism than any other type of dwelling place for the working classes. The heaviest concentration was found in northern industrial towns, notably Leeds, Bradford and Manchester, but the back-to-back was also translated to other districts, including London. A detailed study of housing in Leeds by Beresford showed that as late as 1920 no less than 70 per cent of the total housing stock was back-to-back, mainly brick-built. The distinctive features of the back-to-back are the lack of a back door, back windows, and indeed of any through ventilation since the houses were built so closely together that houses in adjoining streets often shared the same back wall. Back-to-backs were invariably built in rows,

Plate 92   Workers' housing at Forge Row, Cwmavon, South Wales, (*above*) a front view and (*below*) a rear view.

giving fairly high densities of one-up, one-down units, rather like double cottages. The urban cottage type was readily adapted to this layout and, using cheap bricks, could be economically constructed to match the low purchasing power of the working-class tenants. Despite condemnation by nineteenth-century reformers and a general ban in the Housing Act of 1909 back-to-backs continued to be built in Leeds until the 1930s. In recent years an urban clearance programme has demolished virtually every back-to-back that appears in the Ordnance Survey plan of 1850, but fieldworkers can still find examples of later date.[16]

Another major concentration of back-to-back housing was found in Birmingham. Much of it was built up in the 1860s and 1870s, yet the general layout preserved the familiar traditions of the old workshop courts. The long mid-Victorian terraces therefore gave a superficial impression of space, but the tunnel entries between alternate front houses led to numbered courts of six to eight back-to-back houses. Further inspection disclosed that the 'front houses' were also built back-to-back. A single street might contain more than twenty courts; the layout of the whole block reveals ingenious planning for the maximum use of available space combined with cheapness of construction. Heaton Street showed the courtyard style layout, with walls separating courts, tiny gardens and washhouses—facilities which many back-to-back houses could not boast.[17]

Tenement housing is typically Scottish and still represents a high proportion of working-class dwellings in the major cities of Glasgow, Edinburgh, Dundee and Aberdeen as well as in other industrial towns. The history of the tenement has been fairly fully charted, particularly in Glasgow where the largest concentration of the type was to be found.[18] Multiple occupancy was a common enough feature in growing industrial towns during the nineteenth century, but in Scotland high densities were already common in tenement-type property built in multi-storey blocks even in the seventeenth century. Many were larger units which had been sub-divided, so that a single room might be occupied by one family. The typical tenement property is of four storeys, with a back court (reached through closes) at the centre of each square, barrack-like block. In the earlier tenements the upper floors were reached by a turret staircase built at the rear, while later structures have an internal stairway. Tenements built on main thoroughfares often had their ground floor occupied by shops—a feature that still survives almost everywhere the buildings are to be seen. Some of the best working-class housing of the Industrial Revolution period in Scotland was of the tenement type and can be found at Blantyre and New Lanark. Shuttle Row in Blantyre (NS695585) is an excellent example of early tenement-style factory housing, now preserved as part of the national monument to the missionary-explorer, David Livingstone.[19] The two-storey block has external turret stairs of the kind which can be seen in tenement housing dating from the seventeenth century in the Old Town of Edinburgh. At New Lanark (NS880426) three and four-storey tenements were built by both David Dale and Robert Owen—an expedient adopted because of the constrained nature of the site in the valley of the River Clyde below Lanark. The handsomest buildings there are Caithness Row (built to house Highland immigrants), New Buildings and Nursery Buildings (the only new housing put up in Owen's time), while the remaining dwellings in Braxfield Row, Long Row and Double

Row are austere and plain, all of the tenements having sunk storeys. Owen seems to have exaggerated the benefits his regime brought to the place, though the housing provision at New Lanark undoubtedly compared favourably with the norm in urban environments.[20]

Terraced housing has already been variously described in the previous categories, though it is most commonly associated with the cottage and back-to-back types and can be seen wherever they occur. The studies by Tarn, Chapman and others, give ample indication of the scope for the investigation of terraced housing. M. D. Freeman, for example, has examined housing in Portsmouth built in terraces for artisans employed in the local dockyards. Most were constructed after the 1840s under civic Improvement Acts which enforced certain minimum standards. The typical house had three downstairs rooms—a kitchen/scullery, living room, and front room—while upstairs were three bedrooms. These units were a great improvement on accommodation for working-class families in the older districts of the city and were of better standard than similar housing being built in the Midlands and the north.[21] Of course, standards varied greatly from one part of the country to another, in much the same way as they did within cities. Only detailed studies by historians and by industrial archaeologists of working-class housing will eventually make possible these sorts of local and regional comparisons. Many aspects of nineteenth-century industrial housing require investigation: the work of Jeremy Lowe and his colleagues at the Welsh School of Architecture provides a good indication of what can be achieved by the marriage of fieldwork with documentary research. The same could be achieved for the history of the building of clubs and workmen's co-operative dwellings, such as those found in Edinburgh, Newcastle, Leeds and London, built mainly for artisans in the latter half of the nineteenth century.[22] So long as the buildings themselves remain the industrial archaeologist can make a major contribution to the study of housing.

Industrial settlements

Industrial settlements and factory villages have long been subjects of detailed study by geographers, historians, architects and planners. Hence the literature on the subject was already extensive before the rise in popularity of industrial archaeology. The main concern of earlier studies was spatial or historical; only the architects and planners had much interest in buildings. Few studies took much account of machinery or other installations, and still fewer were able to set local developments in any sort of national framework. Much has since been done to extend our knowledge of the physical dimension of many industrial communities. The most satisfactory studies are those which relate buildings and other remains to documentary research. Planned industrial communities were logical appendages of many factory and other sites, particularly in the countryside where the provision of housing and other facilities was a prerequisite to acquiring a settled workforce. In the early stages of industrialization most factory or mine masters were interested in exercising control over their labour force and this was most readily achieved in a planned environment. Other entrepreneurs were motivated by philanthropy—a feature seen in varying degrees in many factory villages.[23] At best the planned village provided reasonable housing, a decent store, a school, and facilities for leisure, such as a church, library or evening institute. At worst the industrial settlement might consist of mean housing and little else, save perhaps a company store or truck shop. Industrial settlements are commonly associated with centres of textile manufacture, mining and metallurgy, and transport. Other—often later—communities owe their origins to diverse activities, including the better known examples of Wolverton (railway engineering), Port Sunlight (soap-making), and Bourneville (chocolate-making). The documentation on industrial communities is considerable and we have space here to consider only a representative sample from various parts of the country. Local examples can be readily identified in the regional surveys, where they exist.[24]

Some of the best model communities of the Industrial Revolution period were developed alongside textile mills, mainly but not exclusively those associated with linen, cotton or wool manufacture. Housing was often laid out in a classical Georgian grid street pattern, though in restricted valley sites lack of space dictated more random development. Country textile mills, like the more isolated coal- or metal-mining centres, invariably preserve something of the original community near by. Many still survive much as they must have been in the early part of the nineteenth century. Cromford (Derbyshire), Cronkbourne (Isle of Man) and New Lanark are cases in point.[25] Because of their relative isolation the Scottish cotton mill communities are particularly well preserved; among others are Catrine, Ayrshire (where the mill itself has sadly been demolished), Stanley and Deanston, both in Perthshire (Plate 93), and Gatehouse-of-Fleet

Plate 93   Textile workers' housing at the planned cotton village of
Stanley, Perthshire, a settlement promoted by the Duke of Athol.

in Galloway.[26] The last is a typical example of the planned estate
village that combined industry and land-based activity. There
water power was the prime mover for cotton spinning and a
number of primary processing industries including tanning and
brewing.[27]

Later textile communities include the famous Saltaire, which
like its predecessors originated in the establishment of a new
plant in an open rural site near Bradford. Saltaire was the brainchild of Sir Titus Salt, a successful woollen manufacturer. His
community, begun in 1851, turned out, in the words of Professor
Tarn, 'to be a well-built and sanitary version of any working-
class housing development in any town'. Houses were laid out
in parallel rows, each terrace being 200–300 ft (61–91 m) long.
There are no front gardens and at the rear is a small yard with
privy and coalhouse, separated from the back area of the next
terrace by a lane. The typical workman's house provided fairly
generous accommodation, with a living room, scullery, cellar
below, and three bedrooms on the upper floor. Houses for over-
seers had up to six bedrooms divided between two upper floors.
Salt provided the handsome Congregational chapel, the institute
(guarded by four lions), public baths, almshouses, infirmary,
school, and a fine park.[28]

Mining settlement is more varied, both in chronology and
type, for developments in this field were often continuous from

the seventeenth century to the early part of the present century, and invariably took place in areas with few established communities. The metal-mining districts of the Southern Uplands, the Pennines, Derbyshire, North Wales, Devon, and Cornwall, among others, provide countless interesting settlements built by mine masters to provide housing for their operatives. In the south of Scotland at Leadhills (Strathclyde) and Wanlockhead (Dumfries and Galloway), where large-scale mining dates from the seventeenth century, housing was built along vernacular lines. Some of the cottages are built singly, some in informal groups, others in short rows. The morphology of both settlements, in common with many in upland mining districts, is largely dictated by the surrounding landscape. Housing is built on the valley slopes, with gardens stretching behind to moorland grazing.[29] Further south in Wensleydale and Swaledale the villages cluster on the better ground of the valley bottoms, so that many miners lived a few miles from their work.[30] In Cardiganshire too agricultural settlement formed the core of many mining villages, particularly near mine sites developed before the beginning of the nineteenth century. Later villages of the period 1830–70 were generally built within sight of the mines—such hamlets as Cwmerfin (SN698830), Cwmsymlog (SN699839), and Cwmbrwyno (SN708807) are typical—and consist of a few blocks of semi-detached cottages.[31]

Colliery communities often owed their origin to existing rural settlement. This was clearly the case in the Brampton colliery district of East Cumbria, where old farm settlements were developed as colliery villages. Typical colliers' hamlets can be seen at Hallbankgate (NY580596), Tindale (NY617594), and Halton-lea-Gate (NY653585). Other settlements in the area consisted of little more than an isolated terrace of perhaps ten or a dozen houses, together with allotments and a piece of grazing land near by.[32] The great coal-mining districts of Northumberland and Durham offer considerable scope for the study of settlement, the best examples having been investigated and recorded by Atkinson in his regional study. He points to the fact that if little has been recorded about the machinery of the coal trade still less has been noted about miners' housing. Again, the older housing was built close to the mines in the style of local agricultural labourers' dwellings. The basic two-room plan persisted throughout the nineteenth century, and behind the terraces were closets, allotments and space for pigsties and pigeon 'crees'. Leasingthorne, Durham (NZ256301), preserves some interesting mid-nineteenth-century colliery housing in Stone Row, which curves round to

Plate 94   Colliery housing at Siddick, near Workington, Cumbria.

follow the road line and slope. Originally the front doors there opened straight into the bedroom and out of this room opened a door to the living room cum kitchen. More commodious accommodation was provided at Coundon (NZ243296) which consists of a series of terraces dating from 1870. These dwellings have two downstairs rooms and one upper room with a dormer window. Finally, Esh Winning (NZ195425) is a good example of a rectangular planned village, with the former colliery buildings making up most of the south side. The colliery was opened in 1866 and the village is of the same period. Within the centre of the village are the omnipresent allotments and pigeon houses.[33] Plates 94 and 95 show other good examples of colliery housing from Cumbria and Leicestershire.

Transport towns were products of the Transport Revolution which created the features described in greater detail in Chapters 9 and 10. Many new communities grew up at seaports, inland harbours along the canals, at new railway junctions, and engineering centres. Harbour and seaport towns exist in great numbers; the most impressive completely new communities include Milford Haven, Pembroke Dock, Maryport (Cumbria), and Ardrossan (Strathclyde), although there are numerous interesting lesser examples all round the coast.[34] Milford Haven was planned

Plate 95   Barrack Row, a miners' terrace at Coalville, Leicestershire.

in precise Georgian style and mainly built between 1795 and 1810. Its naval dockyard prospered as long as strategic demand for shipping during the French and Napoleonic Wars made it profitable to build there.

A number of completely new towns and settlements were brought into being by the canals, including the well-known examples of Shardlow (Nottinghamshire), Stourport on the River Severn, and Goole on the Yorkshire Ouse. Stourport grew up after the Staffordshire and Worcestershire Canal reached its junction with the Severn in 1771. It was built on land surrounding the canal basins, the street plan following existing roads, contours and the canal itself, somehow suggesting that the town was not a new foundation at all. Stourport is well preserved, with some fine canalside warehousing and splendid period dwellings.[35] Goole was the last of the canal towns, developed by the Aire and Calder Navigation Company after 1822 as a new terminal for the export of South Yorkshire coal. Its history has been documented in some detail by Porteous and Duckham, their studies paying due attention to what still survives following extensive urban renewal in the 1960s. Yet a great deal remains, including the principal thoroughfare, Aire Street, and the finest building in Goole, the Lowther Hotel.[36]

The great railway settlements of Wolverton, Crewe and Swindon were new communities built to house the mechanics of the Railway Age. All three preserve much of original interest to the industrial archaeologist or architectural historian. Wolverton was an engineering centre for the London and Birmingham Railway developed after 1838, and by 1849 its population was 1,400. It consisted of rows of small brick-built terraced houses, with narrow streets, small backyards and back lanes. The railway company built the school, library, reading-room, and (suprisingly) pubs.[37] Crewe was also built in the 1840s and served as the base for the Grand Junction Railway's works. The scale was more ambitious than Wolverton, with a wide variety of houses, ranging from widely-spaced blocks of four houses for engineers to 'neat cottages of four apartments' for labourers. The latter was closely packed together, but still with back areas and a lane separating each terrace. The North Western Railway Company constructed the school, public baths and church. It was also responsible for emptying cesspools draining the backyard privies.[38] Finally, Swindon, created by the Great Western Railway Company, probably came closest to the later-nineteenth-century view of a planned workers' community. Great attention was paid to detail in the planning of the streets and houses: vernacular styles and local stone were used in most of its terraced cottages. The streets were spacious, the façade brightened by gardens, though the backs of the houses were more cramped. Though sanitation and water supply presented initial problems, the railway company provided excellent social and recreational facilities, including a cottage hospital, school, Mechanics Institution, and library.[39]

Later model communities include Port Sunlight (Merseyside) begun after 1888 by the first Viscount Leverhulme, and Bourneville (West Midlands) created by the Cadbury family after 1895 around housing which had been constructed in 1879 when the firm first moved from central Birmingham. Port Sunlight was, in the words of Professor Tarn, 'quite different in concept and execution from anything built before'. The layout—with wide curving roads, rectangular housing plots, and large areas of grass kept by the company—pointed the way to garden city developments like Letchworth. The Tudor-style cottages are simple and spacious with up to seven apartments in the largest. The Lever Brothers were lavish in their endowment of public buildings: an art gallery, church, hotel, and school. Bourneville in its initial stages was not so formally planned as Leverhulme's Port Sunlight.

The houses were of simple design with economic rental in mind. This is not to say that Bourneville did not provide good low-density housing, but at the same time it showed local authorities what could be done economically with good planning. After 1900 when Cadbury founded the Bourneville Village Trust greater attention was paid to a coherent plan for the community.[10]

These developments inspired others. Sir William Hartley built a model village for his workers at his jam factory, organizing a design competition which attracted no fewer than 85 entries. The community was built at Aintree and was something of an imitation of Leverhulme's work across the Mersey. A group of 71 cottages, built in short terraces, was placed around a central recreation green near the factory. The terraces had predictable names like Cherry Row, Strawberry Street and Red Currant Court! Joseph Rowntree began the construction of another model village about 1903 at New Earswick (SE6155) near York, and later in 1908 the Brodsworth Main Colliery Company built Woodlands (SE5307) near Doncaster to house their colliers. Yet as Tarn and others have indicated, the isolated philanthropist had all but given way to central government and local authorities by the turn of the present century. In most of the major cities private housing companies had been building housing for those of the working class who could afford it since the 1880s. Working-class housing provision still depended heavily on the legacy of the previous century, owing much of what was best to industrialists of vision and humanity who created model communities in advance of their time.[11]

Workhouses, gaols, etc.

Industrial archaeology can play an important role in the under-standing and operation of nineteenth-century Poor Law legislation and penal codes through the study of surviving workhouses, poorhouses, gaols and bridewells. Some useful work in this relatively neglected field has already been undertaken in several localities by social historians and industrial archaeologists. This has produced much interesting data on general conditions, accommodation and levels of occupancy in both workhouses and gaols. Workhouses were by no means uncommon before the Industrial Revolution, especially in England, but numbers grew as poverty became more widespread among an expanding work-force. The majority of those surviving to the present time as hospitals, old folks' homes or similar institutions are products of the new Poor Laws of 1834 and later. The reorganization of poor relief with its more rigorous emphasis on indoor relief brought about the progressive construction of numerous 'model' workhouses. Though differing in scale from locality to locality, many workhouses are of standard design. Celebrated for their barrack-like appearance, it is hard to mistake former workhouses or poorhouses, despite long-changed functions. The workhouse offered a minimum level of comfort in order to discourage permanency on the part of the luckless inmates. One study of the Poor Law in Amesbury (Wiltshire) devoted attention to the architectural layout and physical conditions of a typical workhouse. Constructed in 1836–8, the Amesbury workhouse was a two-storey barrack-styled building with additional wings incorporating segregated dormitories for males and females, sick wards, hospital, chapel, school, boardroom for governors' meetings, washhouses and various outbuildings, including earth closets. The workhouse remained substantially intact until as recently as 1967, when it was demolished.[42]

Several studies of workhouses elsewhere have been undertaken by industrial archaeologists, notably those of Stafford and at Stone (also Staffordshire). The Stafford Union New Workhouse was completed and occupied in 1838, when it was described as 'a very substantial structure' with 'an ornamental and imposing appearance'. The workhouse is still in use as an old people's home, and the external character of the building is almost unaltered. The buildings are grouped round four yards, the main façade on the east consisting of a three-storey block surmounted by a clock tower. The remaining blocks provided accommodation for the inmates, as infirmary, a chapel, dining-rooms, and school-rooms.[43] The workhouse in Stone (now incorporated in a hospital) dates from 1793 and was later greatly extended following reorganization of local administration under the Poor Law Amendment Act of 1834. The original structure incorporated 'the Scullery, Privies, Colonades, Workshops, Brewhouse, Washhouse and Infirmary' and a sewer 'to carry off the filth from the Scullery and Privies and sufficient drains from the Washhouse, Brewhouse and Infirmary including the Bath therein'. There was a 'Manufactory' which made mop-heads and rugs and, though only on a small scale, provided more useful employment than the stone-breaking common in many workhouses of the period (including those at Stafford).[44]

In a similar category of essentially social interest are gaols and prisons, the objects of some concern during the Industrial Revolution and after. John Howard's prison reform campaign had three principal aims: to preserve the physical health of prisoners; to prevent their further moral corruption: and, where appropriate, to promote repentence and reformation. In existing prisons, planned with no precise requirement save security, the physical and moral health of prisoners could not be much improved. To achieve such objects a new functional architecture was needed. Unreformed gaols and debtors' prisons (commonly located in the Town House or Tolbooth) held every class of prisoner, including men and women awaiting trial or under sentence of imprisonment, transportation or execution, vagrants, petty criminals, and debtors (confined on application by their creditors). There was no attempt to reform or improve the criminals and debtors, although vagrants were always given the nastiest accommodation in the half-hearted belief that discomfort might make them mend their ways or at least go somewhere else. More enlightened authorities maintained bridewells or reformatory prisons, where vagrants and petty villains were to be set on the paths of righteousness by compulsory labour. These provided the basis for improved gaols advocated by Howard and other reformers.

The early nineteenth century therefore saw the construction in many parts of the country of new prisons, whose architects invariably strove to combine strict functionalism of plan with appropriateness of stylistic expression. A wide range of styles and plan-types still survive, though few have yet been the subject of detailed investigation. One which has—at Jedburgh, Roxburghshire (NT647202)—is now restored as a historic prison and is open to visitors. The plans were prepared by Archibald Elliot (who designed Edinburgh's Calton Gaol) and the prison opened in 1823. The design incorporated most of the principles of reform, with three detached prison blocks radiating from a central gaoler's house.[45]

Worship, leisure and entertainment

The industrial archaeologist is inevitably more concerned with workplaces than venues of leisure-time activities, but much can nevertheless be learned about the social fabric of the community from relics of worship and entertainment. By far the most common are centres of worship, found in even the smallest industrial community. The landowner-industrialist had a natural enthusiasm for discipline and good order among his workforce and was generally only too anxious to encourage worship and even to provide the church or chapel if none existed. Dissenting sects and particularly Methodism and Congregationalism rapidly established themselves in industrial communities during the latter half of the eighteenth and early part of the nineteenth centuries. Dissenting chapels and meeting houses are generally much less pretentious in appearance than the fabrics of established churches and are as utilitarian as the factory villages and towns they were built to serve. Churches and churchyards of every denomination can be useful sources of information to the industrial archaeologist: vital starting points for social investigation of many kinds both within and beyond the communities under study.[16] The same can be said of facilities like the school, Mechanics' Institute or library—reflections both of traditional enthusiasm for education among certain sections of the working class and to a lesser degree of economic maturity and rising standards of living in the communities concerned. As we have already seen, some nineteenth-century planned industrial communities proudly sported these and other facilities, in most instances provided by the local industrialist, or occasionally raised by public subscription.

Excepting the church, probably the warmest place in many industrial communities was the pub: it goes without saying that these can form a fascinating study for the industrial archaeologist. The pub was the meeting place for the community and for most organizations such as friendly societies, trade unions and political groups. Pub names, like street names, are of great interest and often reflect local industries or crafts.

Many other nineteenth- and early-twentieth-century leisure facilities have attracted the attention of the industrial archaeologist, though some purists might maintain that these are wholly within the ken of the architectural historian. In public parks (often the gift of a successful industrialist) one finds many monuments to Victorian technology in ornamental cast-iron work, ranging from the humble railing or drinking fountain to the functional majesty of the bandstand or the conservatory. At the seaside there are many subjects worthy of study and record, including boarding houses and pleasure piers. Theatres and cinemas have been recorded by industrial archaeologists in some parts of the country, but many more have escaped record completely.

Centres of worship, such as churches, chapels and meeting houses, often played a significant role in the life of industrial communities. Philip Jones regards the Nonconformist chapels as 'foci of the emerging industrial culture' and though he is speaking with reference to the South Wales coalfield his description applies far more widely.[17] The industrial archaeologist can therefore learn a great deal about local history and workfolk in and around these places. Chapels in particular are dotted about all over the larger industrial towns, and were generally contemporaneous with them. Yet, as Kenneth Lindley has observed, even the simplest of chapels can impart scale to a landscape consisting mainly of terraced rows of workmens' cottages—as any town or village in South Wales can prove.[18] The typical chapel or meeting house is readily recognized by its box-like proportions, sometimes so plain it might be mistaken for a steam engine house. The minimum of decoration can be seen in the windows or door, above which might be set a plaque or date-stone. Lindley's survey covers a wide range of chapels and meeting houses, many in industrial districts. Good examples can be found all over the country, but in parts of Wales the original simple chapel façade is seen to advantage. In the mining valleys of the south, or the northern slate-quarrying villages, the dominant Nonconformist communities, particularly the Baptists, produced a tremendous range of chapels. Most are gable-ended with a plaque at the centre, often with a long inscription in Welsh, though numerous arrangements of doors and windows were tried. The Zion Independent Chapel at Cwmaron (West Glamorgan), 'Built 1821 Rebuilt 1883', is larger than most, with an adjoining schoolroom, but retains the features of its smaller counterparts. Apart from the Welsh valleys, good chapels and meeting houses can be found in Yorkshire, West Cumbria, Derbyshire, Lincolnshire and Shropshire: Lindley's survey provides details of the most interesting in these and other areas.[19] As monuments of an important but short-lived phase of social history the old chapels and meeting houses are fascinating. Many are abandoned or derelict and it would be sad if such an important part of our heritage were to be allowed to pass unnoticed and unrecorded. Industrial archaeology can play a part in recording these interesting relics of religious life in former industrial centres.

Kenneth Lindley has also indicated the fascinating range of monuments and tombstones associated with trade, industry, transport and shipping. Many tombstones are carved with motifs of craftsmen, such as the anvil for the blacksmith or cogged wheels and hammers representing the millwright. Plenty of industrial examples can be found, including most of the trades associated with the Industrial Revolution. At Saddleworth, West Yorkshire, there are some fine monuments to woollen mill-masters and operatives. One—to a millowner—was paid for by his employees. Another shows in carved panels all the processes which went into the treatment of wool from the sheep to the finished product. A great many tombstones of the industrial era inevitably record death by accident or misadventure. A monument to child miners—the oldest was seventeen and the youngest seven—stands in the churchyard at Silkstone near Barnsley (South Yorkshire). It commemorates an accident in 1838 which claimed 36 young lives. Church and chapel-yard relics connected with transport and shipping are also of considerable interest and often indicate the increased mobility brought about by the opening of canals and railways. It was quite usual during the eighteenth and nineteenth centuries to record the death of a man away from his birthplace, even if he died abroad, and erect a gravestone in his home parish. Great engineering works like tunnels or bridges often caused fatalities. At Chapel-le-Dale in North Yorkshire are the graves of more than a hundred navvies killed while building the Settle to Carlisle Railway. In the churchyard at Otley (West Yorkshire) a monument in the form of a miniature tunnel was built by the railway company to commemorate workmen killed during the construction of Bramhope Tunnel on the North Eastern Railway between Leeds and Harrogate. One particularly striking monument in Bromsgrove, Hereford and Worcester, was erected to commemorate railwaymen killed when a boiler exploded in 1840. The two engines in the oval entablatures are exact in every detail, though someone has tried to correct the one on the right-hand stone by painting in a steam dome. Drawings in the Science Museum show that the original sculptor was right to leave it out![50]

A search of graveyards can often be the starting point for social and demographic study in a locality. For example, the cemeteries at both Leadhills and Wanlockhead, former leadmining centres high in the Lowther Hills between Lanarkshire and Dumfriesshire, have numerous headstones which indicate the high level of death by accident in the mines over the past two hundred years. A survey of tombstones at the former cotton mill village of New Lanark provided a great deal of information unavailable from documentary sources (Plate 96). In the graveyard overlooking the River Clyde about a dozen tombstones were discovered, mostly of late-eighteenth- and early-nineteenth-century origin. Seven legible inscriptions provided a wealth of new information about a few of New Lanark's workers. There were many Highland names and birthplaces—at least half of the initial workforce of 1,500 people were expatriate Highlanders driven from their holdings during the Clearances. The survey also indicated the high mortality among juveniles.[51]

Plate 96   Tombstone in the graveyard at New Lanark.

Much else about crafts and industries of the past can be learned in and around churches and chapels. The variety of local building materials—stone, flint, slate, brick, tile, timber, and iron—is often seen to advantage in church buildings and memorials. Because churches and gravestones are invariably dated it is possible to trace the development of local building-stone quarrying. If on the other hand, stone was not locally available or perhaps unsuitable for sculpture or carving, it might well be transported from a distant quarry. Slate was very popular for tombstones because it did not weather easily: quarries in North Wales, Devon, Cornwall, the Lake District, and Argyll supplied many other parts of the country. Slate from North Wales found its way into many graveyards in the Midlands, transported by canal as far north as Derbyshire and east into Lincolnshire. Cast iron became increasingly popular for all kinds of ornamental work, including gravestones and memorials. Not surprisingly the best examples are found in Shropshire, where iron from Coalbrookdale was extensively used to cast monuments. One of the finest examples can be seen at Madeley near Coalbrookdale. Like other monuments of cast iron it is painted and hence has resisted corrosion. Examining and recording such artefacts is clearly not for the morbid, but it can be very worthwhile for the industrial archaeologist who wants to know more about the social context of his discipline.[52]

A wide variety of buildings associated with entertainment and recreation have been recorded by industrial archaeologists and architectural historians. Cinemas have attracted considerable attention, though the validity of such study to industrial archaeology was the subject of debate in early issues of the journal *Industrial Archaeology*. Both Richard Storey and Aubrey Wilson regard cinemas as items of interest.[53] Wilson wrote that to regard the service industries as non-industrial is a mistake likely to lead to the loss of many important industrial items. In any event, he continued, if one looks beyond the 'software' of its exhibition side, there can be little doubt that the cinema is indeed an industry and well worth investigation. A considerable amount of work has since been undertaken and at least two major studies are available. C. W. Ceram undertook a pioneer study, which in a sense ends with the beginning of the modern film industry.[54] Dennis Sharp reviews the history of cinemas and their architecture, from buildings of the pre-movie era through cinema buildings in Britain before 1914 to cinema design and buildings in the 1920s and 30s. He provides a detailed outline of styles and also a select list of cinemas surviving at the time of his survey.[55] Many of the oldest cinemas were formerly music halls, few of which now survive. Cinemas of the 1920s and 30s have mostly been modernized, but many original and interesting buildings still exist. The common fate of some urban cinemas as bingo halls or accommodation for light industry is at least better than that of so many which have been demolished.

Many features of interest can be found in public parks and by the seaside. Much has already been written about decorative wrought-iron work and the use of cast iron in Victorian ornamental architecture, but there is certainly considerable scope for the industrial archaeologist in this field. The major features—like glass-houses at Kew Gardens, London, or the Kibble Palace in the Botanic Gardens, Glasgow—are well enough known, but it is the forgotten or lesser monuments of the Victorian era which can escape record. Fortunately, the Victorian Society is ever vigilant in this field and has done much to encourage and educate local civic and preservation groups on the importance of the simple and mundane. There is a growing literature on cast-iron architecture and ephemera in Britain and Ireland. Among many studies is one of the Palm House of the Botanic Garden in Belfast, which also examines cast-iron and glass buildings elsewhere in Ireland.[56] Leisure facilities by the seaside are likewise a legitimate concern. Kenneth Lindley has been responsible for the most comprehensive study so far undertaken in this field of architectural history. His survey of promenades, piers and pavilions, amusement centres, hotels, boarding houses, and seaside transport, includes a comprehensive list of pleasure piers and cliff railways.[57] Undoubtedly there is great scope here, though seaside architecture has featured in few of the regional studies in industrial archaeology. The notable exception is the Isle of Man, where the architectural development of the boarding house has been examined in some detail.[58] Pleasure piers—features of major architectural importance—have been the subject of considerable study, presumably because they are under obvious threat.[59]

With the exception of housing and settlement studies the whole field of social archaeology is as yet in its infancy. Perhaps the initial emphasis on industrial buildings and machinery was only proper in the early days of industrial archaeology. It has certainly resulted in a certain degree of imbalance in the subject. To our mind there seems every justification for extending the boundaries of industrial archaeology to include the features described in this concluding chapter. There are purists, no doubt, who will see this as an attack on what they regard as the technological basis of the subject. It is wrong to draw lines in this way, because to us it seems impossible to understand technical and economic changes if they are divorced from their social and historical contexts. Industrial archaeology itself has a long way to go. The basis already established is firm—though perhaps not rock-solid. The regional and local studies on which this book is based all have a variety of approaches to their subject matter. Each is as valid as the next and collectively they point the way forward for a new and exciting inter-disciplinary study which holds a tremendous fascination for all who become involved in it.

Gazetteer

The following gazetteer covers sites of interest in England, Wales, Scotland and Ireland, arranged on a county basis. It is a highly selective exercise in compression and our choices may well not please all, particularly those whose expertise and local knowledge may be offended by either our generalizations or our brevity. The selection is not necessarily of what might be considered *outstanding* (though many notable sites are included) but of what might be considered *typical* of each area. National or Irish Grid References are indicated, where appropriate.

ENGLAND

Avon
Avonmouth: docks.
Bath: Bath Spa Station, ST753643.
Bristol: Clifton suspension bridge, 564731.
   Cumberland basin, 568723.
   Soap factory, 597729.
   Temple Meads Station, 595724.
   Tobacco warehouses, 570723.
Claverton pumping station: ST792644.
Kelston: brassworks, 694680.
Kennet and Avon canal: many features.
Keynsham: Albert mills (dyewood), ST657679.
New Rock: colliery, ST647505.
Old Mills: colliery, ST694680.
Swineford: copper mills, ST691689.

Bedfordshire
Leighton Buzzard: Grange mill, SP910273.
Luton: workers' housing; East Hyde, Hyde mill, TL133170.
Stevington: windmill (post mill), SP992527.

Berkshire
Berkshire and Wiltshire canal: many features.
Frilsham: brickworks, SU552727.
Pitstone: windmill, SP945147.
Wickham: brickworks and kilns, SU403717.
Woolley Park: horse mill, SU410802.

Buckinghamshire
Grand Union canal: many features.
Tingewick: mill, SP662341.
Wolverton: railway works, housing.

Cambridgeshire
Bottisham Lode: staunch, TL516651.
Bourn: windmill (post mill).
Great Chishill: windmill (post mill).
Wood Walton: Lotting Fen mill, windpump. 249876.

Cheshire
Birmingham and Liverpool Junction Canal: many features.
Crewe: railway workshops, housing.
Ellesmere Port: canal, warehouses.
Macclesfield: silk and other mills, housing.
Nantwich: salt workings, canal, warehouses, maltings.
Nether Alderley: corn mill, SJ840765 (Plate 97).

Cleveland
Boulby: alum works, NZ761191.
Ingleby: incline and wagonway, NZ609025.
Langthwaite: lead mines, NY997035.

Plate 97   Alderley Edge Mill, Cheshire.

Lunehead: lead-crushing plant, NY847207.
Middlesbrough: many features.
Port Mulgrave: harbour, miners' housing, NZ799177.
Rosedale: ironstone mines, SE7098.

Cornwall
Calstock: quarries, mines, kilns, brickworks and other features.
Camborne: many mines and engine houses.
Fowey: harbour, shipyards, lighthouse.
Hayle: foundry (SW558372), Copperhouse canal dock, metalworks, housing.
Luxulyan: railway viaduct (Treffry Aqueduct), SX055572.
Nancegollan: engine house, SW648333.
Porthleven: harbour (SW628258), many engine houses.
Redruth: mining remains, stacks, engine houses, tin works, foundry, Mining Exchange.
St Austell: china-clay workings and other features.
St Ives: harbour and lighthouse.
St Just/Pendeen: numerous metal mines and engine houses, notably Bottallack and Levant.
Wadebridge: quays and warehouses, SW9972.
Zennor: mining remains and engine houses, SW438382, 422625, 407359.

Cumbria
Alston: leadmining remains.
Barrow-in-Furness: docks, shipyard, housing.
Carlisle: Citadel Station, brewery, mills.
Cleator Moor: ironstone mines, housing.
Dalton-in-Furness: iron mines, tramroads.
Duddon: charcoal iron furnace, SD197884.
Egremont: mines, housing.
Kendal: woollen mills, SD515935.
Maryport: harbour, warehouses, housing, NY0336.
Silloth: docks, railways, planned town.
Stott Park: bobbin mill, SD373882.
Ulverston: canal, SD313777–293785.
Whitehaven: harbour, docks, warehouses, collieries.
Workington: harbour, collieries.

Derbyshire
Alfreton: Golden Valley, ironworkers' housing, SK4351.
Belper: cotton-spinning mills, SK345478.
Buxworth: Peak Forest canal basin, SK022821.
Calver: cotton mill, SK248745.
Cromford: cotton mills and village, SK295570; Cromford Canal, many features.
Derby: railway station, canal.
High Peak Trail: abandoned railway Cromford–Dowlow, SK313560.

Lathkilldale: lead mines; engine house at Mandale Mine, SK2066.
Long Eaton: lace mills, especially Britannia Mill, SK4933.
Matlock Bath: cotton mills, Masson Mills, SK292582.
Morley Park: ironworks with furnaces, SK380492.
Sheldon: lead mines, SK172687.
South Wingfield: railway station (N. Midland Railway), SK385556.
Wirksworth: Middleton Top engine house, SK275552.

Devon

Exeter: canal, basin, warehouses, SX921918.
Grand Western Canal: many features.
Haytor: granite tramway, ten miles long, but especially at Holwell quarry, SX751778.
Lee Moor: clay works and tramway, SX567625.
Morwellham: harbour and industrial museum, SK445695.
Ottery St Mary: circular weir and former serge mills, SY095953.
Plymouth: many features, notably Royal Naval Dockyard, SX448552.
Rolle Canal, Torrington–Bideford: many features.
Saltash: Royal Albert Bridge, SX435587.
Sticklepath: Finch Foundry and Museum of Rural Industry, SX639940.
Tamar valley: mines, quarries, tramways and other features.
Wheal Betsy: mine and engine house, SX510813.
Woodbury: cider presses, SY012873.

Dorset

Bridport: brewery, mill, ropewalk, SY4693.
Corfe: quarries.
Poole: pottery, quay, warehouses.
Portland: quarries, housing.
Weymouth: harbour, warehouses, SY6778.

Durham

Annfield Plain: collieries, wagonway, NZ144525.
Beamish: Open Air Industrial Museum.
Esh Winning: colliery village, NZ195425.
Seaham: harbour, housing, NZ433495.
Stanhope: lime-kilns, wagonway, NY989401.
Stockton and Darlington Railway: many features.
Tanfield Arch, NZ201559.

Essex

Aythorpe Roding: windmill (post mill).
Burnham-on-Crouch: quay, TQ9595.
Colchester: quays, warehouses, and other features.
Dedham: mill, lock, TM057335.
Felsted: grain mill, TL6720.
Harwich: harbour, TM2532.
Heybridge: mill, basin, TL8508.

Mistley: quay, warehouses, maltings, TM1231.
Mountnessing: windmill (post mill), TQ6297.
Witham: grain mill, TL8114.

Gloucestershire
Ebley: woollen mill, SO825045.
Forest of Dean: many iron and coal workings, e.g. Fairplay Pit, 659165, and Lightmoor, 641121.
Gloucester: docks, warehouses, canal.
Leckhampton: quarries, SO9418.
Severn navigation: many features.
Stroud: woollen mills on R. Frome; Butterrow, tollhouse, 856042.
Tewkesbury: corn mills, bridge, quay, Avon lock, SO8933.
Thames and Severn Canal: many features.
Whitecliffe: iron furnace, 568103.

Hampshire
Basingstoke Canal: many features.
Botley: toll-house, SU509137.
Eling: tidemill, SU365125.
Funtley: ironworks (associated with Henry Cort), SU550082.
Portsmouth: H. M. Dockyard, many features; Rudmore, gasholder, SU644018.
Southampton: docks, warehouses and other features; electricity station, SU422113.
Twyford: pumping station, SU493248.
Upham: manor house, treadwheel and well, SU537206.
Winchester: City Mill.
Whitchurch: silk mill, SU463479.

Hereford and Worcester
Bewdley: bridge (Telford, 1801).
Bromsgrove: parish churchyard, tombstones to railway workers; Stoke Prior, Avoncroft Museum of Buildings, SO9568.
Kidderminster: carpet mills and related buildings.
Stourport-on-Severn: Staffordshire and Worcester Canal, basin, wharfs, bridges.
Worcester: many features, including electric power station, canal.

Hertfordshire
Ardeley: post windmill at Cromer, TL300286.
Baldock: good town for maltings: Seven Roes off the High Street; Lion in Mansfield Road.
George and Dragon, a coaching inn.
Berkhamsted: King's Arms, a coaching inn and post office in late eighteenth and early nineteenth century.
Bishop's Stortford: maltings in South Mill Road (1843, 1856 and 1897) and in Station Road (one 1819); most others converted to other purposes.

Bovingdon: tandem compound steam engine (1926) at Bourne End, TZ019061.

Broxbourne: New River waterworks pumping station, TL374076.

Cheshunt: New River Pumping Station, Canada Lane, Turnford, TL360044, with Boulton and Watt side-lever engine (1845), compounded in 1882.

Chorleywood: Solesbridge Mill, TQ042970, operated as a paper mill 1746–1902.

Codicote: corn mill and originally fulling mill, TL226169.

Hertford: number of maltings converted to other purposes.

Hitchin: Charlton House, TL179281, birthplace of Sir Henry Bessemer.

King's Langley: brick and flint maltings built for Groome's brewery in 1826 converted to church hall.

Letchworth: Garden City, the first planned town in England by Sir Ebenezer Howard in 1903.

North Mimms: Bell Bar, TL252054, good area for milestones erected by turnpike trusts (list given by Branch Johnson, 1970, Appendix 2).

Potters Bar: two coal duty markers, TL260021, of 44 in the county (Johnson, 1970, Appendix 1, pp. 183–4).

Rickmansworth: Croxley Mills, TQ084954, with Egyptian façade built by John Dickinson as a paper mill in 1830.

Stocker's Bridge, TQ052935, over Grand Junction (Union) Canal.

Stevenage: first sponsored new town after 1946 Act.

Tring: canal cutting through Chilterns 1¼ miles long for Grand Junction completed 1800; wharf at Dudswell SP966097 has original canal warehouse; cutting for London and Birmingham Railway, late 1830s, 2½ miles long, SP940137; silk mill in Brook Street established 1824 by William Kay, now converted to other industrial uses but retains water wheel.

Ware: many maltings converted to other uses.

New River pumping stations at Amwell Hill (1847), Amwell End (1867) and Amwell Marsh (1883).

Welwyn: good coaching inns, e.g. Wellington and White Hart; early toll-house, 1725, opposite Ayot Green TL223130; railway viaducts over Mimram Valley, 40 arches 1,560 ft (475 m) long at TL245148, 7 arches at Robbery Bottom TL253183 and Woolmar Green TL251188.

Welwyn Garden City: founded in 1920 by Sir Ebenezer Howard and intended to avoid mistakes at Letchworth.

Wigginton: Low Roast Lock, SP959103, on Grand Junction Canal.

Humberside

Goole: canal, warehouses, planned town.

Grimsby: docks, Dock Office, warehouses.

Hull: docks, warehouses, oil mills, waterworks.

New Holland: pier, railway station.

Pocklington: canal, many features; Devonshire Mill, SE801478.

Sutton upon Derwent: corn mill, SE704474.

Isle of Wight
Bembridge: windmill, SZ639875.
St Catherine's Point: lighthouse, SZ497753.

Kent
Bagham: mill, TR077534.
Beltring: Whitbread's hop farm, oast-houses.
Chegworth: mill, TQ850527.
Cranbrook: smock windmill, TQ779360.
East Farleigh: bridge and oast-houses.
Faversham: gunpowder mill, TR009613.
Royal Military Canal: many features.
Sheerness: naval dockyard, housing, TQ9075.

Lancashire
Blackburn: cotton mills, SD687288; housing, 688251.
Burnley: cotton mills, collieries.
Chorley: mills, SD5818.
Haslingden: cotton mills and housing, SD7922.
Helmshore: Higher Mill (wool finishing), SD777217.
Lancaster Canal: many features, notably Rennie's aqueduct, SD484639.
Nelson: cotton mills, SD861379.
Preston: mills, dock and other features, SD5229.

Leicestershire
Foxton: locks and inclined plane, Grand Union Canal, SP691895.
Hinckley: framework knitters' cottages, Lower Bond St, SP4294.
Kegworth: framework knitters' workshop, SK4826.
Leicester: textile factory, canal, hosiery works, SK5904.
Loughborough: Taylor's Bell Foundry, Chapman St, SK5319.
Moira: ironworks with blast furnace, brickworks, SK314152.
Morcott: tower windmill, SK931002.
Wigston: framework knitters' house, Bull's Head Yard, SP608991.

Lincolnshire
Alford: railway station (E. Lincs. Railway), TF4475.
Boston: quays and warehouses on R. Witham, TF330430; basin and
  bridges.
Burgh-le-Marsh: tower windmill, TF503650.
Dogdyke: land drainage pumping house, with beam engine, TF206558.
Heckington: tower windmill with 8 sails, TF145437.
Lincoln: St Mark's Station, Midland Railway, SK972707.
Louth Navigation: now drainage course, TF3488–TA3402.
New Bolingbroke: planned village of 1820s, TF308579.
Pinchbeck: land drainage pump, TF261261.
Sleaford maltings, TF075452.

Greater London

Bromley: atmospheric railway flyover, TQ352708.
Camden: King's Cross Station, 303830; St Pancras Station, 301828.
City of London: Liverpool St Station, 333817; Whitbread brewery, 326819.
Croydon: waterworks engine house, 322654.
Greenwich: Royal Woolwich Dockyard, 427792; Deptford East generating station, sewage pumping station, 3777.
Hillingdon: Grand Junction Canal, 046932–105792.
Hounslow: Kew Bridge waterworks, 188780.
Islington: Regent's Canal, 303835–322833.
Lambeth: Brixton windmill, 305744.
Tower Hamlets: St Katherine dock, 339805.
  Thameside warehouses, Wapping.
  Spitalfields silk weavers' workshops, 338818.
  Truman's brewery, Brick Lane, 338820.
Wandsworth: Battersea power station, 290775; Ram brewery, 256747.

Greater Manchester

Ashton-under-Lyne: Peak Forest and Ashton canals, many features.
Bolton: mills, bleachworks, canal.
Bury: Chesham Fold, mill and weavers' cottages, SD819113.
Manchester: Pin mill works (calico printing), SJ855978.
  Levenshulme printworks, SJ883946.
  Bridgewater Canal basin, 831975.
  Rochdale Canal, many features.
  Liverpool Road Station, 831978.
Oldham: many mills of interest.
Rochdale: Smallbridge, domestic workshops, SD911151.
Wigan: Leeds and Liverpool Canal, basin, SD577053.
Worsley: Bridgewater Canal, SD748005.

Merseyside

Birkenhead: Bidston windmill, SJ287894.
  Mersey pumping station, 328892.
  Woodside, ferry landing stage, 329892.
Leasowe: lighthouse, 253914.
Liverpool: Albert Dock, many features, 340897.
  St Martin's cottages, housing, 344921.
  Liverpool and Manchester Railway, many features.
Port Sunlight: workers' housing and planned community, 338845.
Ravenhead: Pilkington glassworks, 502944.
Sankey Canal, 511951–585934.

Midlands West

Birmingham: canals, warehouses, and numerous other features, notably Brindley Walk, SP060870; Curzon Street Station, 085873.
Coventry: Hillfields, silk weavers' workshops, SP345795; Cash Brothers' factory, housing, 336806.

Coventry Canal: many features, especially Hawkesbury pumping house, SP362846.
Dudley: canal tunnel, SO968917.
Moseley: Sarehole Mill (corn).
Wednesbury: Willingsworth, colliery, ironworks, SO968943.

Norfolk
Burham Overy: tower windmill.
East Dereham: maltings.
Haddiscoe: steam pump.
Horsham St Faith: foundry, TG218153.
Ludham: Turf Fen, drainage mill, TG3618.
Norwich: mills, warehouses; City Station.
Rougham: brickworks, TF826208.

Northamptonshire
Billing: corn mill and museum, SP815615.
Braunston: canal basin at junction of Grand Union and Oxford canals, SP540659.
Bugbrooke: reconstructed turnpike, Holyhead Road, SP656563.
Harringworth: railway viaduct, SP9197.
Heyford: ironworks with blast furnace hearths, SP654580.
Hunsbury Hill: ironstone quarries and tramways, SP738584.
Kettering: maltings, railway station, SP8678.
Northampton: boot and shoe factories (Victoria and Palmerston Roads), maltings, breweries, SP7560.
Ravensthorpe: waterworks with engine house, SP682704.

Northumberland
Allendale Town: lead mine and smelt mill, NY8356.
Allenheads: lead-dressing plant, NY803455.
Amble: coal staithes and harbour, NU269049.
Beadnell: lime-kilns, NU238285.
Berwick-upon-Tweed: harbour, granaries, icehouse.
Hexham: Fourstones Farm, steam threshing mill, NY892680.
Morpeth: East Mill, NZ205864.
Ridsdale: ironworks, NY909848.
Seaton Sluice: harbour, NZ339769.
Tweedmouth: brewery, NT994522.

Nottinghamshire
Beeston: textile mills, especially Anglo-Scotian Mills and Swiss Mills, SK5336.
Bestwood: vertical colliery winding engine, SK549510.
Calverton: framework knitter's cottage, especially Windles Square, SK6149.
Cuckney: cotton mill and village, SK5671.
Gonalston: cotton mills, New Mills, SK680475.

Mansfield: the Hermitage Mill, SK5461.
Nottingham: many features including canal, framework knitting shops, lace and hosiery factories.
Papplewick: pumping station: SK549510.
Ruddington: framework knitters' museum and cottages, SK5733.

Oxfordshire
Aston: wheelwright's shop.
Banbury: Hunt Edmunds brewery, foundry, workers' housing.
Buscot Park: industrialized farm.
Chipping Norton: Hitchman's brewery.
Combe: Blenheim Estate, mill, SP416151.
Highmoor: parish pump, SU700843.
Nettlebed: brick kiln, SU703868.
Oxford Canal: many features, especially bridges.
Wiltshire and Berkshire Canal: many features.
Wroxton: ironstone quarries.

Shropshire
Bridgnorth: Severn Valley Railway.
Coalbrookdale: Derby furnace, Great Warehouse, museum and other features, SJ667047.
Coalport: Coalport china works, bridge, Blists Hill Open Air Museum (SJ693033), Hay inclined plane (695027), tar tunnel (694026).
Ellesmere: canalside features.
Ironbridge: the famous bridge, housing and other features, SJ673034.
Madeley: Bedlam furnaces.
Montford: bridge, SJ432153.
Snailbeach: lead mines, engine houses, SJ374023.

Somerset
Bridgewater: quay, warehouses, brickwork.
Bridgewater and Taunton Canal: many features.
Chapel Allerton: Ashton windmill, ST414504.
Charterhouse-on-Mendip: lead mines and smelting plant, ST507561.
Milverton: Fitzhead, lime-kilns, ST127700.
Shepton Mallet: silk mills.
Street: Clark's shoe factory.
Trull: Sweethay Court, cider press and horse mill, ST205213.
Wellington: Tone Bridge, woollen mills, housing, ST125218.
Wells: Wookey Hole, paper mill, ST532477.

Staffordshire
Burton upon Trent: Albion brewery, SK231233, Bass brewery, 2423, Clarence Street brewery, 241225.
Caldon Canal: many features.
Cheddleton: flint mill, SJ972526.
Dudley: canal tunnel, SO932892–947917.

Hanley Deep Pit: SJ885484.
Ipstones: flint mill, SK004484.
Leek: Albion Mills (silk) and housing, SJ9856.
Stafford: mill, maltings, SJ921229.
Staffordshire and Worcestershire Canal: many features.
Stoke-on-Trent: Etruria Works, SJ869473, Etruscan bone and flint mill, 872468, Gladstone Pottery Museum.

Suffolk
Flatford: mill, TM077333.
Framsden: post mill, 192598.
Ipswich: quays, warehouses, maltings.
Saxtead Green: windmill, TM253645.
Wickham Market: Deben mill, 305565.
Woodbridge: tide mill, 278488.

Surrey
Basingstoke Canal: many features.
Farnham: maltings, SU850470; Willey Mill, 817452.
Tilford: mill, SU868444.

Sussex East
Ashburnham: iron furnace, TQ685170; brickworks, 684161.
Ashcombe: toll-house, TQ389093.
Battle: railway station, TQ755155.
Brighton: Palace Pier, West Pier; railway station, TQ310049.
Eastbourne: Polegate windmill, TQ581041.
Hove: Goldstone pumping station, TQ814178.
Lewes: breweries, TQ4110.
Newhaven: harbour, lighthouse, warehouse, TQ4401.
Royal Military Canal: Winchelsea–Rye–Sandgate, many features.
Rye: Town Quay and warehouses, TQ928203.
Upper Ouse Navigation: locks and other features.

Sussex West
Arun Navigation: many features but particularly Orfold aqueduct (TQ058246), and Hardham tunnel (TQ032175–033171).
High Salvington: post mill, TQ013063.
Horsham: St Leonard's Forest, hammer ponds at TQ217292, 219289, 248281.
Littlehampton: maltings, pier, shipyard, timber yards, TQ0201.
Patching: horse gin, TQ087066.
Trotton: Terwick Mills, SU830222.

Tyne and Wear
Houghton-le-Spring: brewery, NZ342497.
Jarrow: shipyard.

Newcastle upon Tyne: High Level railway bridge, NZ251637.
  Swing bridge, 252637.
  Tyne quay and warehouses.
  Jesmond Dene, flint mill.
  Victoria Tunnel, NZ249651.
North Shields: quay, lighthouse, curing houses.
Ryhope: pumping station with beam engines, NZ404525.
Sunderland: docks, warehouses; Monkwearmouth Railway Station
  Museum, NZ396577.
Washington: colliery winding engine, NZ302575.

Warwickshire
Avon Canal: many features, especially locks at Stratford-on-Avon.
Nuneaton: Coventry Canal, many features; collieries and tramways.
Rugby: railway station, workers' housing.
Stockingford: brick and tile works, SP3392.
Warwick and Napton Canal: many features.

Wiltshire
Avebury: cider press.
Box Tunnel, ST840690.
Kennet and Avon Canal: many features, notably Dundas and Avoncliffe
  aqueduct (ST786626, 805600), Devizes locks (ST976614) and Crofton
  pumping station.
Littleton Mill: with working turbine, ST914607.
Malmesbury: Avon Mill (woollen), ST936869.
Stowford: fulling mill, clothiers' workshops, housing, ST811578.
Swindon: railway workshops, community, G.W.R. museum, SU1485,
  1585.
Trowbridge: woollen mills, brewery, ST854575.
Wiltshire and Berkshire Canal: several features, notably at Wootton
  Bassett locks (SU034811), Cricklade tunnel (095934) and Marston
  Meysey, lock-keeper's cottage (132962).

Yorkshire North
Farndale: Hollins Farm, horse threshing mill, SE661985.
Glaisdale: Mountain Ash Farm, horse threshing mill, NZ749025.
Masham: brewery, SE223812.
Skipton: Leeds and Liverpool Canal, warehouses, mills.
Thirsk: corn mills, maltings, breweries, tanneries.
Wensleydale: many lead mines, smelt mills, housing.
Whitby: harbour, lighthouse, bridge, warehouses.

Yorkshire South
Catcliffe: glass cone, SK425886.
Elsecar: colliery, atmospheric engine, housing, SK388999.
Sheffield: cutlers' workshops; Abbeydale forge and housing, SK325820.
Wortley Top: forge, SK293998.

Plate 98   Marshall's (linen) Mill, Leeds.

Yorkshire West
Almondbury: weaving village, SE159158.

Hebden Bridge: cotton mill, housing, SD989291.

Huddersfield Canal: many features, notably Standedge Tunnel, north end, SE040120.

Keighley: station and light railway.

Leeds: many features, especially Burley Mill; Marshall's flax mill, SE295326 (Plate 98); Middleton colliery railway.

Leeds and Liverpool Canal: many features, notably Bingley Five-Rise Locks, SE108400.

Linthwaite: weavers' workshops and housing, SE094148.

Saltaire: woollen mills, planned village, SE140381.

ISLE OF MAN
Ballasalla: cotton mills, SC275696.

Bradda: lead, copper mines, engine houses, SC180707, 186697.

Castletown: harbour, brewery, mill.

Cronkbourne: planned village.
Douglas: harbour, brewery, horse tramway.
Foxdale: many mining remains, engine houses etc.
Isle of Man Railway: many features.
Laxey: 'Lady Isabella' water wheel, lead mines, harbour.
Peel: harbour, fish processing plant.
Port Cornaa: lime-kiln, SC474877.
St John's: Tynwald Mill (woollen), SC2882.

WALES

Clwyd
Dyserth, Cwm: iron mine, SJ072777.
Holywell: cotton mills, SJ190769; copper smelting works, SJ189767.
Llangollen Canal: many features.
Mold, Afonwen: paper mills, SJ131714.
Mostyn Quay: harbour, SJ1580, 1581.
Ruabon, Cefn-y-bedd: wiremill, SJ312557.
Wrexham: forge, SJ349488: brewery, SJ336499.

Dyfed
Aberaeron: forge with water wheel, SN459627.
Ammanford: colliery, SN639123.
Carew: tidemill, SM041038.
Cydweli: tinplate works, SN421079.
Eglwysfach, Dyfi: iron furnace, SN685952.
Kilgetty, Stepaside: ironworks, SN142073.
Llandovery, Nantymwyn: lead mine, SN788447.
Llandybie, Pantyllyn: lime-kilns, SN614166.
Llanelli: docks.
Porth-gain: quarries, SM8132.
Tal-y-bont, Leri: woollen mill, SN654891.

Glamorgan Mid
Aberdare Canal: many features; Bwllfa, colliery, SN986026; Merthyr
    Dare, colliery, 982026.
Caerphilly: railway workshop ('the Welsh Swindon'), ST165865.
Maesteg: tramroad, SS859880.
Merthyr Tydfil: many ironworks, furnaces; Glamorganshire Canal at
    ST090963; Penydarren tramroad, ST085950–056069; collieries.
Pontypridd: foundry, ST078901.
Porthcawl: harbour, warehouses, tramroad, SS8176.
Rhondda: collieries.

Glamorgan South
Barry: docks, ST1167.
Cardiff: docks (much altered); tinplate works at Melingriffith, ST142802; many other features.
Glamorganshire Canal.

Glamorgan West
Neath Abbey: ironworks, SS738977.
Port Talbot: docks, SS7588.
Swansea: docks, warehouses, tinplate works and related features.

Gwent
Abersychan: Cwmbrygwm: colliery and water balance headgear, SO251033.
Abertillery: tinplate and iron works, ST216039.
Blaenavon: ironworks, housing, tramroad, SO2409.
Ebbw Vale: ironworks, collieries, housing.
Monmouth: brewery and maltings, SO510129.
Newport: docks, warehouses, ST3187.
Pontypool: Glyn pits, ST265999.

Gwynedd
Amlwch: Parys Mountain, copper mine, SH4490.
Beaumaris: Penmon granite quarries, lime-kilns, SH635806.
Bethesda, Penrhyn: slate quarry, SH6265.
Blaenau Ffestiniog: slate quarries, dressing sheds, engine houses at SH6946, 7046, 7345 and elsewhere.
Conway: bridge, SH787777.
Dolbenmaen: copper mines at SH531418, 525478, 541507: slate-dressing works, quarries and tramroad, 550434.
Dolgellau: gold mines and processing plant, SH7020, 7019.
Holyhead: harbour, railway station.
Llanberis, Dinorwic: slate quarries and workshops, SH5960.
Llanlleiana: copper mine, SH388951.
Menai Bridge.
Portmadoc: harbour, warehouses, railway.
Tal-y-sarn, Dorothea: slate quarry and engine house, SH4953.

Powys
Abercrave, Hen Noyadd: ironworks, SN811125.
Brecon and Abergavenny Canal: many features.
Clydach: ironworks, housing, SO232128.
Hirwaun: ironworks, tramroad, SN957057.
Llanelly: charcoal iron furnace, SO236140.
Llanidloes: lead mines, SN9186.
Montgomeryshire Canal: many features.
Newtown: woollen mills, SO1091.
Ysradgynlais: ironworks, housing, SN782094.

SCOTLAND

Borders
Chirnside: paper mill, NT853561.
Eyemouth: harbour, warehouses, NT947642; mill, 941634.
Galashiels: tweed mills and finishing works. Hawick: hosiery mills.
Hutton: Union Suspension Bridge and toll-house, NT934511.
Innerleithen: St Ronan's Mill (woollen), NT335379; Ballantyne's Mill
    (woollen), 360371.
Jedburgh: Laidlaw's Mill (woollen), NT650199.
Peebles: woollen mills.
Selkirk: Ettrick mill, NT473293; Forrest mill, 467288; Yarrow mill,
    470292.
Traquair: Scots mill (corn), NT274393.

Central
Alloa: glassworks, NS881923; Thistle brewery, maltings, 888927; Cambus
    distillery, 854942; Devon colliery, engine house, 898958.
Alva: Strude mill (woollen), 887975; housing.
Bridge of Allan: Inverallan mill (corn), NS788977.
Edinburgh and Glasgow Union Canal: many features.
Falkirk: Bonnybridge, firebrick works, NS839796; Rosebank distillery,
    876803; Springfield railway goods yard (Scottish Railway Preservation
    Society), 890803.
Forth and Clyde Canal: many features.
Grangemouth: docks, shipyard, NS9282.
Larbert: Carron ironworks, 880824.
St Ninians: Royal George mill (woollen), NS810904; Cambusbarron,
    lime-kilns, 770930; nailers' cottages, Chartershall, 793903; Milnholm,
    threshing mill with early turbine, 784877.

Dumfries and Galloway
Annan: Annandale distillery, NY194683; harbour, warehouses, 187660;
    boiler works, 183652.
Dalbeattie: paper mill, NX835614; Maidenholm forge, 841613.
Dumfries: Town mill (corn), NX970758; Kingholm quay and tweed mill,
    975735; Nithsdale and Rosefield tweed mills, 9775; Heathhall, former
    motor-car factory (1913), 989791.
Garlieston: harbour, warehouses, planned village, NX4846.
Gatehouse-of-Fleet: cotton mills, brewery, tannery, toll-house, workers'
    housing, NX5956.
Hoddam, Shortrigg: windmill and horse gin, NY162744.
Kirkpatrick-Durham: planned village; Old Bridge of Urr, corn and saw
    mill, NX777677.
Langholm: gas works, NY364844; woollen mills, 363843.
Portpatrick: harbour, lighthouse, NW998542.
Port William: mill, harbour, warehouses, NX337437.
Wanlockhead: lead mines, water-bucket engine (NS873125), housing.

Fife
Auchtertool: distillery, NT217907.

Burntisland: Binnend oil works, housing, 241873.

Crail: harbour, NO612073.

Culross: collieries, NT004885, 010683.

Cupar: railway station, corn mills; Springfield flax mill, NO353119.

Dairsie: weavers' cottages, NO415175.

Dunfermline: linen works, NT0986; lime-kilns NT065835, linked by tramway to Charlestown harbour, 064833.

Ferryport-on-Craig: harbour, NO459291.

Inverkeithing: paper mill, harbour, NT1382.

Kirkcaldy: Frances colliery, NT310939; flint mills, NT265902; linoleum works, 287927.

Markinch: Cameron Bridge distillery, NO346002; Thornton, beam engine house, NT292973.

St Andrews: harbour, brewery, NO5116.

Wemyss, East Wemyss: colliery, housing, NT332967.

Grampian
Aberdeen: harbour, lighthouse, NJ9705, 9505, 9405; Bridge of Don, NJ945094.

Aberlour: distilleries, NJ259399, 246411.

Alford: Montgarrie meal mill, NJ576177.

Banff: harbour, granaries, brewery NJ6864; Whitehills, Blackpotts, brick and tile works, NJ660658.

Craigellachie: bridge (Telford, 1815), NJ286452.

Croy: Cantray Mill, NH801480.

Elgin: woollen mill, NJ215634.

Fraserburgh: harbour, NK0067.

Huntly: woollen mill, NJ532393; Knockdhu distillery.

Inverurie: Port Elphinstone, formerly on Aberdeenshire Canal, NJ7720.

Kemnay: many granite quarries.

Lossiemouth, Branderburgh: harbour, housing, NJ2371.

Peterculter: Culter paper mill, corn mill, NJ835005.

Portsoy: harbour, warehouses, NJ590664; distillery and windmill, 562658.

Highland
Brora: colliery, woollen mill, distillery, harbour, NG9004.

Caledonian Canal: many features.

Cromarty: harbour, hempworks, ropewalk, brewery, ice-house, housing, NH7867.

Dornoch: The Mound (causeway by Telford, 1815), NH768977–774983

Forss: meal mill, ND036687.

Foyers: aluminium plant and hydro-electric station.

Helmsdale: harbour, planned village.

Inverness: Caledonian Canal, Muirtown basin, NH649465; distilleries; Kingsmills (corn), 678447.

Laggan: military road and bridges.

Lybster: harbour, fish stores.

Spinningdale: cotton mill, NH675892.

Tain: Aldie mill, NH787804; Glenmorangie distillery, 766837.

Tarbat, Portmahomack: harbour (Telford), fishing village, NH9184; Tarbat Ness, lighthouse, 947876.

Ullapool: planned village, harbour.

Watten: Achingale mill, NH241535.

Wick: harbour, curing houses, planned community at Pultneytown.

Lothian

Currie, Balerno: paper mills, NT164663.

Dalmeny: Forth railway bridge, NT1379.

Dunbar: Belhaven brewery, NT665784; harbour, maltings, 680792; Cat-craig, lime-kilns, 715772.

East Linton: Preston mill, NT595779; Tyninghame, saw-mill, 611790.

Edinburgh: Caledonian brewery, NT231720; Haymarket Station, 240731; Leith harbour, many features, 2777; Moray Park maltings, 274745; St Ann's brewery, 269741; Waverley Station, 258738.

Edinburgh and Glasgow Union Canal: many features.

Haddington: Gimmers' mills, NT518740; Simpson's maltings, 514733.

Linlithgow: St Magdalene distillery, NT008771.

Musselburgh: Esk net mills, NT339723.

North Berwick: Balgone Barns, windmill, NT553828.

Penicuik, Valleyfield: paper mills, NT238598.

Prestonpans, Prestongrange: pumping engine, NT373737; Saltworks, 385746.

Tranent: Cockenzie harbour and waggonway, NT398757–403734.

Orkney

Dounby: Click Mill (horizontal mill), HY325227.

Kirkwall: harbour, HY448114; Scapa distillery, 434089.

St Margaret's Hope: harbour, ND445943; Mill of Kirkhouse, 434914.

Stenness: Tormiston mill, HY319126.

Shetland

Dunrossness, Troswick: Norse mill, HU4017.

Strathclyde

Ardrossan: harbour, NS2342; beam engine house, 257414.

Ayr: harbour, warehouses, lighthouses, bridges, NS3322.

Beith: Giffen limeworks, NS364507.

Biggar: country gas works, NT040378.

Bonawe: charcoal ironworks, housing, quay, NN010318.

Bonhill: Argyll motor-car factory, NS390807.

Carluke: windmill, NS849508.

Dalmellington: ironworks, NS442083.

Darvel: lace factories and bleachworks, NS5637.

Douglas: Folkerton mill, NS856359.
Dumbarton: Leven shipyard, NS402748.
Easdale: slate quarries, workers' housing, quay, NM7317.
Forth and Clyde Canal: many features.
Furnace: charcoal ironworks, NN025002.
Glasgow: Central Station, NS587652; Eagle pottery, 614638; Fairfield shipbuilding yard, 548660; Kingston grain mills, 584648; Lancefield cotton works, 576652; Port Dundas distillery, 593668; Queen's Dock, 570653; Templeton's carpet factory, 603641; James Watt St warehouses, 585650.
Gourock: ropeworks, NS244773; pier and station, 243779.
Greenock: Shaws waterworks, NS2672; sugar refineries, 2775/76.
Hamilton: Avon bridge, toll-house (Telford), NS735547.
Houston: cotton mills, tannery, NS3865.
Lanark, New Lanark: cotton mills and village, NS8842; Bonnington power station, 883417; Cartland bridge, 869444.
Leadhills: leadmining remains and village, NS8815.
Muirkirk: Glenbuck ironworks, NS750295.
Paisley: Anchor mills (thread), NS490635; Ferguslie mills, 467634; Saucel brewery and distillery, 485636; Gilmour St Station, 483642.
Port Glasgow: Gourock ropeworks, NS326745.
Rothesay: cotton mill remains, NS086643.
Shotts: ironworks, NS879598.
Sorn: Catrine village, NS5225.

Tayside
Aberfeldy: Wade's bridge.
Arbroath: flax spinning mills, NO6441.
Blairgowrie: flax mills, NO1745.
Deanston: cotton mills, housing, NN7101.
Dundee: many jute mills, warehouses, bleachfields; docks, NO4030; Tay railway bridge.
Glamis, Jericho: weavers' cottages, NO408478.
Glenisla: lime-kilns at NO228596, 230597.
Montrose: distillery, NO718615.
Perth: waterworks, railway station, City Mills.
Stanley: cotton mills, housing, NO114328.

Western Isles
Leverburgh: harbour, housing, NG0186.
Shawbost: Norse mill, NB2446.
Stornoway: paraffin works, NB403327; brickworks, 508330.

NORTHERN IRELAND

Antrim
Antrim: Islandbane, beetling mill; Muckamore, dyeworks, J1685.
Ballycastle: colliery remains, D1542.

Ballynure: beetling mill, J3193.
Belfast: linen mills, bleaching works, harbour, bridges, housing.
Bushmills: distillery, corn, flax mills, C9340.
Carnlough: harbour, lime-kilns, D2817.
Culleybackey: Old Maine, finishing works, D0505.
Cushendall: corn mill, Glendun viaduct, D2132.
Dunadry: paper, flax mills, J1984.
Dunminning: Hill Mount, bleaching works.
Kilbridge: Cogry, flax mill, J2691.
Lisburn: linen mills, Lagan navigation, warehouses, lock-keeper's cottage.
Moira: railway station, J1561.
Portrush: railway station.

Armagh
Armagh: Tullyelmer, linen mills, H8645.
Bessbrook: linen mills, planned village, J0428.
Portadown: linen mills.
Ulster Canal: many features.

Down
Ballycopeland: windmill, J5761.
Ballynahinch: Round Hill, bleachworks, J4847; Whitepark, manufacturer's premises, J3646.
Castlewellan, Annsborough: bleachworks and spinning mills.
Coose: linen-spinning mills, J1049.
Donaghadee: harbour, lighthouse, J5980.
Downpatrick: Ballydugan, flour mill, J4642.
Lagan navigation: many features.
Newry navigation: many features.
Rostrevor: Valley dyeworks, beetling mill, J1920.
Ulster Folk Museum: numerous features including Spade Forge (Plate 99).

Fermanagh
Ballinamallard: saw-mill with turbine, H2652.
Belleek: pottery.
Enniskillen: artisan housing.
Rosslea: spade mill, H5432.

Londonderry
Kilrea: bridge over R. Bann, C9313.
Limavady: Dog Leap power station (R. Roe), C6819.
Millbrook: corn mill, C9090.
Upperland: flax and bleaching mills, C8705.

Plate 99   Spade Forge, Ulster Folk Museum, County Down.

Tyrone

Benburb: flax and corn mill with turbine, H8152.
Coalisland: colliery workings, canal, warehouses, brickworks, H8466.
Cookstown: railway station.
Donaghmore: brewery, H7665.
Lindesayville: bleachworks.
Omagh: Bell's bridge.
Strabane: Sion mills, H3493.
Wellbrook: beetling mill.

REPUBLIC OF IRELAND

Carlow

Barrow Navigation, Carlow – St Mullins: many features.
Carlow: canal warehouses, bridge.
Milford mills: saw-mill, tannery, S7070.
St Mullins: quay, S7238.

Cavan
Ballyhaise: Humphrey's Flour Mill, H4612.
Ballynallon: corn and flax mills, H5012.
Cullies Crossroads: Foy's corn mill, H6806.
Knockaghy: Sloane's Millbrook mill, N3294.
Lisboduff: Foy's Bunnoe corn mill, H5114.

Clare
Anagore: woollen mill, R4866.
Ballintlea: oil mill, R4865.
Ballyvergin: lead mine, engine house chimney, R4283.
Clarecastle: woollen mill, R3674.
Ennistymon: Lysagh's Derry mill, R1292.
Killaloe: Shannon Navigation, locks, basin, canal buildings, R7073.
Kilrush: harbour, Glynn's mill, remains of W. Clare Railway, Q9955.
Liscannor: harbour, stores, ice-house, R0688.
O'Briensbridge: mill, quay, R6667.
Sixmilebridge: woollen mill, R4866.

Cork
Allihies: copper mine, engine houses, Cornish Village, V5844.
Ballincollig: Royal Gunpowder Mills, W5970.
Cobh: harbour.
Cork: Beamish and Crawford's brewery; Murphy's brewery.
Clonakilty: brewery, W3840.
Dripsey: woollen mill, W4873.
Kinsale: harbour, W6350.
Midleton: distillery, W8874.
Monard: spade mill, W6476.
Old Head of Kinsale: lighthouse and signal tower, W6339.
Skibbereen: brewery.

Donegal
Braade: windmill, C3301.
Burns Mountain: millstone quarries, G9584.
Carrowtrasna: soapstone quarries, C0619.
Corcreggan: corn mill, B0036.
Inver: Milltown corn mill, G8378.
Kilcar: Drumnafinnagle mill, G8378.
Newmills: corn and flax mills, H2394.
St Johnston: Milltown mill, C3310.
Stranagappoge: Carrowmore Farm, horse mill, C4837.

Dublin
Ballycorus chimney and lead-smelting remains.
Belview maltings: Islandbridge.
City of Dublin maltings.

Connolly Station.
Custom House dock and warehouses.
Dublin – Dun Laoghaire Railway, especially bridges.
Grand Canal, especially Spencer Dock.
Guinness brewery.
Heuston Station.
Killakee: ice-house.
Liffey St, flint glass factory.
Pearse Station.
Power's distillery.
Ringsend: gasworks.
Royal Canal.
Sir John Rogerson quay and cold store.
Thomas St: windmill.
Watkin's brewery.

Galway
Aughinish: Corranroo Bay tidemill, M3312.
Dalgin: corn mill, M4462.
Galway City: Bridge Mill, M2925.
Killaguile: horizontal mill, M1538.
Kilroe: Lynch's mill, M3241.

Kerry
Caherdaniel: Hog's Head lighthouse, V4761.
Causeway: Ballynoe corn mill and creamery, O8030.
Dingle: Milltown, Fitzgerald's saw-mill, Q4302.
Dunloe: St John's Mills, V8891.
Kenmare: woollen mills at V9072 and V93070; Clontoo copper mine, shafts, engine house and chimney, V9874.
Kerry: woollen mills, V8596.
Portmagee Bridge: ruin of Anglo-American cable house, V3574.
Tralee: corn and meal mill, warehouses, Blennerville Canal, Q8314.
Valencia Island: slate quarries, haulage engine house, workers' housing, V3877.
West Cove, Coad Mountain: copper mines, V5862.

Kildare
Athgarvan: maltings, N8212.
Ballymore Eustace: woollen mill, N9310.
Castledermot: Cope's Prumplestown corn mill, S7683.
Grand Canal, Leixlip – Monasterevan: many features.
Leixlip: Ryevale distillery, O0136.
Maynooth: Manor Mills, N9437.
Monasterevan: Grand Canal harbour, warehouses, Cassidy's distillery, N6211; Ballykelly, maltings, N6312.
Robertstown: Grand Canal harbour, hotel, warehouses, N7824.
Royal Canal, Leixlip – Moyvalley: many features.

Kilkenny
Castlecomer: colliery, coal pits, S5175.
Goresbridge: Barracore mills, S6856.
Kells: Hutchinson's mill, S4943.
Kilkenny: Smithwicks brewery.
Nore Navigation, Inistioge to confluence with Barrow: many features.

Laois
Ballykilcavan: mill.
Donaghmore: corn mill.
Grand Canal (Barrow branch), Ballybrittas – Athy: many features, notably Gratton aqueduct, N6103.
Mountmellick, Irishtown: mills, N4507.
Mountrath: mill, S3594.
Portarlington: railway station, Grand Canal, N5411.
Stradbally: maltings, N5796.

Leitrim
Ballinamore and Ballyconnell Canal: many interesting features.
Cloone: Killyvehy mill, H1400.
Dromahair: mill, G8031.

Limerick
Askeaton: mill, R3450.
Glin: harbour.
Limerick: Shannon Navigation, canal, warehouses, railway station.
Stoneville: forge and smithy.

Longford
Cloondara: Richmond Harbour, Royal Canal, dock, warehouses, mill, N0675.
Lanesborough: windmill, N0169.
Mostrim: Lissanure corn mill, N2769.
Royal Canal, Abbeyshrule – Cloondara: many features.
Shrule Bridge: mills, N1355.

Louth
Annagassan: flour mill, O0994.
Castlebellingham: brewery, saw-mill, O0605.
Drogheda: mills, granaries, Cairnes's brewery.
Dundalk: brewery.
Peppertown: windmill, N9694.
Ravensdale: linen mills and spade mill, J0913.
Stancarry: maltings, J0410.

Mayo
Ballinrobe: Moran's Dunadober mill, horizontal mill, M1663.
Cong: canal and mill, M1555.

Meath
Martry: Finnegan's mills, N8072.
Millbrook: John Henry's flax mill, N5578.
Navan: mills, N8668.
Royal Canal: many features, notably Boyne aqueduct.
Slane: bridge and corn mill, N9673.

Monaghan
Clontibert: Ballagh's corn and flax mill, H7431.
Glaslough: Boylan's flax mill, H7338.
Newbliss: Wright's corn mill, H5725.
New Mills: Wallace's corn and flax mills, H7239.
Scotstown: mill, H6237.

Offally
Banagher: maltings, N0015.
Bellmount: mills.
Edenderry: canal harbour, warehouses, N6231.
Grand Canal, Edenderry – Shannon Harbour: many features.
Killeigh: Gorteen Bridge, forge, N3317.
Shannon Harbour: N0318.
Tullamore: Grand Canal, warehouses, bridges, distillery, maltings, N3325.

Roscommon
Arigna: colliery and old coal pits, G9055, 9160, 9258, 9259.
Cloonfad: Gammon's mill, horizontal mill, M5270.

Sligo
Ballysadare: bridge over Owenmore River.
Sligo: railway station, quays, warehouses.

Tipperary
Ballinunty: Mardyke colliery, mining remains, S2447.
Carrick-on-Suir: quay, warehouses.
Holycross: Abbey Mill, S0854.
Killaloe: slate quarries.
Kylecrue: Burke's mill, S0362.
New Birmingham: colliery village, S2451.
Newtown: Armitage's grist mill, R8181.
Silvermines: mines and engine houses, R8371.
Templemore: Fogarty's Whitefield mills, S1169.

Waterford
Aglish: Cooneen mills and quay on River Blackwater, X0890.
Clashmore: distillery, X1384.
Dungarvan: brewery.

Helvick Head: harbour and coastguard houses, X3188.
Lismore: Ballyrafter, mills and Blackwater navigation.
Portlaw: industrial village, cotton mill, brickworks, S4615.
Tallowbridge: quays on River Bride at X0393 and X0692.
Waterford: Fairbrook woollen factory.

Westmeath
Ballykeeran: Glassan mill, N0947.
Kilbeggan: Locke's distillery, N3334.
Royal Canal: many features, notably at Mullingar, warehouses etc.

Wexford
Castlebridge: Garrylough mill, T0506.
Enniscorthy: Fairfield distillery, S9400.
Kilcarbry Bridge: mill, S9736.
Kiltealy: Mocurry Bridge, carding and tuck mill, S8646.
New Ross: brewery.
Tacumshin: windmill, T0807.

Wicklow
Avoca: copper and sulphur mines, engine houses, chimneys, T1981, 1982.
Ballinglen: mill.
Rathdrum: mills.

Notes

Chapter 1. Introduction: Scope and Definitions
1 cf. *Journals of Iron and Steel Institute*; Journals of the Institutes of Civil, Mining and Mechanical Engineers.
2 Hamilton, 1964, 74–5.
3 Wailes, 1954.
4 Postlethwaite, 1877.
5 Raistrick, 1972, xi–xii.
6 Discussion with Professor W. H. Chaloner; cf. also Harris, 1970, 129.
7 cf. Rix, 1967a.
8 Cossons, 1975, 28–9.
9 Storer, 1975, 172.
10 cf. Morgan Rees, 1969; Feather, 1975, 113–21; McCutcheon, 1977, Introduction; Wood, 1973, 400–2.
11 Atkinson, 1964, 3–8; Browning, 1965, 7–12; Linsley and Smith, 1975, 55–68; Atkinson, 1972; Cossons, 1973; Atkinson and Holton, 1973; Cossons and Sowden, 1977.
12 cf. *Industrial Archaeology*, Notes and News columns.
13 Cossons, 1975, 30–6; Wartnaby, 1975, 69.
14 Linsley, 1973.
15 *Industrial Archaeology* Supplement, Nov. 1967.
16 Rolt, 1971 and 1977.
17 Hudson, 1963, 11–21; cf. e.g. Hudson, 1974, 72–7; Buchanan, 1970, 281–7; Riden, 1973, 210–16; Harris, 1970, 129–34; Tann, 1969.
18 Lewis, 1973, 574–7.
19 Raistrick, 1972, 1–14; cf. also Buchanan, 1972, 19–31.
20 Buchanan, 1968.
21 Riden, 1973, 210.
22 Raistrick, 1972, 196–7, 215–16.
23 *Bulletin of the Historical Metallurgy Society*.
24 Barker, 1977, 486.
25 Bartlett and Brooks, 1970.
26 Griffin, 1969, 392–7.
27 Crawford, 1953.

Chapter 2. Sources and Techniques
1 Hudson, 1963, 1976; Buchanan, 1972; Raistrick, 1972; Cossons, 1975.
2 Bracegirdle, 1973; Burton, 1974; Powell, 1962.
3 Pannell, 1966, 2nd ed. with Major, 1973.
4 Major, 1975.
5 Harley, 1972.
6 Harley, 1975.
7 Ford, 1972.
8 Green, 1963; Donnachie, 1971a.

9 See, for example, Hey, 1973, on the use of probate inventories for industrial archaeology.
10 Major, 1975, 142.
11 Bracegirdle, 1971.
12 Major, 1975, ch. 9; Bracegirdle, 1970; Hodgkiss, 1970.

Chapter 3. Power and Prime Movers
1 See, for example, Atkinson, 1960-1, and Brunner and Major, 1972.
2 On windmills in general see Freese, 1971, and Wailes, 1954.
3 Hoare and Upton, 1972; information from Eastbourne and District Preservation Society.
4 Donnachie and Stewart, 1967.
5 Lennox, 1973.
6 For a comprehensive list of national and local studies on windmills see Lindsey, 1974.
7 Nixon, 1969, 99-101.
8 Hoare and Upton, 1972.
9 On wheel types see Syson, 1965, 74-91.
10 See Thomas, 1969, on the recording of a typical water-power site.
11 Wailes, 1938-9; Syson, 1965, 92-9.
12 See, for example, Ellis, 1968, on Hampshire; Minchinton and Perkins, 1971, on Devon and Cornwall.
13 Ellis, 1975, 7.
14 Downs-Rose and Harvey, 1973; Hume, 1976a, 105.
15 Hume, 1976a, 16.
16 Atkinson, 1974, II, 258.
17 Davies-Shiel and Marshall, 1969, 247, 260.
18 Gribbon, 1969.
19 Rolt and Allen, 1977.
20 The following section is based on Watkins, 1967.
21 Hume, 1976a, 122.
22 Linsley, 1973.
23 Rees, 1975, 107-8.
24 Thompson, 1975, 37.
25 See p. 00.
26 Buchanan, 1972, 270.

Chapter 4. Agriculture, Processing and Rural Crafts
1 Raistrick, 1970b, ch. 4; Davies-Shiel and Marshall, 1969.
2 Fenton, 1976, ch. 5.
3 Harvey, 1970.
4 Robinson, 1976.
5 Peters, 1969, 238-9.
6 Gray, 1971.
7 Atkinson, 1974, I, 187-90.
8 East Lothian County Planning Dept, 1970.
9 Atkinson, 1960-1; Harrison and Harrison, 1973; many refs. in regional studies elsewhere. See also Macdonald, 1975, on chronology.
10 Nixon, 1969, 209-10, for Derbyshire example; Donnachie, 1971a, 21, 40, for Galloway.
11 Cruden, 1974.
12 Bowie, 1973.

13 Allison, 1970, 30, 50, plate 2.
14 Hume, 1976a, 122.
15 Rhodes, 1962; Green, 1963, 53, fig. 3.
16 Work on a national basis has been undertaken over a period of years by Wailes, Jones, Major and others. There are many useful local and regional studies.
17 Signet Library, Edinburgh, Session Papers, 415/54, Anthony Sloan *v.* John Milroy, 1800.
18 Davies-Shiel and Marshall, 1969, 168–70.
19 Starmer, 1970, 17–21; Hudson, 1965, 102–7; Hume, 1976a, 25–6.
20 Gittins, 1977.
21 Starmer, 1970, 20–1.
22 Ashdown, *et al.*, 1969, 15, 50, 54, 56.
23 Sherlock, 1976, 153–5.
24 Hume, 1976a, 184–93.
25 Corran, 1968 and 1975.
26 Butt, 1967.
27 Donnachie, 1971a, 215–16.
28 Bowie, 1974.
29 Minchinton, 1973, 20.
30 Davies-Shiel and Marshall, 1969, 161–79.
31 Grant, 1976.

Chapter 5. Textiles

1 cf. Coleman, 1973, 1–21.
2 cf. Thirsk, 1961.
3 Mann, 1964; id. 1971, 89–119.
4 Rogers, 1973, 141.
5 Rogers, 1976a, 24 ff.
6 Smith, 1965, 27–53.
7 Butt, 1967, 57, 226, 255, 298–9.
8 Ashmore, 1969, 27–37.
9 Smith, 1971, 247–75.
10 Warner, 1921, Chaloner, 1953, 778–85.
11 Ellis, 1975, 8.
12 Butt, 1976a, 116 ff.
13 Wadsworth and Mann, 1931; Lord, 1903; Chaloner, 1965, 9–12; Fitton and Wadsworth, 1958; Catling, 1970, 1–30.
14 Aspin and Chapman, 1964.
15 French, 1859; Catling, 1970, 31–40.
16 Hills, 1970, 66–7; Tann, 1970, 47–9.
17 Chapman, 1967; Butt, 1967, 67–72; id. 1971, ch. 7; Brook, 1977, 99, 101, 102, 140–2.
18 Chapman, 1972, 22.
19 Chapman, 1971b; Chapman and Butt, 1979.
20 Gatrell, 1977, 106–18.
21 Chapman and Butt, 1979; Dickson, 1976, 100–15; Chapman, 1971b; Butt, 1976a.
22 Baines, 1835, 193; Butt, 1967, 67, 69–70; Cooke (ed.), 1977, 11 ff.
23 The following paragraphs are heavily dependent on Hume, 1971, 215–53.
24 Chaloner, 1954, 78–102; Butt, 1971, 168 ff; Owen, 1858.
25 cf. essays by Treble, Browning, Fraser, and Ward in Butt, 1971.

26 Hay, 1974, 92–101.
27 We are grateful to William Thompson of Bolton for this information and many other acts of kindness.
28 Jenkins, 1973, 247–80; id. 1975; Wilson, 1973, 225–46.
29 Balgarnie, 1877.
30 Tann, 1967b.
31 Rogers, 1976a, cf. also Mann, 1971.
32 Ponting, 1971, plates 29–33; Moir, 1971, 28–56.
33 Gulvin, 1973; Butt, 1967, 79 ff.
34 Hume, 1976a, 97, 239, 242.
35 Hume, 1977, 231; Butt, 1967, 77.
36 Hume, 1976a, 170.
37 Butt, 1967, 59; Hume, 1977, 39, 266.
38 Hume, 1977, 171.
39 Green, 1963, 15; McCutcheon, 1977, 51 ff.
40 Lythe and Butt, 1975, 170–1, 178–83.
41 Butt, 1967, 64; Hume, 1977, plate 16.
42 Hume, 1977, 257–8; Butt, 1967, 62–3.
43 Green, 1963, 18–19.
44 Gauldie, 1969; Warden, 1867.
45 Hume, 1977, 130.
46 ibid., 122–3, 127, 142, 257; Butt, 1967, 60–3.

Chapter 6. Metallurgy and Engineering

1 Schubert, 1957; Tylecote, 1962.
2 Gale, 1967.
3 Phillips, 1977, 1–34; Fell, 1908; Davies-Shiel and Marshall, 1969, 29 ff.; Morton, 1965; Raistrick, 1972, 25.
4 Flinn, 1959; Hammersley, 1957, 136–61; id., 1973; Phillips, 1977.
5 Ashton, 1963, 162 ff.; Hyde, 1977, 48, 126 ff.
6 Schubert, 1957, 243; Riden, 1977, gives an average output of 300 tons p.a. for 78 furnaces in the decade 1690–9.
7 Schubert, 1957, 244.
8 Crossley, 1972; Crossley and Ashurst, 1968, 10–54; Phillips, 1977; Atkinson, 1974, I, 84 ff.; Butt, 1967, 105–6.
9 Crossley, 1975; id., 1972.
10 Cossons, 1975, 151.
11 Rees, 1975, 29–36.
12 ibid., 36–7; Burton, 1974, 28–9 and plate II.
13 Hyde, 1977, 12–13.
14 Davies-Shiel and Marshall, 1969, 42–3; Morton, 1962, 444–52.
15 Davies-Shiel and Marshall, 1969, 43.
16 Morton, 1963a, 259–68.
17 Davies-Shiel and Marshall, 1969, 45.
18 Fell, 1908, 343–415.
19 Murray, 1883, 64.
20 Hume, 1977, 46, 146.
21 ibid., 46–7, 150–1; Butt, 1967, 106–7.
22 Hume, 1977, 151; Butt, 1967, 107–8.
23 Brook, 1977, 21.
24 ibid., 22; Morton and Wanklyn, 1967, 48–65.
25 Raistrick, 1970a, 1–46; Cossons and Sowden, 1977, 11.

26 Ashton, 1963, 24–38; Gale, 1967, 33; Schubert, 1957, 331; Raistrick, 1970a, 68.
27 Hyde, 1977, 23–41.
28 Raistrick, 1970a, 57, 90–2, 129–47, 151, 177, 179–81, 193–9.
29 Morton, 1963 a and b.
30 Hulme, 1928–9, 16.
31 Hildebrand, 1958, 3–52; Flinn, 1973, viii ff.; Birch, 1955, 23–33.
32 Hyde, 1977, 77–81.
33 Mott, 1957–9, 52 ff.; Morton and Mutton, 1967, 722–8.
34 Flinn, 1961–2, 55–71; Hyde, 1977, 82–4.
35 Hyde, 1977, 84–6.
36 Freeman, 1971, 63–8; Riley, 1971, 69–76.
37 Gale, 1977, 12–13 and plates 38–43.
38 Brook, 1977, 80; Gale, 1977, plate 9.
39 Palmer, 1976, 63–9; and reply with C. P. Griffin, 1977, 85–7.
40 Rees, 1975, 51, 58–60.
41 Mackenzie, 1928; Butt, 1976b, 67–79.
42 Birch, 1967, 121–77.
43 Butt, 1967, 111–12; Hume, 1976a, 179–80 and plate 6.
44 Gale, 1977, plate 9; Brook, 1977, 80.
45 Gale, 1977, plate 80.
46 Barraclough, 1976, 12.
47 Flinn, 1962, 46 ff.
48 Atkinson, 1974, 92.
49 Barraclough, 1976, 12–13 and plates 29–52.
50 Gale, 1977, 13 ff. and plates 56–61.
51 ibid., 14.
52 Barraclough, 1976, 14.
53 Gale, 1977, 14 and plates 63–72.
54 Hume, 1976a, 177.
55 Scrivener, 1854, 92.
56 Musson and Robinson, 1969, 427 ff.
57 Hume, 1976b, 158–80; Butt, 1969, 1–16; Butt, Hume and Donnachie, 1968, 80.
58 See, for example, illustrations in the *Catalogue of Machine Tools prepared for Craig & Donald c. 1900;* also those in Hume's paper (1976b) which lists many of the major engineers.
59 Smith, 1965, 145–51; e.g. Butt, 1967, ch. 5; Ashmore, 1969, ch. 3; Hume, 1974, ch. 4.

Chapter 7. Mining and Quarrying

1 Nef, 1934.
2 Nef, 1932; Ashton and Sykes, 1929; Galloway, 1882; A. R. Griffin, 1977.
3 Spring, 1951 and 1952; Ward and Wilson, 1971, 31–8, 63–107, 174 ff.; Morris and Williams, 1958, ch. 5; Ward, 1963; Atkinson, 1966; Lythe and Butt, 1975, 131; Duckham, 1970, 141–69; A. R. Griffin, 1977, 21–4.
4 Nef, 1932, I, 347–428, II, 3–134; Duckham, 1970, 170–99; Anderson, 1975, 149 ff.; Namier, 1969, 76 ff.; John, 1950, 25 ff; A. R. Griffin, 1977, 24–8.
5 Duckham, 1970, 240–313; Hair, 1965; Scott, 1947; Handley, 1945, 118–24; Deane and Cole, 1969, 220.
6 Minchinton, 1969, xxviii ff.; B. Thomas, 1969, 37–56.
7 Duckham, 1970, 21–8.
8 Deane and Cole, 1969, 216–20; Rees, 1975, 88.
9 Cossons, 1975, 126–7.

10 Ashmore, 1969, 99.
11 Butt, 1967, 83-4; Brook, 1977, 120.
12 Rees, 1975, 84-7; for Carmarthenshire p. 240 and for Glamorgan p. 256.
13 A. R. Griffin, 1977, 4; Ashton and Sykes, 1929, 16; Duckham, 1968; Duckham, 1970, 59 ff.; Ashmore, 1969, 101.
14 Ashmore, 1969, 101; A. R. Griffin, 1977, 4; Ashton and Sykes, 1929, 17-18; Duckham, 1970, 64; Rees, 1975, 100 ff.
15 Smith, 1957; Nef, 1932, I, 245, 353, II, 72, and Appendix N.
16 British Patent No. 2822, 12 Feb. 1805.
17 c.f. Anderson, 1975, 51 ff.; Cossons, 1975, 130.
18 Holland, 1841, 180.
19 Butt, 1967, 84-7.
20 Duckham, 1970, 56; Cossons, 1975, 130; Anderson, 1975, 55.
21 Ashton and Sykes, 1929, 14 ff.; Anderson, 1975, 52.
22 Galloway, 1882, I, 311 f.
23 Nef, 1932, I, 48, 49, 51, 70, 135, 298, 333, 343, 353-7; A. R. Griffin, 1977, 3, 5, 6, 7, 18, 22, 23, 24, 26; Ashton and Sykes, 1929, 33 ff.
24 Anderson, 1975, 71 ff.
25 Sir John Clerk's phrase, c.f. Duckham, 1970, 73-7.
26 e.g. Butt, 1967, 85-6; Ashmore, 1969, 101 ff., 270.
27 Duckham, 1970, 77-8.
28 Atkinson, 1974, 34; Anderson, 1975, 79; Ashmore, 1969, 106.
29 Banks and Schofield, 1968.
30 Duckham, 1970, 68, 80.
31 Rolt and Allen, 1977, 24-30; British Patent No. 356, 25 July 1698.
32 Rolt and Allen, 1977, 45 ff.
33 Brook, 1977, 183.
34 Rolt and Allen, 1977, 146-7.
35 Harris, 1967; Hughes, 1949; Ashmore, 1969, 109; Duckham, 1970, 81-8; Whatley, 1977, Raistrick 1936-7.
36 Duckham, 1970, 83.
37 Ashmore, 1969, 109; Rolt and Allen, 1977, plate 87.
38 Rolt and Allen, 1977, 134 and plates 91-2.
39 Whatley, 1977, 69-77.
40 Rolt and Allen, 1977, 128-30; Clayton, 1962-3.
41 Duckham, 1970, 90.
42 ibid.; Morgan Rees, 1975, 99; Anderson, 1975, 101.
43 Royal Commission on Mining Accidents, 1881.
44 Anderson, 1975, 133-8; Duckham, 1970, 94-101.
45 Duckham, 1970, 103.
46 ibid., 102-9; Morgan Rees, 1975, 86, 91-3.
47 Deane and Cole, 1969, 214.
48 Rolt and Allen, 1977, 85, 148, 150; Rogers, 1976b.
49 Minchinton, 1957.
50 Todd and Laws, 1972, ch. 4 and p. 236; Barton, 1967; Buchanan and Watkins, 1976, 24-6.
51 Deane and Cole, 1969, 56-7; Harris, 1964; Hamilton, 1967; Richardson, 1974, 76-106; Day, 1973; Bainbridge, 1970.
52 Davies-Shiel and Marshall, 1969, 140-8; Booker, 1967, 129-203; Barton, 1967.
53 Ward, 1971, 88-92.
54 Richardson, 1974, 107.
55 Bird, 1977, plate 18.

56 Booker, 1967, 256.
57 Rees, 1975, 131–2; Bird, 1977, plate 35.
58 Rees, 1975, 133–6; Bird, 1977, plate 37; Richardson, 1974, 133.
59 Rees, 1975, 136; Bird, 1977, plates 49, 50; Richardson, 1974, 136; Morrison, 1971.
60 Rees, 1975, 137–9.
61 Allbutt and Brook, 1973a and 1973b, 40–63.
62 Brook, 1977, 92 ff.; Bird, 1977, plates 67–71; Richardson, 1974, 138–9.
63 Richardson, 1974, 42, 46, 122–4; Bird, 1977, plates 90–102; Bawden *et al.*, 1972, 51–98.
64 Richardson, 1974, 46, 110, 119–22; Kirkham, 1968; Nixon, 1969, 17, 18, 23–48; Rieuwerts, 1972.
65 Raistrick and Jennings, 1965; Raistrick, 1973; Raistrick, 1975; Raistrick, 1977; Clough, 1962; Hunt, 1970; Dunham and Hobbs, 1976.
66 For Scotland cf. Butt, 1967, 91–4; Donnachie, 1971a, 116–33, 226 ff.; Hume, 1976a, 105, 160; Hume, 1977, 52, 147; Richardson, 1974, 43, 45, 46, 110–14; Downs-Rose and Harvey, 1973.
67 cf. Richardson, 1974, 13–31, 161–9; Davies-Shiel and Marshall, 1969, 120, 134; Todd and Laws, 1972, 27, 30, 43, 64, 101, 249, 250; Donnachie, 1971a, 131–2; Butt, 1967, 92, 94–5; Morrison, 1975; Booker, 1967, 13–14, 23, 162–4, 249.
68 Donnelly, 1974; Butt, 1967, 98–9; Hume, 1977, 197.
69 Donnachie, 1971a, 111–16.
70 Lindsay, 1974, but esp. 308–33; Barton, 1966; Hudson, 1966; Donnelly, 1974.
71 Viner, 1976.
72 Lindsay, 1974; Davies-Shiel and Marshall, 1969, 154–60; Butt, 1967, 95–8.
73 Lindsay, 1974, 310, 315, 317–18, 328; Rees, 1975, 161–71.
74 cf. Butt, 1967, 99–100; Donnachie, 1971a, 141–50; Rees, 1975, 171–8.
75 Brook, 1977, 107, 108, 183.
76 Davis, 1934; Dodsworth, 1972.

Chapter 8. Chemicals, Ceramics and Glass

1 Martin, 1925; Campbell, 1971; Hardie and Pratt, 1966; Taylor, 1957, I; Clow and Clow, 1952.
2 Atkinson, 1974, I, 114–16; Telford, 1974, 189–90.
3 Butt, 1967, 132–5; Adams, 1965, 153–62.
4 Ellis, 1975, 9; Cossons, 1975, 274–5.
5 Cossons, 1975, 275.
6 Gibbs, 1939; Clow and Clow, 1952, 116–29; Wilson, 1954, I, 34–8; Musson, 1965, 13 ff.
7 Gittins, 1977, 274.
8 Brook, 1977, 195–6.
9 Butt, 1967, 135–7; Higgins, 1924; Clow and Clow, 1952, ch. IX; Firth, 1977, 52 ff.; Dickinson, 1937; Clow and Clow, 1945, 44–55.
10 Musson and Robinson, 1969, 251–337; Butt, 1967, 137–8.
11 Chapman, 1972, 12 ff.
12 Ashmore, 1969, 58 ff.
13 Green, 1963, 3–35.
14 Musson and Robinson, 1969, 338–51; Butt, 1967, 144–7.
15 Ponting, 1978, 154–9; Fairlie, 1964–5, 488–510.
16 Clow and Clow, 1952, 199–233; Musson and Robinson, 1969, 348–51; Butt, 1967, 146–7.
17 Ashmore, 1969, 64 ff.; Green, 1963, 28, 35.

18 Raistrick, 1972, 62–4, 214–15; Ashmore, 1969, 132, 297; Butt, 1967, 144–5.
19 Hart, 1971, 338–69; Davies-Shiel and Marshall, 1969, 75–85, 162; Butt, 1967, 144–5; Hume, 1977, 158.
20 Percival, 1969.
21 Hume, 1977, 150, 152; Davies-Shiel and Marshall, 1969, 38, 76, 78, 80, 81, 171, 226, 244; Harris, 1968, 14, 128–33, 161, 162.
22 Butt, 1965, 511–21; Clow and Clow, 1952, 389 ff.; Hume, 1976a, 157.
23 Butt, 1967, 147–50; Rees, 1975, 227 ff.
24 Trinder, 1973a, 126–7.
25 cf. Young, 1970 and 1972.
26 Leslie, 1970–1.
27 Hammond, 1977.
28 Cossons and Sowden, 1977, 140–3.
29 Copeland, 1972.
30 Brears, 1971, 83–152.
31 Shaw, 1829; Thomas, 1971.
32 Weatherill, 1971, xv ff.; Sherlock, 1976, 29–44.
33 Brook, 1977, 105–6; Copeland, 1969.
34 Sherlock, 1976, 164.
35 Barker, 1960, 33–45.
36 Lewis, 1964; Atkinson, 1974, I, 167, 173–5; Barker, 1960, 21–54; Ashmore, 1969, 123–30; Logan, 1972, 177–87; Butt, 1967, 150; Hume, 1976a, 85 and plate 22.
37 Atkinson, 1974, II, 246.
38 Hey, 1973, 202.
39 Lewis, 1965, 206–11.
40 Logan, 1972, 177–87.
41 Brook, 1977, 27, 175, 193 and plate 64; Sherlock, 1976, 28–9.

Chapter 9. Transport: Roads and Canals

1 Dodd and Dodd, 1974; Hodgson, 1969.
2 Haldane, 1968; Marshall, 1971.
3 Haldane, 1962; W. Taylor, 1976; Donnachie and Macleod, 1974.
4 Albert, 1972.
5 Butt, 1967; Williams, 1975.
6 Cullen, 1972; Green, 1963.
7 Hudson, 1963, 132–6 indicates the scope for investigation of roads through excavation.
8 Bird, 1973, especially ch. 4 on road construction.
9 Rolt, 1958; Haldane, 1968, on the Highland roads; Rees, 1975.
10 Graham, 1975.
11 Trinder, 1973b; Bracegirdle and Miles, 1974.
12 Hague, 1968.
13 Butt, 1967, 236; Chisholm, 'Suspense Story of a Border Bridge', *The Scotsman*, 7 Jan. 1976.
14 The scope is particularly well illustrated in E. de Mare, *Bridges of Britain* (new rev. ed. 1975).
15 Stephen, 1967; Hoare and Upton, 1972, 6–9.
16 Ellis, 1975, 26.
17 Awdry, 1973, 5; Cox, 1967.
18 Thompson, 1975, 19, 49.
19 Raistrick, 1972, 133.

20 Cossons, 1968; Rees, 1972.
21 Stephen, 1967–8; cf. also his unpublished Ph.D. thesis.
22 Cox, 1969 and 1964.
23 Some still survive in country districts, though they have not, so far, been recorded in any detail.
24 Bone, 1973, 25, 27.
25 Donnachie, 1971a, 236.
26 Storey, 1968, indicates the wider implications of rapid change in this field.
27 Cross, 1968, describes such artefacts as 'roadside furniture'; cf. also his contribution in Ponting, 1971.
28 Early motor garage architecture has attracted some attention in the United States, cf. B. A. Lohof, 'The Service Station in America: the Evolution of a Vernacular Form', *Industrial Archaeology*, 11/12 (1974).
29 Lewis, Slatcher and Jarvis, 1969; see also their 'Flashlocks: an Addendum', *Industrial Archaeology*, 7/2 (1970).
30 Minchinton, 1973, 6–7; Chitty, 1974, 19–25; Hall and Yates, 1974.
31 Ellis, 1975, 34–5; Cross, 1970.
32 Course, 1967.
33 Green, 1963, 64–70.
34 Hadfield, 1966a, 29–32.
35 Minchinton, 1973, 6; *I.W.A.A.C.*, 1971, 30; Hall and Yates, 1973.
36 Minchinton, 1973, 6.
37 Booker, 1967, 103–28; see also his *The Story of Morwellham*, 1970, 15–19; Hughes, 1970.
38 Hadfield, 1967.
39 Rees, 1975, 184–97, 234, 250, 269–70.
40 *I.W.A.A.C.*, 1974, 6.
41 *I.W.A.A.C.*, 1971, 35–8; Wilson, 1975.
42 Hadfield, 1969; Vine, 1966; Clew, 1968.
43 Ashdown *et al.*, 1969, 17–18, 22.
44 Ellis, 1975, 36–7.
45 Ponting, 1971, 3–4.
46 Awdry, 1973, 7–10.
47 Hadfield, 1966b and 1966c; Broadbridge, 1974.
48 *I.W.A.A.C.*, 1974, 2–4.
49 Smith, 1965, 157–66, 228, 246, 263, 273; Sherlock, 1976; Thompson, 1975, 20–5; Broadbridge, 1973b.
50 Hadfield and Biddle, 1970; Hadfield 1972; Ashmore, 1969, 165–80.
51 Wilson, 1968.
52 Davies-Shiel and Marshall, 1969, 184–5, 263.
53 George, 1973.
54 Lindsay, 1968; Butt, 1967, 162–75.
55 Hume, 1976a, 32–4, 106, 156, 162, 182, 259.
56 McCutcheon, 1965a; Delany and Delany, 1966. The best industrial archaeology study is in Green, 1963, 64–75.
57 Seen in the many planning studies and surveys of An Fora Forbartha, National Institute for Physical Planning & Construction Research.
58 Pratt, 1976.

Chapter 10. Transport: Railways and Shipping

1 Baxter, 1966; Lewis, 1970.
2 On canal wagonways and inclines see Hadfield, 1966a. 9.
3 Rees, 1975, 173, 195–6.

4 D. M. Rees, 1969, 69–70; Rattenbury, 1964–5.
5 Lewis, 1970, 110–25, 137 ff.
6 Atkinson, 1974, I, 41; II, 256, 305.
7 A. Harris, 1972.
8 Thompson, 1975, 26–7, 30.
9 Atkinson, 1974, I, 135–8; II, 278, 299, 308–9.
10 ibid., II, 276.
11 Ashmore, 1969, 188–207.
12 Chitty *et al.*, 1974, 9, 17–18; Rees, 1976.
13 Davies-Shiel and Marshall, 1969, 185–94.
14 George, 1973.
15 Rees, 1975, 197–205.
16 Minchinton, 1973, 8–10.
17 Harris, 1972, 77–81.
18 Todd and Laws, 1972, 133–9.
19 The museum in Birmingham has a particularly impressive transport collection.
20 Smith, 1965, 166–75.
21 E. Midlands Tourist Board, 1976.
22 Ashdown *et al.*, 1969, 20, 52; Wilson, 1967b, 46–7.
23 Ashdown *et al.*, 1969, 11, 20–1; Wilson, 1967b, 116–19.
24 Hoare and Upton, 1972, 10–14.
25 Ellis, 1975, 30–3.
26 The Journal of the Irish Railway Record Soc. contains many papers of interest to the industrial archaeologist.
27 Biddle, 1973; Lloyd, 1967, provides perhaps the best survey by an industrial archaeologist.
28 P. T. L. Rees, 1969.
29 Pudney, 1975; Ashdown *et al.*, 1969, 14–15, 52–3.
30 Chitty, 1974, 4–5, 12–14.
31 Pannell, 1964–5; Buchanan and Cossons, 1969; Jackson, 1972; Hume, 1976a.
32 Bainbridge, 1972; Atkinson, 1974, II, 232.
33 Martins, 1971.
34 Atkinson, 1974, I, 121–9, II, 260–1, 298; Telford, 1974.
35 Davies-Shiel and Marshall, 1969; Rees, 1975, 205–15.
36 Minchinton, 1973, 30; Booker, 1967 and 1970.
37 Todd and Laws, 1972, 139–48; Rees, 1975, 205–15.
38 Hudson, 1965, 75–6; Ellis, 1975, 39–41.
39 Minchinton, 1973, 12.
40 Taylor, 1977.
41 Donnachie, 1971a, 180–4, 238.
42 Green, 1963, 75–7.

Chapter 11. Public Services and Utilities

1 McNeill, 1972, 96–108; Buchanan and Watkins, 1976; Brunner and Major, 1972, 117–51.
2 Buchanan and Watkins, 1976, 112 ff.; Warren, 1968, 327–34.
3 Brook, 1977, 107, Buchanan and Watkins, 1976, 158.
4 Brook, 1977, 111, 114, 119, 140; Bradbury, 1971.
5 Buchanan and Watkins, 1976, 159; Brook, 1977, 119–20; Sherlock, 1976, 186–7.
6 Sherlock, 1976, 165.

7 *Journal of Herefordshire Waterworks Museum Trust.*

8 Smith, 1965, 149–50, 234, 267–8, 272–3.

9 Linsley, 1973, Atkinson, 1974, I, 155, 165.

10 Buchanan and Watkins, 1976, 138, 143, 144, 145, 149; Ellis, 1975, 18–19.

11 Nicol, 1891, 109–18.

12 McNeil, 1972, 96 ff.

13 Briggs, 1959, 33–4, 277–8, 334–5, 441–2; Rolt, 1970, 138 ff.; Buchanan and Watkins, 1976, 30–1, 120, 146, 150, 177; Veale, 3rd ed., 1956, ch. 1.

14 Wood, 1973, 400–2; Buchanan and Watkins, 1976, 148.

15 Brook, 1977, 88; Buchanan and Watkins, 1976, 157; *Industrial Archaeology,* 1972, 87.

16 Buchanan and Watkins, 1976, 144; Ellis, 1975, 19–20.

17 Buchanan and Watkins, 1976, 139, 158; Brook, 1977, 102.

18 Buchanan and Watkins, 1976, 139, 147; Bracegirdle, 1971, 20–1, 99.

19 Tucker, 1977a, 5–27.

20 Ashworth, 1960, 78–9, 86.

21 Tucker, 1977b, 126–63.

22 cf. also Tyson, 1972, 48–57.

23 Buchanan and Cossons, 1969, 167–9; Tucker, 1972, 11–18.

24 Tucker, 1977c, 8–28.

25 Warburton, 1974, 46–52.

26 Hannah, 1977; Parsons, 1939.

Chapter 12. Social Archaeology

1 Hudson, 1975.

2 ibid.

3 Chapman 1971a; Gauldie, 1974. Professor J. N. Tarn's work, cited below, has also recorded many survivals.

4 The Welsh School of Architecture, UWIST, has played a leading role in its surveys of iron industry housing in South Wales.

5 Alcock, 1972.

6 Smith in Chapman, 1971a.

7 Bodey, 1971; Taylor, 1966.

8 Chapman in Chapman, 1971a.

9 Smith, 1965.

10 Barnsby, 1975, 6–11.

11 Morton, 1972.

12 Hey, 1972.

13 Silvester, 1972; Melton, 1972.

14 Lowe and Anderson, 1972, 9.

15 Lowe and Anderson, 1972, 6.

16 Beresford in Chapman, 1971a, 93–132.

17 Chapman and Bartlett in Chapman, 1971a, 223–46.

18 Butt in Chapman, 1971a, 55–92; Kellett, 1961.

19 Butt, 1967, 277; Hume, 1976a, 158.

20 Hume in Butt, 1971, 215–53.

21 Freeman, 1973.

22 Tarn, 1971; see also his more detailed study, 1973.

23 Tarn, 1973; Bell and Bell, 1969, 163–213.

24 Not all of the surveys have been as attentive as they might have been to industrial villages.

25 Arkwright Soc., 1971; Garrad, 1972, 200–2; Hume in Butt, 1971.

26 Butt, 1967, 230, 67, 296.
27 Butt, 1966; Donnachie, 1971a, 96–8, 223.
28 Tarn, 1973, 145–8.
29 Hume, 1976a, 105, 160.
30 Raistrick, 1975, 106–14.
31 Morrison, 1973.
32 Harris, 1974.
33 Atkinson, 1974, 277, 282, 293–4.
34 Bell and Bell, 1969, 111–62; Aston and Bond, 1976, 136–40.
35 Aston and Bond, 1976, 141–4; Porteous, 1977.
36 Porteous, 1969a; see also his 1969b on later developments; Porteous 1977.
37 Tarn, 1971, 33.
38 Tarn, 1973, 149–51.
39 Hudson, 1968.
40 Tarn, 1971, 35–6, 85–6.
41 For a detailed account of surviving private housing for the working class, see Tarn, 1973.
42 Goodhugh, 1970.
43 Bailey, 1971.
44 Broadbridge, 1973a.
45 McIvor, 1973; Dunbar, 1966, 194, 207.
46 Rix, 1967b; Walker, 1971.
47 Jones, 1976.
48 Lindley, 1969.
49 ibid.
50 Lindley, 1972.
51 Donnachie, 1971b.
52 Lindley, 1972.
53 Storey, 1966; Wilson, 1967a.
54 Ceram, 1965.
55 Sharp, 1969.
56 McCraken, 1972.
57 Lindley, 1973.
58 Garrad, et al., 1972, 99–124.
59 Lindley, 1973.

Bibliography

Except where obvious, the only abbreviations used are:

B.I.A.S.—*Journal of the Bristol Industrial Archaeology Society*
Bull. Hist. Met. Group—*Bulletin of the Historical Metallurgy Group*
Ec.H.R.—*Economic History Review*
I.A.—*Industrial Archaeology*
I.A.R.—*Industrial Archaeology Review*
I.W.A.A.C.—*Inland Waterways Association Publication*
J.I.A.—*Journal of Industrial Archaeology*
P.S.A.S.—*Proceeding of the Society of Antiquaries of Scotland*
T.N.S.—*Transactions of the Newcomen Society*
T.H.—*Transport History*

Adams, I. H. 1965. The Salt Industry of the Forth Basin, *Scottish Geog. Mag.* **81**, 153–62.

Albert, W. 1972. *The Turnpike Road System in England 1663–1840*.

Alcock, N. W. 1972. *Dartington Houses: a Survey*. Exeter I.A. Group, University of Exeter.

Allbutt, M. and Brook, F. 1973a. *The Shropshire Lead Mines*.

Allbutt, M. and Brook, F. 1973b. The South Shropshire Lead Mines, *I.A.*, **10/1**, 40–63.

Allison, K. J. 1970. *East Riding Water-Mills*, East Yorks. Local History Soc., York.

Anderson, D. 1975. *The Orrell Coalfield, Lancashire 1740–1850*.

Arkwright Society. 1971. *Arkwright and the Mills at Cromford*.

Ashdown, J., Bussell, M. and Carter, P. 1969. *A Survey of Industrial Monuments of Greater London*. Thames Basin Archaeological Observers' Group.

Ashmore, O. 1969. *Industrial Archaeology of Lancashire*.

Ashton, T. S. 1963. *Iron and Steel in the Industrial Revolution*.

Ashton, T. S. and Sykes, J. 1929. *The Coal Industry of the Eighteenth Century*.

Ashworth, W. 1960. *An Economic History of England 1870–1939*.

Aspin, C. and Chapman, S. D. 1964. *James Hargreaves and the Spinning Jenny*. Helmshore Local History Society.

Aston, M. and Bond, J. 1976. *The Landscape of Towns*.

Atkinson, F. 1960–1. The Horse as a Source of Rotary Power, *T.N.S.*, **33**.

Atkinson, F. 1964. An Open-Air Museum for the North-East, *I.A.*, **1/1**, 3–8.

Atkinson, F. 1966. *The Great Northern Coalfield*. Barnard Castle.

Atkinson, F. 1972. Open Air Museums and Environmental Conservation, *Museums Journal*, **72/3**.

Atkinson, F. 1974. *The Industrial Archaeology of North East England*. 2 vols.
Atkinson, F. and Holton, M. 1973. Open Air and Folk Museums, *Museums Journal*, **72/4**.
Awdry, W. (ed.) 1973. *I.A. in Gloucestershire*. Gloucestershire Soc. for I.A.
Bailey, J. E. 1971. The Stafford workhouse, *Journal of Staffordshire I.A. Soc.*
Bainbridge, J. W. 1970. A nineteenth-century copper working: Tomnadashan, Lochtayside, *I.A.*, **7/1**, 60–74.
Bainbridge, J. W. 1972. Stocking Northumbrian Icehouses: an Exercise in Relating Climate to History, *I.A.*, **9/2**.
Baines, E. 1935. *History of the Cotton Manufacture*.
Balgarnie, R. 1877. *Sir Titus Salt*.
Banks, A. G. and Schofield, R. B. 1968. *Brindley at Wet Earth Colliery: an Engineering Study*.
Barker, T. C. 1960. *Pilkington Brothers and the Glass Industry*.
Barker, T. C. 1977. *The Glassmakers*.
Barker, T. C. and Savage, C. I. 1975. *An Economic History of Transport in Britain*.
Barnsby, G. J. 1975. *A History of Housing in Wolverhampton 1750–1975*.
Barraclough, K. C. 1976. *Sheffield Steel*.
Bartlett, J. and Brooks, D. 1970. *Hull Pottery*. Kingston-upon-Hull Museums Bulletin No. 5.
Barton, D. B. 1966. *A History of Copper Mining in Cornwall and Devon*.
Barton, D. B. 1967. *A History of Tin Mining and Smelting in Cornwall*.
Barton, R. M. 1966. *A History of the Cornish China-Clay Industry*.
Bawden, T. A., Garrad, L. S., Qualtrough, J. K. and Scatchard, J. W. 1972. *The Industrial Archaeology of the Isle of Man*.
Baxter, B. 1966. *Stone Blocks and Iron Rails*.
Bell, C. and Bell, R. 1969. *City Fathers: the Early History of Town Planning in Britain*.
Biddle, G. 1973. *Victorian Stations: Railway Stations in England and Wales 1830–1923*.
Birch, A. 1955. Foreign Observers of the British Iron Industry during the Eighteenth Century, *Journal of Economic History*, 23–33.
Birch, A. 1967. *The Economic History of the British Iron and Steel Industry, 1784–1879*.
Bird, A. 1973. *Roads and Vehicles*.
Bird, R. H. 1977. *Yesterday's Golcondas*.
Bodey, H. A. 1971. Coffin Row, Linthwaite, *I.A.*, **8/4**.
Bone, M. 1973. *Barnstaple's Industrial Archaeology: a Guide*. Exeter I.A. Group.
Booker, F. 1967. *The Industrial Archaeology of the Tamar Valley*.
Booker, F. 1970. *The Story of Morwellham*. Dartington Amenity Research Trust, Totnes.
Bowie, G. 1973. *Two Mills Worked by Horizontal Waterwheels*. An Foras Forbartha Teoranta, Dublin.
Bowie, G. 1974. Two Stationary Steam Engines in Power's Distillery, John's Lane, Dublin, *I.A.*, **11/3**.

Bracegirdle, B. 1970. *Photography for Books and Reports.*
Bracegirdle, B. 1971. Aids to Recording (7). Industrial Archaeology and Photography: an Account of a Course at Flatford Mill, *I.A.*, **8/1**.
Bracegirdle, B. 1973. *The Archaeology of the Industrial Revolution.*
Bracegirdle, B. and Miles, P. H. 1974. *The Darbys and the Ironbridge Gorge.*
Bradbury, J. J. 1971. Sandfields Pumping Station, *I.A.*, **8/2**, 117–21.
Brears, P. C. D. 1971. *The English Country Pottery: its History and Techniques.*
Briggs, Asa. 1959. *The Age of Improvement.*
Broadbridge, S. R. 1973a. The workhouse in Stone, *Journal of Staffordshire I.A. Soc.*, **4**.
Broadbridge, S. R. 1973b. Water Supply on the Birmingham Canal Navigation, 1769–1830, *I.A.*, **10/3**.
Broadbridge, S. R. 1974. *The Birmingham Canal Navigations, Vol. 1, 1768–1846.*
Brook, F. 1977. *The West Midlands.*
Browning, A. S. E. 1965. The Museum of Transport, Glasgow, *I.A.*, **2/1**, 7–12.
Browning, M. 1971. Owen as an Educator, in Butt, J. (ed.), *Robert Owen, Prince of Cotton Spinners*, 52–75.
Brunner, Hugo and Major, J. Kenneth. 1972. Water-raising by Animal Power, *I.A.*, **9/2**, 117–51.
Buchanan, R. A. 1969. *The Theory and Practice of Industrial Archaeology.*
Buchanan, R. A. 1970. Industrial Archaeology: Retrospect and Prospect, *Antiquity*, **XLIV**, 281–7.
Buchanan, R. A. 1972. *Industrial Archaeology in Britain.*
Buchanan, R. A. and Cossons, N. 1969. *The Industrial Archaeology of the Bristol Region.*
Buchanan, R. A. and Watkins, G. 1976. *The Industrial Archaeology of the Stationary Steam Engine.*
Burton, A. 1974. *Remains of a Revolution.*
Butt, J. 1965. Technical Change and the Growth of the British Shale Oil Industry (1680–1870), *Ec.H.R.*, **XVII**, 511–21.
Butt, J. 1966. The Industrial Archaeology of Gatehouse-of-Fleet, *I.A.*, **3/2**.
Butt, J. 1967. *The Industrial Archaeology of Scotland.*
Butt, J. 1969. Extracts from a Catalogue of Machine Tools prepared for Craig & Donald, Engineers of Johnstone *c.* 1900, *I.A.* (Supplement), 1–16.
Butt, J. (ed.) 1971. *Robert Owen, Prince of Cotton Spinners.*
Butt, J. 1976a. The Scottish Cotton Industry during the Industrial Revolution, in Cullen, L. M. and Smout, T. C. (eds.), *Comparative Aspects of Scottish and Irish Economic History and Social History 1600–1900*, 116–28.
Butt, J. 1976b. Capital and Enterprise in the Scottish Iron Industry, 1780–1840, in Butt, J. and Ward, J. T. (eds.), *Scottish Themes*, 67–79.
Butt, J., Hume, J. R. and Donnachie, I. L. 1968. *Industrial History in Pictures: Scotland.*
Campbell, W. A. 1971. *The Chemical Industry.*
Catling, H. 1970. *The Spinning Mule.*
Ceram, C. W. 1965. *Archaeology of the Cinema.*

Chaloner, W. H. 1953. Sir Thomas Lombe (1685–1739) and the British Silk Industry, *History Today*, 778–85.

Chaloner, W. H. 1954. Robert Owen, Peter Drinkwater and the Early Factory System in Manchester, 1788–1800, *Bulletin of the John Rylands Library*, **37**, 78–102.

Chaloner, W. H. 1965. The Textile Inventor, John Kay, *Bulletin of the John Rylands Library*, **48**, 9–12.

Chapman, S. D. 1967. *The Early Factory Masters*.

Chapman, S. D. (ed.). 1971a. *The History of Working-Class Housing*.

Chapman, S. D. 1971b. Fixed Capital Formation in the British Cotton Industry, in Higgins, J. P. P. and Pollard, S. (eds.), *Aspects of Capital Investment in Great Britain 1770–1850*.

Chapman, S. D. 1972. *The Cotton Industry in the Industrial Revolution*.

Chapman, S. D. and Butt, J. 1979. The Cotton Industry, in Pollard, S. (ed.), *Capital Formation in the Industrial Revolution 1750–1850*.

Chitty, M. 1974. *Industrial Archaeology of Exeter: a Guide*. Exeter I.A. Group.

Chitty, M. *et al.* 1974. *A Guide to the Industrial Heritage of Merseyside*.

Clayton, A. K. 1962–3. The Newcomen-type Engine at Elsecar, West Riding, *T.N.S.*, **XXXV**.

Clew, K. R. 1968. *The Kennet and Avon Canal*.

Clough, R. T. 1962. *The Lead Smelting Mills of the Yorkshire Dales*.

Clow, A. and Clow, N. L. 1945. Vitriol in the Industrial Revolution, *Ec.H.R.*, **XV**, 44–55.

Clow, A. and Clow, N. L. 1952. *The Chemical Revolution*.

Coleman, D. C. 1973. Textile Growth, in Harte, N. B. and Ponting, K. G. (eds.), *Textile History and Economic History*, 1–21.

Cooke, A. (ed.). 1977. *Stanley: its History and Development*.

Cooksey, A. J. 1970. The Wren & Hopkinson Horizontal Cross Compound Engine *c.* 1870, *I.A.*, **7**, 165–70.

Copeland, R. 1969. Cheddleton Flint Mill, *North Staffs. Journal of Field Studies*, **9**.

Copeland, R. 1972. *A Short History of Pottery Raw Materials and the Cheddleton Flint Mill*.

Corran, H. S. 1968. The Guinness Museum, Dublin, *I.A.*, **5/3**.

Corran, H. S. 1975. *A History of Brewing*.

Cossons, N. 1968. Turnpike Roads of the Bristol Region: a Preliminary Study. *B.I.A.S.*, **1**.

Cossons, N. 1973. The Ironbridge Project, *Museums Journal*, **72/4**.

Cossons, N. 1975. *The BP Book of Industrial Archaeology*.

Cossons, N. and Sowden, H. 1977. *Ironbridge: Landscape of Industry*.

Course, E. 1967. The Itchen Navigation, *Proc. Hants. Field Soc.*, **XXIV**.

Cox, C. 1964. Milestones of the Stroud District, *Trans. Bristol & Gloucester Arch. Soc.*, **XXXIII**.

Cox, C. 1967. Turnpike Houses of the Stroud District, *Trans. Bristol & Gloucester Arch. Soc.*, **XXXVI**.

Cox, C. 1969. Aids to Recording (2), Some Problems of Dating Milestones, *I.A.*, **6/1**.

Crawford, O. G. S. 1953. *Archaeology in the Field*.

Cross, D. A. E. 1968. The Development of Traffic Signs, *I.A.*, **5/3**.

Cross, D. A. E. 1970. The Salisbury Avon Navigation, *I.A.*, **7/2**.

Crossley, D. W. 1972. A Sixteenth Century Wealden Blast Furnace: a Report on Excavations at Panningridge, Sussex 1964–1970, *Post-medieval Archaeology*, 42–68.

Crossley, D. 1975. *The Bewl Valley Ironworks*. Royal Arch Arch. Inst.

Crossley, D. W. and Ashurst, D. 1968. Excavations at Rockley Smithies. . . , *Post-medieval Archaeology*, 10–54.

Cruden, S. 1974. *Click Mill, Dounby, Orkney*. H.M.S.O., Edinburgh.

Cullen, L. M. 1972. *An Economic History of Ireland Since 1660*.

Daunton, M. J. 1977. *Coal Metropolis: Cardiff, 1870–1914*.

Davies-Shiel, M. 1971. Terminology of Early Iron Smelting in Lakeland, *Trans. Cumberland & Westmorland Soc.*, **LXXI**.

Davies-Shiel, M. and Marshall, J. D. 1969. *The Industrial Archaeology of the Lake Counties*.

Davis, A. C. 1934. *Portland Cement*.

Day, J. 1973. *Bristol Brass*.

Deane, P. and Cole, W. A. 1969. *British Economic Growth*.

Delany, V. T. H. and Delany, D. R. 1966. *The Canals of the South of Ireland*.

Dickinson, H. W. 1937. History of Vitriol Manufacture in England, *TNS*, **1**.

Dickson, D. 1976. Aspects of the Rise and Decline of the Irish Cotton Industry, in Cullen L. M. and Smout, T. C. (eds.), *Comparative Aspects of Scottish and Irish Economic and Social History 1600–1900*, 100–15.

Dodd, A. E. and Dodd, E. M. 1974. *Peakland Roads and Trackways*.

Dodsworth, C. 1972. The Early Years of the Oxford Cement Industry, *I.A.*, **9/2**, 285–95.

Donnachie, I. 1971a. *The Industrial Archaeology of Galloway*.

Donnachie, I. 1971b. I.A. on Tombstones. *I.A.*, **8/2**.

Donnachie, I. and Macleod, I. 1974. *Old Galloway*

Donnachie, I. and Stewart, N. 1967. Scottish Windmills: an Outline and Inventory, *P.S.A.S.*, **XCVIII**.

Donnelly, T. 1974. The Rubislaw Granite Quarries 1750–1939, *I.A.*, **11/3**, 225–36.

Downs-Rose, G. and Harvey, W. S. 1973. Water-Bucket Pumps and the Wanlockhead Engine, *I.A.*, **10/2**, 129–47.

Duckham, B. F. 1968. Some Eighteenth-Century Scottish Coal Mining Methods: the Dissertation of Sir John Clark, *I.A.*, **5**.

Duckham, B. F. 1970. *A History of the Scottish Coal Industry, Vol. I, 1700–1815*.

Dunbar, J. G. 1966. *The Historic Architecture of Scotland*.

Dunham, R. K. and Hobbs, R. J. 1976. Burtree Pasture Lead Mine, Weardale, *I.A.R.*, **1/1**, 7–17.

Dyos, H. J. and Aldcroft, D. H. 1974. *British Transport: an Economic Survey from the Seventeenth Century to the Twentieth*.

East Lothian County Planning Dept. 1970. *East Lothian Water Mills*. East Lothian County Council, Haddington.

East Midlands Tourist Board. 1976. *Industrial Archaeology.*

Ellis, C. M. 1968. A Gazetteer of the Water, Wind and Tide Mills of Hampshire, *Proc. Hampshire Field Club,* **XXV**.

Ellis, C. M. (ed.) 1975. *Hampshire Industrial Archaeology: A Guide.* Southampton.

Fairlie, S. 1964–5. Dyestuffs in the Eighteenth Century, *Ec.H.R.,* **XVII**, 488–510.

Feather, S. W. 1975. Bradford Industrial Museum, an Interim Report, *Trans. of the First International Congress on the Conservation of Industrial Monuments,* 113–21. Ironbridge.

Fell, A. 1908. *The Early Iron Industry of Furness and District.* Ulverston.

Fenton, A. 1976. *Scottish Country Life.* Edinburgh.

Finch Brothers Foundry, Sticklepath. 1967. *I.A.* Supplement, **4/4**.

Firth, G. 1977. The Development of the Northbrook Chemical Works, Bradford, *I.A.R.,* **2/1**, 52–68.

Fitton, R. S. and Wadsworth, A. P. 1958. *The Strutts and the Arkwrights 1758–1830.*

Flinn, M. W. 1959. The Growth of the English Iron Industry, 1660–1760, *Ec.H.R.*

Flinn, M.W. 1961–2, William Wood and the Coke-smelting Process, *T.N.S.,* **XXXIV**, 55–71.

Flinn, M. W. 1962. *Men of Iron: the Crowleys in the Early Iron Industry.*

Flinn, M. W. (ed.) 1973. *Svedenstierna's Tour of Great Britain 1802–3.*

Ford, P. and Ford, G. 1972. *A Guide to Parliamentary Papers.*

Fraser, W. H. 1971. Robert Owen and the Workers, in Butt, J. (ed.), *Robert Owen, Prince of Cotton Spinners,* 76–98.

Freeman, M. D. 1971. Funtley Iron Mill, Fareham, Hampshire, *I.A.,* **8/1**, 63–8.

Freeman, M. D. 1973. Working-class Housing in Portsmouth, *I.A.,* **10/2**.

Freese, S. 1971. *Windmills and Millwrighting.*

French, G. J. 1859. *Life and Times of Samuel Crompton.*

Gale, W. K. V. 1967. *The British Iron and Steel Industry: a Technical History.*

Gale, W. K. V. 1977. *Iron and Steel.*

Galloway, R. L. 1882, reprint 1969. *A History of Coal Mining in Great Britain.*

Gatrell, V. A. C. 1977. Labour, Power and the Size of Firms in Lancashire Cotton in the Second Quarter of the Nineteenth Century. *Ec.H.R.,* **XXX**, 95–139.

Gauldie, E. (ed.) 1969. *The Dundee Textile Industry.*

Gauldie, E. 1974. *Cruel Habitations: a History of Working Class Housing 1780–1918.*

George, A. D. 1973. The Industrial Archaeology of Carlisle, *I.A.,* **10/3**.

Gibbs, F. W. 1939. The History of the Manufacture of Soap, *Annals of Science,* **IV**.

Gittins, L. 1977. Soapmaking and the Excise Laws 1711–1853, *I.A.R.,* **1/3**, 265–75.

Godfrey, E. S. 1975. *The Development of English Glassmaking 1550–1660.*

Goodhugh, P. 1970. The Poor Law in Amesbury, *Wilts. I.A.,* **2**.

Graham, F. 1975. *The Bridges of Northumberland and Durham.*

Grant, A. 1976. The Cooper in Liverpool, *I.A.R.*, **1/1**.

Gray, J. R. 1971. An Industrial Farm Estate in Berkshire, *I.A.*, **8/2**.

Green, E. R. R. 1963. *The Industrial Archaeology of County Down.* H.M.S.O., Belfast.

Gribbon, H. D. 1969. *The History of Water Power in Ulster.*

Griffin, A. R. 1969. Bell-Pits and Soughs: some East Midlands Examples, *I.A.*, **6/4**, 392-7.

Griffin, A. R. 1977. *The British Coal Mining Industry.*

Griffin, C. P. 1977. Three Generations of Miners' Housing at Moira, Leicestershire, 1811-1934, *I.A.R.*, **1/3**, 276-82.

Griffin, C. P., Palmer, D., and Palmer, M. 1977. Historical Discussion: the Moira Furnace, *I.A.R.*, **2/1**, 85-8.

Gulvin, C. 1973. *The Tweedmakers: a History of the Scottish Fancy Woollen Industry 1600-1914.*

Hadfield, C. 1966a. *British Canals: an Illustrated History.*

Hadfield, C. 1966b. *The Canals of the West Midlands.*

Hadfield, C. 1966c. *The Canals of the East Midlands.*

Hadfield, C. 1967. *The Canals of South Wales and the Border.*

Hadfield, C. 1969. *The Canals of South and South-East England.*

Hadfield, C. 1972. *The Canals of Yorkshire and North-East England.*

Hadfield, C. and Biddle, G. 1970. *The Canals of North-West England.*

Hague, D. B. 1968. *Conway Suspension Bridge.* The National Trust.

Hair, P. E. H. 1965. The Binding of Pitmen of the North-East, 1800-9, *Durham Univ. Journal.*

Haldane, A. R. B. 1962. *New Ways through the Glens.*

Haldane, A. R. B. 1968. *The Drove Roads of Scotland.*

Hall, J. and Yates, J. 1973. *The Grand Western Canal.* Devon County Council.

Hall, J. and Yates, J. 1974. *Exeter Canal and Quays.* Exeter I.A. Group.

Hamilton, H. 1967 edn. *The English Brass and Copper Industries.*

Hamilton, S. B. 1964. The Newcomen Society and Industrial Archaeology, *J.I.A.*, **1**, 74-5.

Hammersley, G. 1957. The Crown Woods and their Exploitation in the Sixteenth and Seventeenth Centuries, *Bull. Inst. Hist. Research*, 136-61.

Hammond, M. D. P. 1977. Brick Kilns: an Illustrated Survey, *I.A.R.*, **1/2**, 171-92.

Handley, J. E. 1945. *The Irish in Scotland.*

Hannah, L. 1977. A Pioneer of Public Enterprise: the Central Electricity Board and the National Grid, in Supple, B. (ed.), *Essays in British Business History.*

Hardie, D. W. F. and Pratt, J. D. 1966. *A History of the Modern British Chemical Industry.*

Harley, J. B. 1972. *Maps for the Local Historian. A Guide to British Sources.* National Council of Social Service.

Harley, J. B. 1975. *Ordnance Survey Maps: a Descriptive Manual.* Ordnance Survey, Southampton.

Harris, A. 1972. The Tindale Fell Waggonway, *Trans. Cumberland & Westmorland Soc.,* **LXXII**.

Harris, A. 1974. Colliery Settlements in East Cumberland, *Trans. Cumberland & Westmorland Soc.,* **LXXIV**.

Harris, H. 1968. *The Industrial Archaeology of Dartmoor.*

Harris, J. R. 1964. *The Copper King.*

Harris, J. R. 1967. The Employment of Steam Power in the Eighteenth Century, *History,* **62**.

Harris, J. R. 1970. Industrial Archaeology and its Future, *Business History,* **XII**, 129–34.

Harris, R. 1969. *Canals and their Architecture.*

Harrison, A. and Harrison, J. K. 1973. The Horse Wheel in North Yorkshire, *I.A.,* **10/3**.

Hart, C. 1971. *The Industrial History of Dean.*

Hartley, R. 1964–5. Industrial Archaeology and Schools of Architecture, *I.A.,* **1/4**, 225–30.

Harvey, N. 1970. *A History of Farmbuildings in England and Wales.*

Hay, G. D. 1974. Houldsworth's Cotton Mill, Glasgow, *Post-Medieval Archaeology,* **8**, 92–101.

Hey, D. 1972. *The Rural Metal Workers of the Sheffield Region: a Study of Rural Industry before the Industrial Revolution.*

Hey, D. G. 1973. The use of Probate Inventories for Industrial Archaeology. *I.A.,* **10/2**, 201–12.

Higgins, S. H. 1924. *A History of Bleaching.*

Hildebrand, K. G. 1958. Foreign Markets for Swedish Iron in the Eighteenth Century, *Scandinavian Ec. Hist. Review,* **VI**, 3–52.

Hills, R. L. 1970. *Power in the Industrial Revolution.*

Hinde, K. S. G. 1973. Windpump Remains in the Fens, *Cambridge Industrial Archaeology.*

Hoare, J. and Upton, J. 1972. *Sussex Industrial Archaeology: A Field Guide.*

Hodgkiss, A. G. 1970. *Maps for Books and Theses.*

Hodgson, H. W. 1969. Packhorse Roads in Todmorden, *I.A.,* **6/4**.

Holland, J. 1841, reprint 1968. *History and Description of Fossil Fuel, the Collieries and Coal Trade of Great Britain.*

Hudson, K. 1963. *Industrial Archaeology: An Introduction.*

Hudson, K. 1965. *The Industrial Archaeology of Southern England.*

Hudson, K. 1966. *The History of English China Clays.*

Hudson, K. 1968. The Early Years of the Railway Community in Swindon, *T.H.,* **1/2**.

Hudson, K. 1974. Monuments to Whom? The State of Industrial Archaeology, *Encounter,* 72–7.

Hudson, K. 1975. *Exploring our Industrial Past.*

Hudson, K. 1976. *Industrial Archaeology: a New Introduction.*

Hughes, B. D. 1970. Aids to Recording (6). The Rolle Canal, *I.A.,* **7/1**.

Hughes, E. 1949. The First Steam Engines in the Durham Coalfield, *Archaeologa Aeliana,* **27**.

Hughes, J. 1972. Cumberland Windmills, *Trans. Cumberland & Westmorland Soc.,* **LXXII**, 112–41.

Hulme, E. W. 1928–9. Statistical History of the Iron Trade of England and Wales, 1717–50, *T.N.S.*, **IX**, 12–35.

Hume, J. R. 1971. The Industrial Archaeology of New Lanark, in Butt, J. (ed.), *Robert Owen, Prince of Cotton Spinners*.

Hume, J. R. 1974. *The Industrial Archaeology of Glasgow*.

Hume, J. R. 1976a. *The Industrial Archaeology of Scotland: 1. The Lowlands and Borders*.

Hume, J. R. 1976b. Shipbuilding Machine Tools, in Butt, J. and Ward, J. T. (eds.), *Scottish Themes*.

Hume, J. R. 1977. *The Industrial Archaeology of Scotland: 2. The Highlands and Islands*.

Hunt, C. J. 1970. *The Lead Mines of the Northern Pennines*.

Hyde, C. K. 1977. *Technological Change and the British Iron Industry*.

I.W.A.A.C. 1971. *Remainder Waterways*.

I.W.A.A.C. 1974. *Upgrading of Remainder Waterways: A Report to the Secretary of State for the Environment*.

Jackson, G. 1972. *Hull in the Eighteenth Century*.

Jenkins, D. T. 1973. Early Factory Development in the West Riding of Yorkshire, 1770–1800, in Harte, N. B. and Ponting, K. G. (eds.), *Textile History and Economic History*, 247–80.

Jenkins, D. T. 1975. *The West Riding Wool Textile Industry 1770–1835, A Study in Fixed Capital Formation*.

John, A. H. 1950. *The Industrial Development of South Wales*.

Johnson, W. B. 1970. *The Industrial Archaeology of Hertfordshire*.

Jones, P. N. 1976. Baptist Chapels as an Index of Cultural Tradition in the South Wales Coalfield before 1914, *Journal of Hist. Geography*, **2**.

Journal of Herefordshire Waterworks Museum Trust. 1975.

Kellett, J. R. 1961. Property Speculators and the Building of Glasgow, 1780–1830, *Scot. Journal of Political Economy*, **7**.

Kirkham, N. 1968. *Derbyshire Lead Mining through the Centuries*.

Lennox, R. G. 1973. The History of W. W. Dickie & Sons, Implement Makers and Agricultural Engineers, East Kilbride, *I.A.*, **10/4**.

Leslie, K. C. 1970–1. The Ashburnham Estate Brickworks 1840–1968, *Sussex Industrial History*, **1**.

Lewis, G. D. 1964. *The South Yorkshire Glass Industry*, Sheffield City Museum.

Lewis, G. D. 1965. The Catcliffe Glassworks, *I.A.*, **1/4**, 206–11.

Lewis, M. J. T. 1970. *Early Wooden Railways*.

Lewis, M. J. T. 1973. Industrial Archaeology, in Cipolla, C. M. (ed.), *The Fontana Economic History of Europe*, 574–603.

Lewis, M. J. T., Slatcher, W. N. and Jarvis, P. N. 1969. Flashlocks on English Waterways: a Survey, *I.A.*, **6/3**.

Lindley, K. 1969. *Chapels and Meeting Houses*.

Lindley, K. 1972. *Graves and Graveyards*.

Lindley, K. 1973. *Seaside Architecture*.

Lindsay, J. 1968. *The Canals of Scotland*.

Lindsay, J. 1974. *A History of the North Wales Slate Industry*.

Lindsey, C. F. 1974. *Windmills: A Bibliographical Guide*.

Linsley, S. and Smith, S. B. 1975. On Site Preservation of Industrial Monuments, *Trans. First International Congress on the Conservation of Industrial Monuments*, 55–68. Ironbridge.

Linsley, S. M. 1973. *Ryhope Pumping Station: A History and Description.*

Lloyd, D. 1967. Railway Station Architecture, *I.A.*, **4/3** and **4/4**.

Logan, J. C. 1972. The Operations of a Glassworks in the Industrial Revolution, *I.A.*, **9/2**, 177–87.

Lord, J. 1903. *Memoir of John Kay of Bury.*

Lowe, J. B. and Anderson, D. N. 1972. *Iron Industry Housing Papers.* Welsh School of Architecture.

Lynch, P. and Vaizey, J. 1960. *Guinness's Brewery in the Irish Economy, 1759–1876.*

Lythe, S. G. E. and Butt, J. 1975. *An Economic History of Scotland.*

McCraken, E. 1972. *The Palm House and Botanic Garden.* Ulster Architectural Heritage Society, Belfast.

McCutcheon, W. A. 1965a. *The Canals of the North of Ireland.*

McCutcheon, W. A. 1965b. The Application of Water Power to Industrial Purposes in the North of Ireland, *I.A.*, **2/2**, 69–81.

McCutcheon, W. A. 1977. *Wheel and Spindle.*

MacDonald, S. 1975. The Progress of the Early Threshing Machines, *Agric. Hist. Rev.*, **23**.

McIvor, I. 1973. Jedburgh Castle and the Architecture of Prison Reform, *Papers on the Borders in the Nineteenth Century.*

Mackenzie, T. B. 1928. *Life of James Beaumont Neilson, F.R.S.*

McNeil, I. 1972. *Hydraulic Power.*

Major, J. K. 1975. *Fieldwork in Industrial Archaeology.*

Mann, J. (ed.) 1964. *Documents illustrating the Wiltshire Textile Trades in the Eighteenth Century.*

Mann, J. 1971. *The Cloth Industry in the West of England from 1640 to 1880.*

Marshall, J. D. 1971. *Old Lakeland.*

Martin, G. 1925. *Industrial Chemistry.*

Martins, S. 1971. Aids to Recording (8). A Small Fish-processing Community in Great Yarmouth, Norfolk: A Training Course in Field Techniques, *I.A.*, **8/3**.

Mathias, P. 1959. *The Brewing Industry in England 1700–1830.*

Melton, V. L. 1972. *Social Conditions in Mid-Nineteenth-Century Sheffield.* Sheffield City Museums.

Minchinton, W. E. 1957. *The British Tinplate Industry.*

Minchinton, W. E. (ed.) 1969. *Industrial South Wales.*

Minchinton, W. E. 1973. *Industrial Archaeology in Devon.* Dartington Amenity Research Trust, Totnes.

Minchinton, W. E. and Perkins, J. 1971. *Tidemills of Devon and Cornwall.* Exeter I.A. Group.

Moir, E. 1971. Marling & Evans, King's Stanley and Ebley Mills, Gloucestershire, *Textile History*, **2/1**, 28–56.

Morris, J. H. and Williams, L. J. 1958. *The South Wales Coal Industry 1841–1875.*

Morrison, T. A. 1971. Some Notes on the Van Mine, Llanidloes, Mont-gomery, *I.A.*, **8/1**, 29–51.

Morrison, T. A. 1973. The Initiation of Mining Settlement on the Cardiganshire Orefield, *I.A.*, **10/2**.

Morrison, T. A. 1975. *Goldmining in Western Merioneth.*

Morton, G. R. 1962. The Furnace at Duddon Bridge, *Journal of the Iron and Steel Institute*, 444–52.

Morton, G. R. 1963a. The Products of Nibthwaite Ironworks, *Metallurgist*, II, 259–68.

Morton, G. R. 1963b. An Eighteenth-Century Ironworks, *Metallurgist*, II, 299–300.

Morton, G. R. 1965. The Use of Peat in the Reduction of Iron Ore, *Iron and Steel*, Sept. issue.

Morton, G. R. 1972. The Industrial History of Darlaston, *Journ. of West Midland Studies*, **5**, 11–15.

Morton, G. R. and Mutton, N. 1967. The Transition to Cort's Puddling Process, *Journ. of the Iron and Steel Institute*, 722–8.

Morton, G. R. and Wanklyn, M. 1967. Dud Dudley. A Reappraisal, *Journal of West Midlands Regional Studies*, 48–65.

Mott, R. A. 1957–9. Abraham Darby (I and II) and the Coal Iron Industry, *T.N.S.*, **XXXI**, 49–93.

Munmer, A. 1937. *New British Industries in the Twentieth Century.*

Murray, D. 1883, reprinted 1973. *The York Buildings Company.*

Musson, A. E. 1965. *Enterprise in Soap and Chemicals: Joseph Crosfield & Sons Limited 1815–1965.*

Musson, A. E. and Robinson, E. 1969. *Science and Technology in the Industrial Revolution.*

Namier, L. B. 1969. Anthony Bacon, M.P., an Eighteenth-Century Mer-chant, in Minchinton, W. E. (ed.), *Industrial South Wales*, 59–106.

N.C.B. 1958. *A Short History of the Scottish Coal-Mining Industry.*

Nef, J. U. 1932. *The Rise of the British Coal Industry*, 2 vols.

Nef, J. U. 1934. The Progress of Technology and the Growth of Large-Scale Industry in Great Britain, 1540–1640, *Ec.H.R.*, **5**.

Nichol, James. 1891. *Statistics of Glasgow 1885–1891.*

Nielson, V. G. 1968. Cheese Making and Cheese Chambers in Glouces-tershire, *I.A.*, **5/2**.

Nixon, F. 1969. *The Industrial Archaeology of Derbyshire.*

Norris, J. Harold. 1965–6. The Water-Powered Corn Mills of Cheshire, *Trans. Lancs. & Cheshire Soc.*, 75–6.

O'Neill, H. 1965. Iron Tombstones and the Pembrokeshire Coal & Iron Company, *I.A.*, **2/3**, 158–60.

Owen, R. 1858. reprint 1971. *Life by Himself.*

Palmer, M. and Palmer, D. 1976. Moira Furnace, *I.A.R.*, **1/1**, 63–9.

Pannell, J. P. M. 1964–5. Early Loading Places in the Port of Southamp-ton, *I.A.*, **1/1**.

Pannell, J. P. M. 1966. *Techniques of Industrial Archaeology.*

Parsons, R. H. 1939. *The Early Days of the Power Station Industry.*

Percival, A. 1969. *The Faversham Gunpowder Industry.*

Peters, J. E. C. 1969. *The Development of Farm Buildings in Western Lowland Staffordshire up to 1880.*

Phillips, C. B. 1977. The Cumbrian Iron Industry in the Seventeenth Century, in Chaloner, W. H. and Ratcliffe, B. M. (eds.), *Trade and Transport, Essays in Economic History in Honour of T. S. Willan.*

Ponting, K. G. 1971. *The Woollen Industry of South-West England.*

Ponting, K. G. 1978. Important Natural Dyes of History, *I.A.R.*, **2/2**, 154–9.

Porteous, J. D. 1969a. Goole: a Pre-Victorian Company Town, *I.A.*, **6/2**.

Porteous, J. D. 1969b. A New Canal Port in the Railway Age: Railway Projection to Goole 1830–1914, *T.H.*, **2/1**.

Porteous, J. D. 1977. *Canal Ports: the Urban Achievement of the Canal Age.*

Postlethwaite, J. 1877, reprint 1976. *Mines and Mining in the English Lake District.*

Powell, W. R. 1962, reprint 1969. *Local History from Blue Books.* Historical Assoc. pamphlet.

Pratt, F. 1976. *Canal Architecture in Britain.* British Waterways Board.

Pudney, J. 1975. *London Docks.*

Raistrick, A. 1936–7. The Steam Engine on Tyneside 1715–1778, *T.N.S.*, **XVII**.

Raistrick, A. 1970a. *Dynasty of Ironfounders: the Darbys and Coalbrookdale.*

Raistrick, A. 1970b. *The Making of the English Landscape: West Riding of Yorkshire.*

Raistrick, A. 1972. *Industrial Archaeology: an Historical Survey.*

Raistrick, A. 1973. *Lead Mining in the Mid-Pennines.*

Raistrick, A. 1975. *The Lead Industry in Wensleydale and Swaledale.* 2 vols.

Raistrick, A. 1977. *Two Centuries of Industrial Welfare. The London (Quaker) Lead Company.*

Riastrick, A. and Jennings, B. 1965. *A History of Lead Mining in the Pennines.*

Rattenbury, P. G. 1964–5. Survivals of the Brinore Tramroad in Brecknockshire. *J.I.A.*, **1/3**.

Rees, Morgan, D. 1969. *Mines, Mills and Furnaces.* National Museum of Wales, Cardiff.

Rees, Morgan, D. 1975. *The Industrial Archaeology of Wales.*

Rees, P. T. L. 1969. Aids to Recording (5). The East Lancashire Railway, *I.A.*, **6/3** and **6/4**.

Rees, P. 1976. Four Railway Stations, *North Western Soc. for I.A. and Hist. Journal.*

Rees, S. A. 1972. Turnpike Roads of the Bristol Area Survey: Part 2, *B.I.A.S.*, **5**.

Reynolds, J., Burrel, G. and Bignall, D. 1967. Durngate Mill, Winchester, *Proc. Hants Field Club*, **XXIV**.

Rhodes, P. S. 1962. *A Guide to Ballycopeland Windmill.* H.M.S.O., Belfast.

Richardson, J. B. 1974. *Metal Mining.*

Riden, P. 1973. Post-post Medieval Archaeology, *Antiquity*, **XLVII**, 210–16.

Riden, P. 1977. The Output of the British Iron Industry before 1870, *Ec.H.R.*, 442–59.

Rieuwerts, J. 1972. *Derbyshire Old Lead Mines and Miners.*

Riley, R. C. 1971. Henry Cort at Funtley, Hampshire, *I.A.*, **8/1**, 69–76.

Rix, M. M. 1964–5. A Proposal to Establish National Parks of Industrial Archaeology, *I.A.*, **1/3**, 184–92.

Rix, M. M. 1967a. *Industrial Archaeology.* Historical Assoc. pamphlet.

Rix, M. M. 1967b. Industrial Archaeology and the Church, *I.A.*, **4/1**.

Robinson, J. M. 1976. Model Farm Buildings of the Age of Improvement, *Arch. Hist.*, **19**.

Rogers, K. H. 1973. Trowbridge Clothiers and their Houses, 1660–1800, in Harte, N. B. and Ponting, K. G. (eds.), *Textile History and Economic History*, 138–61. Manchester.

Rogers, K. H. 1976a. *Wiltshire and Somerset Woollen Mills.*

Rogers, K. H. 1976b. *The Newcomen Engine in the West Country.*

Rolt, L. T. C. 1944. *Narrow Boat.*

Rolt, L. T. C. 1953. *Railway Adventure.*

Rolt, L. T. C. 1958. *Thomas Telford.*

Rolt, L. T. C. 1970. *Victorian Engineering.*

Rolt, L. T. C. 1971. *Landscape with Machines. An Autobiography.* Vol. 1.

Rolt, L. T. C. 1974. *The Potters' Field: A History of the South Devon Ball Clay Industry.*

Rolt, L. T. C. 1977. *Landscape with Canals. An Autobiography.* Vol. 2.

Rolt, L. T. C. and Allen, J. S. 1977. *The Steam Engine of Thomas Newcomen.*

Schubert, H. R. 1957. *History of the British Iron and Steel Industry from c. 450 B.C. to A.D. 1770.*

Scott, H. 1947. The Miners' Bond in Northumberland and Durham, *Proc. Soc. of Antiq. of Newcastle.*

Scrivener, H. 1854. *History of the Iron Trade.*

Shaffrey, P. 1975. *The Irish Town: An Approach to Survival.*

Sharp, D. 1969. *The Picture Palace and other Buildings for the Movies.*

Shaw, Simeon, 1829, reprinted 1970. *History of the Staffordshire Potteries.*

Sherlock, R. 1976. *The Industrial Archaeology of Staffordshire.*

Short, M. 1971. *Windmills in Lambeth: an Historical Survey.* London Borough of Lambeth.

Silvester, J. W. H. 1972. *Scythe-making at Abbeydale.* Sheffield City Museums.

Simmons, J. 1978. *The Railway in England and Wales 1830–1914: Vol 1, The System and its Working.*

Skinner, B. C. 1965. *The Lime Industry of the Lothians.*

Smith, D. 1965. *Industrial Archaeology of the East Midlands.*

Smith, R. S. 1957. Huntingdon Beaumont: Adventurer in Coalmines, *Rennaisance and Modern Studies*, I.

Smith, W. J. 1971. The Architecture of the Domestic System in South-East Lancashire and the Adjoining Pennines, in Chapman, S. D. (ed.), *The History of Working-Class Housing*, 247–75.

Spring, D. 1951. The English Landed Estate in the Age of Coal and Iron, 1830–1880, *Journal of Economic History.*

Spring, D. 1952. The Earls of Durham and the Great Northern Coalfield, *Canadian Hist. Rev.*

Starmer, G. 1970. *Industrial Archaeology in Northamptonshire*. Northampton Museums and Art Gallery.

Stephen, W. M. 1967. Toll-houses of the Greater Fife Area, *I.A.*, **4/3**.

Stephen, W. M. 1967–8. Milestones and Wayside Markers in Fife, *P.S.A.S.*, 100.

Storer, J. D. 1975. Preservation Progress in Scotland, *Trans. of the First International Congress on the Conservation of Industrial Monuments.* Ironbridge.

Storey, R. 1966. The Archaeology of the Cinema, *I.A.*, **3/4**.

Storey, R. 1968. The Industrial Archaeology of Modern Road Transport: some Initial Considerations, *I.A.*, **5/3**.

Symonds, R. 1972. Preservation and Perspectives in Industrial Archaeology, *History*, **57**, 82–8.

Syson, L. 1965. *British Watermills.*

Tann, J. 1965. Some Problems of Water-Power—a Study of Mill Siting in Gloucestershire, *Trans. Bristol & Gloucestershire Arch. Soc.*, **LXXXIV**, 53–77.

Tann, J. 1967a. A Survey of Thirsk, Yorkshire, *I.A.*, **4**, 232–47.

Tann, J. 1967b. *Gloucestershire Woollen Mills.*

Tann, J. 1969. Industrial Archaeology and the Business Historian, *Business Archives.*

Tann, J. 1970. *The Development of the Factory.*

Tarn, J. N. 1971. *Working Class Housing in Nineteenth-Century Britain.* Architectural Assoc.

Tarn, J. N. 1973. *Five Per Cent Philanthropy: an Account of Housing in Urban Areas Between 1840 and 1914.*

Taylor, J. 1977. John Rennie's Reconstruction of Sheerness Dockyard, *I.A.R.*, **1/3**.

Taylor, P. S. 1957. *A History of Industrial Chemistry.* 2 vols.

Taylor, R., Cox, M. and Dickins, I. 1975. *Britain's Planning Heritage.*

Taylor, R. F. 1966. A Type of Handloom-weaving Cottage in Mid-Lancashire, *I.A.*, **3/4**.

Taylor, W. 1976. *The Military Roads of Scotland.*

Telford, S. J. 1974. Early Industrial Developments on the Northumberland Coast between Seaton Sluice and Cullercoats, *I.A.*, **11/3**.

Thirsk, J. 1961. Industries in the Countryside, in Fisher, F. J. (ed.), *Essays in the Economic and Social History of Tudor and Stuart England.*

Thomas, A. L. 1969. Aids to Recording (3). Surveying an Industrial Ruin: the Abbey Mill, West Ham, *I.A.*, **6/2**.

Thomas, Brinley. 1969. The Migration of Labour into the Glamorganshire Coalfield (1861–1911), in Minchinton, W. E. (ed.), *Industrial South Wales*, 37–56.

Thomas, J. 1971. *The Rise of the Staffordshire Potteries.*

Thompson, E. P. 1968. *The Making of the English Working Class.*

Thompson, W. J. 1975. *Industrial Archaeology of North Staffordshire.*

Tighe, M. F. 1973. *A Gazetteer of Hampshire Breweries.* Univ. of Southampton.

Todd, A. C. and Laws, P. 1972. *The Industrial Archaeology of Cornwall.*

Treble, J. H. 1971. The Social and Economic Thought of Robert Owen, in Butt, J. (ed.), *Robert Owen, Prince of Cotton Spinners*, 20–51.

Trinder, B. 1973a. *The Industrial Revolution in Shropshire.*

Trinder, B. 1973b. *The Iron Bridge: A Short History of the First Iron Bridge in the World.* Ironbridge Gorge Museum Trust.

Tylecote, R. F. 1962. *Metallurgy in Archaeology.*

Tyson, S. 1972. The Linton Lock Hydro-Electric Power Station, *I.A.*, **9/1**, 48–57.

Tucker, D. G. 1972. The Beginnings of Electricity Supply in Bristol 1889–1902, *B.I.A.S.*, **5**, 11–18.

Tucker, D. G. 1977a. Refuse Destructors and their use for Generating Electricity: A Century of Development, *I.A.R.*, **2/1**, 5–27.

Tucker, D. G. 1977b. Hydro-electricity for Public Supply in Britain, 1881–1894, *I.A.R.*, **1/1**, 126–63.

Tucker, D. G. 1977c. Electricity Generating Stations for Public Supply in the West Midlands 1888–1977, *West Midlands Studies*, **10**, 8–28.

Veale, T. H. P. 1956 (3rd ed.) *The Disposal of Sewage.*

Vine, P. A. L. 1966. *London's Lost Route to the Sea.*

Viner, D. J. 1976. The Marble Quarry, Iona, Inner Hebrides, *I.A.R.*, **1/1**, 18–27.

Wadsworth, A. P. and Mann, J. 1931. *The Cotton Trade and Industrial Lancashire 1600–1780.*

Wailes, R. 1938–9. Tidemills in England and Wales, *T.N.S.*, **19**.

Wailes, R. 1954. *The English Windmill.*

Walker, I. C. 1971. Ecclesiastical Archaeology—a Review Article, *I.A.*, **8/4**.

Warburton, R. 1974. The History of Newton Abbot Power Station, *I.A.*, **11/2**, 46–52.

Ward, J. T. 1963. West Riding Landowners and Mining in the Nineteenth Century, *Yorkshire Bulletin*, **15**.

Ward, J. T. 1971. Owen as Factory Reformer, in Butt, J. (ed.), *Robert Owen, Prince of Cotton Spinners*, 99–134.

Ward, J. T. and Wilson, R. G. (eds.) 1971. *Land and Industry.*

Warden, A. J. 1867 edn. *The Linen Trade, Ancient and Modern.*

Warner, Sir Frank. 1921. *The Silk Industry of the United Kingdom.*

Warren, John. 1968. Beam Pumping Engines at Kew Bridge, *I.A.*, **5/4**, 327–34.

Wartnaby, J. 1975. The Role of the Science Museum in Industrial Preservation, *Trans. First International Congress on the Conservation of Industrial Monuments*, **69**. Ironbridge.

Watkins, G. 1967. Steam Power, *I.A.*, **4/3**.

Weatherill, Lorna, 1971. *The Pottery Trade and North Staffordshire 1660–1760.* Manchester.

Whatley, C. A. 1977. The Introduction of the Newcomen Engine to Ayrshire, *I.A.R.*, **2/1**, 69–77.

Wilcox, R. 1971. Bath Breweries in the Latter Half of the Eighteenth Century, *A Second North Somerset Miscellany.*

Williams, L. A. 1975. *Road Transport in Cumbria in the Nineteenth Century.*
Wilson, A. 1967a. The Archaeology of the Cinema, *I.A.*, **4/3**.
Wilson, A. 1967b. *London,s Industrial Heritage.*
Wilson, C. 1954 and 1968. *Unilever.* 3 vols.
Wilson, E. A. 1975. *The Ellesmere and Llangollen Canal.*
Wilson, P. N. 1968. Canal Head, Kendal, *Trans. Cumberland & Westmorland Soc.*, **LXVIII**.
Wilson, R. G. 1973. The Supremacy of the Yorkshire Cloth Industry in the Eighteenth Century, in Harte, N. B. and Ponting, K. G. (eds.), *Textile History and Economic History*, 225–46.
Wood, J. L. 1973. The Museum of Technology for the East Midlands, *I.A.*, **10/4**, 400–2.
Young, D. 1970. Brickmaking at Sandleheath, near Fordingbridge, Hants, *I.A.*, **7/4**.
Young, D. 1972. Brickmaking at Weymouth, Dorset, *I.A.*, **9/2**, 188–96.

Index

Index